NORTH SOUTH

An Emerging Markets Handbook

Robert Lloyd George

Probus Publishing Company
Cambridge, England
Chicago, Illinois

First published in 1994 by
Probus Europe, 11 Millers Yard, Mill Lane, Cambridge CB2 1RQ, England

Designed, illustrated and typeset by Nick Battley, London, England

ISBN 1 55738 878 4

Printed in the United Kingdom

For Donna

Contents

PART III - South Asia

PART IV - Latin America

PART V - The Mediterranean & North Africa

PART VI - Africa

PART VII - Russia & Eastern Europe

PART VIII - Other emerging markets

Preface

As in my previous two books, *A Guide to Asian Stock Markets* and *The East West Pendulum,* I have tried to look at the historical and cultural background of each nation as a guide to its investment potential and possible risks. No stock market can be looked at separately from its national economy. A country's political history is also a sure guide to its inherent stability. Inflation is an important barometer of that national stability.

It is almost impossible to be fully qualified to write such a comprehensive guide to all global emerging markets. The main concentration of my research in the past decade or more has been in Asia but I have also lived in South America for nearly two years and spent a good deal of time in Southern Africa. Together with the team of analysts who have helped me compile the statistics of this book, we have tried to visit nearly every major stock market described in this book.

I would like to acknowledge a particular debt of gratitude to Kiersten Christensen who spent much of 1993 painstakingly compiling statistics for fifty stock markets. She is also responsible for writing the chapters on Mexico, Argentina and Chile. Jacob Rees-Mogg also contributed much to the sections on Eastern Europe and Africa and, in particular, the chapters on Poland, Hungary, the Czech Republic, Morocco, Tunisia, Israel, South Africa and the other African nations. For the Indian sub-continent I would like to thank Scobie Ward and our Bombay office manager, Mr B N Manjunath, who wrote most of the Indian chapter. Our first hand report from Russia was entirely written by Alex Stewart who visited Novosibirsk, Khabarovsk and Vladivostok in the course of his research. Mark Jaskowiak of the IFC in Washington and Roger Garside were both helpful in arranging this. Among our various sources for research, I would like to acknowledge the help of Baring Securities, Morgan Stanley, and the IFC database from Washington, which is an indispensable source of information for all analysts of emerging markets.

Hong Kong, August 1994 *RLG*

Epigraphs

'.... Little else is requisite to carry a state from the lowest barbarism to the highest degree of opulence, but peace, easy taxes, and tolerable administration of justice...'

Adam Smith, Wealth of Nations

'We should not be so tied down with the inland waterways of Europe that we forget the great interests we have in the countries which lie across the oceans....'

Winston Churchill

'In 1990, 800 million people were living in the advanced industrial nations of the world, amounting to some 15 per cent of the world's population; with the accelerating transfer of technology to the developing world, by 2050 some 3.5 billion people will be living in advanced industrial nations, and will then amount to some 50 per cent of the world's population.'

William Rees-Mogg

'It has been well said in the past that the world today is richer than it has ever been but the communications are choked, so that one half of it is water-logged and the other half a parched desert.'

John Buchan

PART I

Emerging markets: An introduction

Chapter 1

Introduction

The political map of the world in the 1990s is radically different from that of the previous fifty years. The end of the Cold War has changed the power balance in every corner of the globe as the former communist nations have rejoined the world trading system. Democracy has been reborn in Latin America and Southern Africa. Many of the former European colonies in Asia and Africa have, for the first time in a generation, opened up for foreign investment. Capital now flows freely across boundaries in search of the best investment returns, which are usually found in countries with the highest economic growth. With the end of the power struggle between East and West, principally between the United States and the former Soviet Union, the world is assuming a new pattern. The contrast now is between rich and poor, between the old industrial north and the new developing south. Led by the newly-industrialized countries of East Asia, this radical shift in economic activity is spreading fast to Africa and Latin America.

The title of this book, *North South*, portrays the challenge of the next generation to bring the necessary capital resources from the pension funds of North America, Europe and Japan to invest in the fast emerging markets of the new industrial nations. (The 'North South' concept was first expressed in the Brandt Report published in 1978. According to that report the 'South' includes all of Asia except Japan, all of Africa, the Middle East, and Central and South America.)

Health & wealth—the gap between nations

It is a central theme of this book that the gap between the old and the new markets of the world is fast changing. If a true understanding is to be reached, it is of course necessary to gauge the dynamics of this process.

The overall development of a nation is often measured purely in terms of GDP per capita. However, the serious investor should be encouraged to look beyond GDP to other indicators, such as demographics, if a balanced view is to be taken reached on future potential.

For example, if we look at infant mortality (see Figure 1.1), it is striking how much countries such as Japan and Singapore have improved their

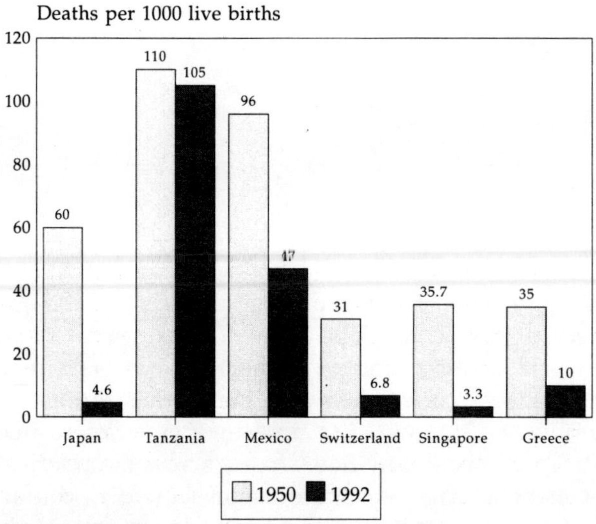

Figure 1.1 Infant mortality

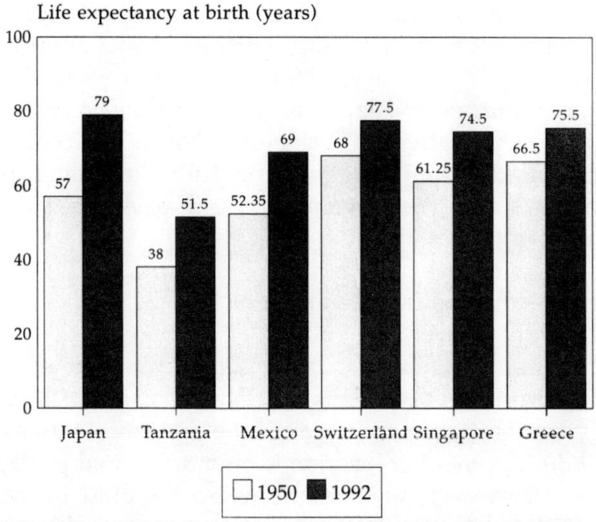

Figure 1.2 Life expectancy at birth

health care in the last forty years and are now ahead of even Switzerland or Greece. Life expectancy (see Figure 1.2) also confirms this picture with the best figures coming from Europe and East Asia.

Another example is that of telephone line diffusion data, as shown in Figure 1.3, which can also provide useful guidance. In no other consumer durable is there such an immediate impact as when a household obtains a telephone or, indeed, a television. (Televisions tend to come first.) In most of the developing countries the number of telephones remains extremely low, less than ten telephones per one hundred people.

Of course, the purely financial wealth of nations remains of primary importance. In the 1970s, the demand of the poor nations of the South was for aid from the rich countries. In 1988, for example, this totalled nearly US$50bn. Following the collapse of communism and the Berlin Wall, however, it became less pressing for the West to finance economic development in Africa, Asia and South America and much European capital was redirected towards Eastern Europe. In the 1990s and in the longer term it is investment, rather than aid, that could provide the much-needed new technology and the growth of free markets. Opinion among the ruling elites of the developing countries is coming around to this more realistic point of view.

Emerging markets defined

What is an emerging market? The normal definition is a developing country with per capita average annual income below US$10,000 or around £7000 in sterling terms. Clearly, some of the Asian economies such as Korea and Taiwan are very close to breaking through this threshold as Hong Kong and Singapore have already done so. However, this definition gives us a 'universe' of stock markets (see Figure 1.4). The overwhelming weight of Asia is due to its rapid growth and to the size of its larger markets such as Korea, Taiwan, Hong Kong (including China) and India. Latin America, at 23.8 per cent of the total emerging markets capitalization, is comparatively smaller but growing fast as the number and size of new issues over the past five years indicates (see Figure 1.5).

An emerging market may be anything outside the recognized and established markets in the United States, Canada, Western Europe and Japan. The fact that these old 'North' countries also possess the lion's share of the world's industrial production is not coincidental. Their established financial markets reflect long traditions of private capital accumulation and the use of savings to finance domestic industries. Therefore Eastern Europe and Russia must be considered as emerging markets along with the with the developing South.

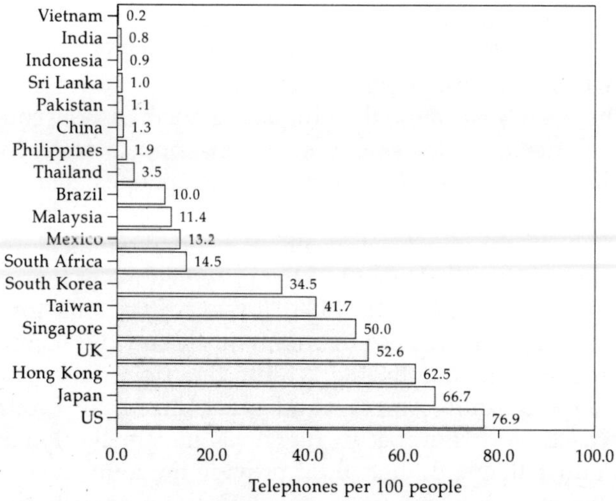

Figure 1.3 Global telephone line diffusion

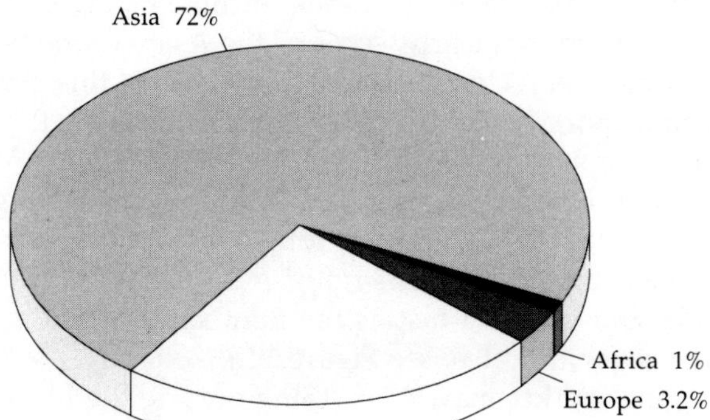

Figure 1.4 The emerging markets universe

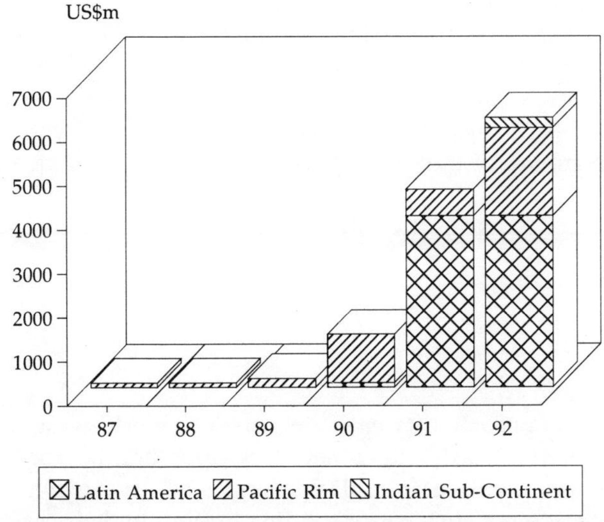

Figure 1.5 International share issuance by emerging market issuers
Source: Euromoney Bondware

Japan is, of course, a unique case in that it has developed very rapidly during the past one hundred years, and particularly since 1950, without recourse to external borrowing. Like other Asian countries, Japan has a high savings rate and this pool of domestic capital has been used to finance the rapid development of her automobile and electronics industries, to take two outstanding examples. Japan's stock market only began to reflect the success of Japan's exports after ten or twenty years, i.e. in the 1980s rather than the 1960s. This time lag between industrial success and stock market performance continues to narrow. Indeed, stock markets in today's emerging markets often predict future industrial and export successes, for example in China. Generally speaking, however, capital markets lag some years behind their economies.

Nonetheless, the debt markets in the developing world are still very large and important. In fact, it is likely that the 1990s will see South East Asia, in particular, develop larger and more important fixed-income markets in, for example, Hong Kong and Singapore—neither of which have had significant debt markets before—while Indonesia, Malaysia, Thailand, the Philippines, Korea and Taiwan may well open up bond markets to foreign investors. For a long-term growth investor, however, bonds will never be as attractive as shares.

Emerging markets include stock markets of developing countries defined as low- and middle-income economies by the World Bank. The total market capitalization of emerging markets has increased eleven-fold over the past decade, while that of the US markets has increased only three-fold over the same period. In spite of the voluminous increase in the market capitalization of emerging markets, it forms only 15.5 per cent of the capitalization of US markets. Rough estimates by experts place the foreign investment in emerging markets at a paltry 5 per cent of international equity holdings. The economic growth of the developing economies as estimated by the IMF is as follows.

	Developing	Developed
1992	5.8	1.7
1993	6.1	1.1
1994	5.5	2.2

This book covers nearly fifty emerging markets world-wide. It is perhaps helpful, therefore, to start with a selective approach by focusing on the major nations—in terms of population and size—those which have the greatest potential to realize a corresponding growth in their capital markets.

Identifying market potential

International Monetary Fund (IMF) figures for China have been used in Figure 1.6. These are not meant to portray its economy, for example, at the

	Population (millions)	GNP (US$bn) Purchasing Power Parity	Market capitalization (US$bn)	Market capitalization (as % of GNP)
China	1150	2870	223*	7.7
India	850	1105	70	6.3
Brazil	150	770	60	7.8
Mexico	90	590	122	20.7
Indonesia	185	510	20	3.9
S. Korea	43	380	107	28.1
Thailand	56	320	58	18.1
Pakistan	123	240	7	2.9
Argentina	33	190	17	8.9
Nigeria	110	190	2	1.0
Egypt	53	180	2	1.1
Philippines	63	155	16	10.3
Malaysia	18	130	97	74.6

**includes Hong Kong*

Figure 1.6 **The real wealth of the developing economies**
Source: IMF

	China	India	USA
Population (millions) 1993^{E}	1175	895	256
Population growth rate	1.4%	2.3%	1.1%
Literacy rate	73.3%	52.1%	95.5%
People per doctor	724	2075	404
People per telephone	89.5	150	1.3
Infant mortality (per 1000)	27	88	8
Modern road system ('000kms)	906	1970	27,413
Televisions ('000s)	206,710	76,800	221,056

Figure 1.7 Vital signs

current dollar exchange rate, but rather the size of its domestic consumption measured according to what a Chinese consumer can buy in terms of housing, clothing, food and consumer goods. Measured in this way, China, along with some of the other major developing nations such as India and the giants of Latin America—Brazil and Mexico—appear to be far wealthier than previously perceived. This may correspond more closely with other important measures of development such as literacy and longevity. For example, China's literacy rate is over 70 per cent (see Figure 1.7) and life expectancy for both men and women is over seventy years. Thus a per capita income of nearly US$2500, as opposed to the usual measure of around US$400, may portray more accurately the real wealth and growing middle-class in countries like China and India. This interpretation is extremely relevant to the development of stock markets which depend so much on the availability of domestic savings. For emerging stock markets, they represent the most telling indicator. The growing wealth of ordinary people in these developing countries quickly spills over into demand for consumer products, savings and investments. More individuals become investors in their own local stock markets, providing a far more solid foundation for long-term performance than the 'hot money' which invested by foreign fund managers. Figure 1.8 shows that eight out of the twelve countries where per capita income has more or less doubled are in East Asia, an area which exemplifies this trend.

Looking at Figure 1.9 which shows the size of the stock markets for each of these major developing economies, it will be seen that, with very rare exceptions, none of them approach even 10 per cent of the size of their respective economies. By contrast, in the developed markets such as New York, London and Tokyo, the corresponding figures average 70 per cent. (In China's case, Hong Kong is included—together with Shanghai and Shenzhen—as the leading capital market of the country. In 1997, of course,

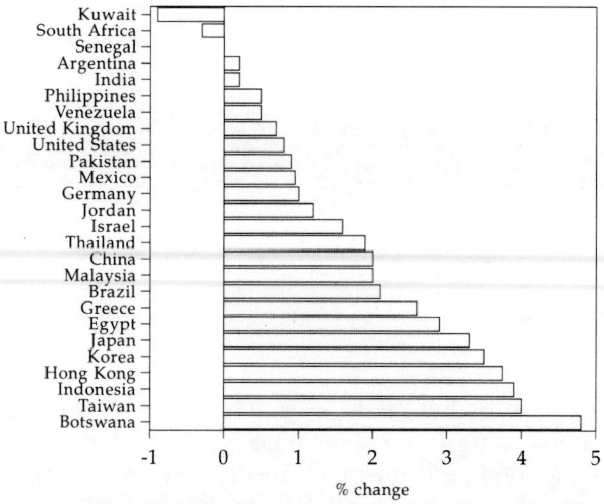

Figure 1.8 Change in GDP per capita, 1965-1985

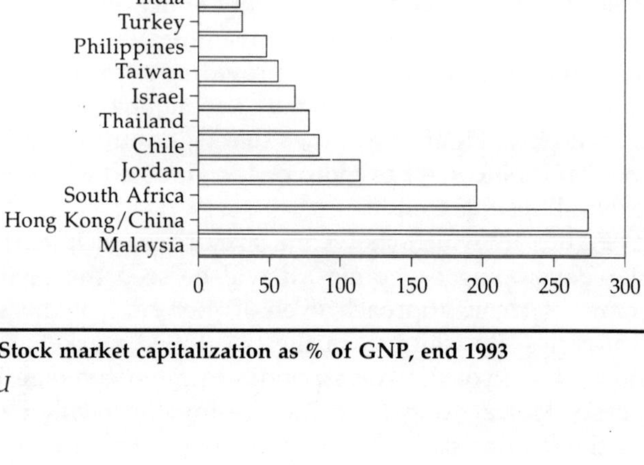

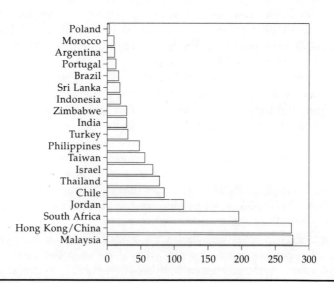

Figure 1.9 Stock market capitalization as % of GNP, end 1993

Source: IFU, EIU

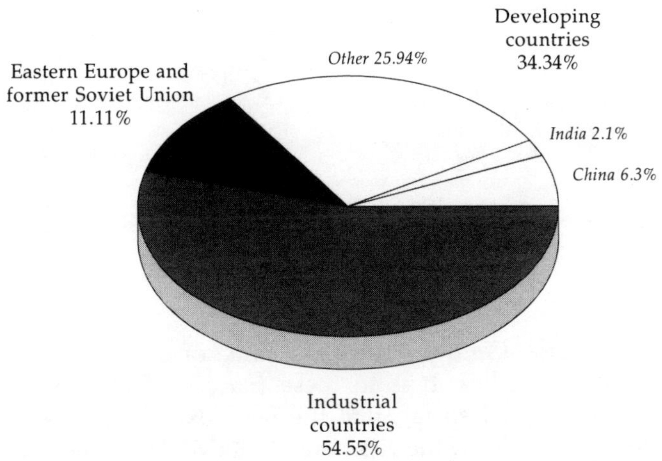

Figure 1.10 Share of world GDP

Hong Kong will form part of China but, even now, mainland Chinese companies are being listed on the Hong Kong Stock Exchange, thus making it an increasingly accurate reflection of China's economic size and growth.)

Figure 1.10 shows also how the former communist countries, despite the deep economic contraction which followed the fall of the Berlin Wall, still have substantial economic weight in the world because of their population and resources. A long-term investor, however, will look not so much at the size of markets and economies, as at their rates of growth. This is the most telling argument for investing in emerging markets. The average growth rate of economies in developing Asia, for example, has been 7 per cent per annum in real terms for the past twenty years, compared with 2.3 per cent in Western Europe and North America. The performance of the emerging capital markets has also been more than double that of the developed markets (see Figure 1.11). As regulations and accounting standards improve, the flow of funds towards the emerging markets is bound to grow.

The key to selecting good investments in emerging markets is not only to take a macroeconomic view of the world and select the likely winners among the developing nations, it is also to spend long days and weeks visiting companies which, despite being in the most unlikely places, nevertheless show great earnings growth potential. In defining emerging markets, therefore, a comprehensive view has been taken and this has resulted in the inclusion of seemingly 'unlikely' places in which to invest. These

	Market capitalization (US%bn)	Average GNP growth (5yr)	Market performance (5yr)
Asia	652	+7.8	+106.1
East Asia	78	+3.2	+98.6
South Asia	249	+3.4	+262.18
Latin America	31	+0.8	+20.6
Africa	7	+0.6	-21.3

Figure 1.11 Emerging markets growth

include Eastern Siberia, Central Africa and some of the smaller nations of Central and South America. It is in these places, which have been untouched by foreign capital so far, that the best investment bargains may, possibly, be found. However, the risks are obviously far higher in terms of currency, political instability and general lack of legal and financial regulations. Furthermore, any investment manager considering investment in such an area must ascertain the existence of a satisfactory local custodian bank. Hence the approach taken by most global emerging market funds has been to diversify broadly and concentrate on the major regions and larger markets.

In this book, the emerging markets have been divided into a 'major league' and a 'minor league'. A characteristic of the major league countries is that they have have large populations with the potential for domestic consumption to grow considerably in the next twenty years. Their strategies will be quite different from those of the 'tiger' economies like Taiwan, Hong Kong, Singapore and Korea in the 1970s which boosted the growth of their exports. China, India, Brazil and Mexico will, in addition, base their growth on the enormous potential for improvement in living standards among their large, growing middle-class populations and the consequent demand for consumer durables which will follow. In a period of slower growth in the developed world, it will also be more difficult for these developing nations to depend solely on export-led growth if export markets are no longer growing at the same rapid momentum.

The **major league** comprises the following nations:

- China, India, Brazil, Mexico, Chile, Argentina, Turkey, Russia, South Africa, Thailand, Korea, Taiwan, Malaysia

The **minor league** comprises:

- The Central American nations, Colombia, Venezuela, Peru, Ecuador, Bolivia, Paraguay, Uruguay, Greece, Portugal, Poland, Hungary, the Czech Republic, Bulgaria, Romania, the Baltic States, Central Asian States, Morocco, Tunisia, Egypt, other African markets including Zimbabwe, Nigeria, Pakistan, Sri Lanka, Bangladesh, Indonesia, the Philippines, Israel, Kuwait, Jordan

Broadly speaking, the major league corresponds to the IMF list of the largest developing economies, although markets with a capitalization of less than US$25bn have been excluded. However, this 'top-down' approach must be complemented by a 'bottom-up' approach to selecting small countries with strong fundamentals and good companies. Examples might include Israel, Costa Rica, Sri Lanka and Jamaica. The fact that there exist large blue-chip companies which account for 20 per cent of market capitalization and trading volume, makes it much more attractive to consider a single investment in a country which might otherwise be looked upon as too small or too risky for a global investor to consider. Another good example was the Philippines which, for many years, was the investment pariah of Asia since it was justifiably considered to have high political, currency and inflation risks. Nevertheless, a purchase of shares in the telephone company, PLDT, or in the brewery company, San Miguel, would have been an extremely good five- to ten-year investment, regardless of the macroeconomic view or political risk analysis.

Requirements for a successful emerging market

Foundations

With the large privatizations and new issues that have come to list in the emerging markets in the past few years, one must consider what listing procedures, accounting standards and rules for investor protection are required. Many developing countries, as already noted, want to have a stock exchange. Some of them have inherited the legal structures from colonial times, whilst others are starting from scratch—particularly those in the communist world. Few have an idea of the legal and accounting procedures which are the *sine qua non* of investor confidence in all stock markets, both established and emerging. The necessary requirements are as follows:

- political stability;
- a sound currency;
- low inflation;

- a welcoming environment for foreign investors with ease of repatriation of dividends and capital;
- international accounting standards;
- proper disclosure of directors' interests;
- regular interim and annual earnings and sales figures;
- full information to share holders;
- a sound and comprehensive system of corporate law for commercial contracts, fund prospectuses, new issue, etc.;
- a liquid and well traded securities market with regular and fair prices.

In my previous work on Asia I attempted to answer the question, 'What are the main elements behind the long-term record of success in Japan and what may, therefore, be the necessary foundations for a similar success in other emerging markets, both in Asia and globally?'. My answer was:

- a strong work ethic;
- a high savings rate;
- an undervalued currency;
- consistent export success;
- strong government support for the stock market;
- some powerful business groups which support share prices;
- asset backing;
- a large and growing population of shareholders;
- strong financial groups, both banks and brokers;

In the final analysis, however, it is the character of a people—their integrity, work ethic and respect for the law—rather than any technical factor which must give the best long-term clues to whether an emerging market will be a winner or not. My approach has always been an historical approach, looking for hints in the past record of a country, its political history, its record as an international borrower and the fluctuations of its currency to make a reliable estimate as to future performance.

Long-term development

What is the longer term potential of each emerging market? In addition to the underlying growth rate of the economy, of exports and of domestic savings, it may be useful to compare the size of the capital market with that of the economy (see Figure 1.12). There are some countries in the world where the capital market already exceeds 100 per cent of GNP—Singapore and Hong Kong are two good examples where there are sound reasons for this apparent over-valuation. Normally, however, we would expect the stock mar-

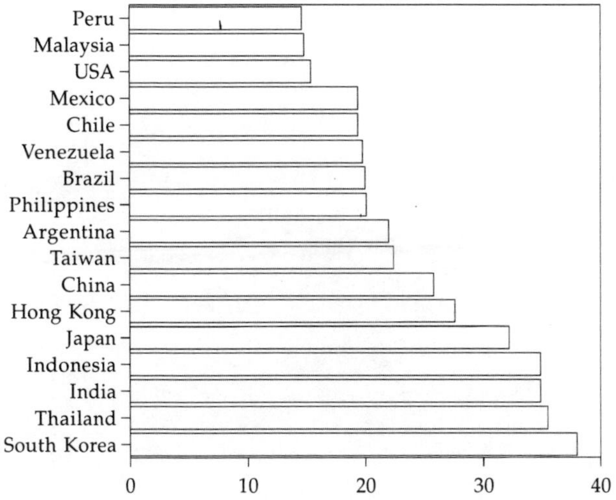

Figure 1.12 Gross capital formation as % of GNP

ket to be roughly equivalent to 50 per cent of GNP. This simple calculation is founded on the following reasoning: if one excludes all the public government sector and one also excludes all the privately-held companies, one ends up with roughly half the economy to be listed on the share market. In some countries, like India, the banking sector is still entirely nationalized and, therefore, it is not surprising to find the market is less than 20 per cent of GNP. Part of the potential for growth lies in the fact that we expect the privatization programme in the next ten years to include the banks. This is also true of China. Wherever one can see a country with sound fundamentals growing at a steady rate, where the stock market is less than 10 per cent of GNP, one must conclude that there is great long-term potential.

In the mid-1990s we are looking at a world population of just over 5.5bn (see Figure 1.13), growing at close to 100m a year, thereby implying that world population will cross the 6bn mark before the year 2000, with an estimated estimated peak of 10bn reached in 2030-40. The growth rate is highest in Africa and Latin America which presently accounts, together, for 20 per cent of the total, a figure which will climb towards 25 per cent as Europe (growing at virtually zero) shrinks below its present 9.5 per cent, to around 5 per cent. North America has only 5 per cent of the world population but has, during this century, accounted for 50 per cent of world industrial production. This is the imbalance which is rapidly being changed as industry moves south and east. The overwhelming portion of world popu-

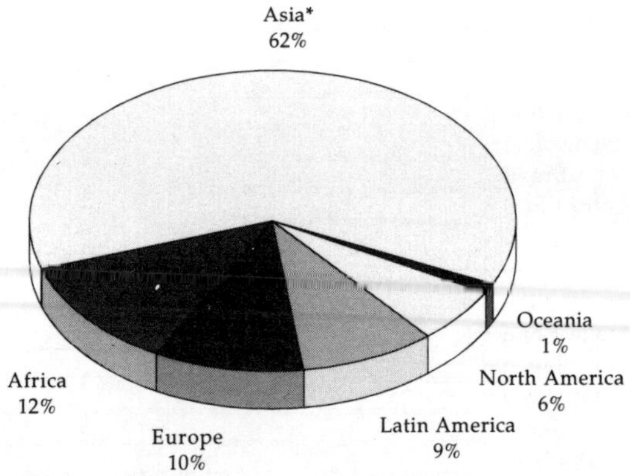

*) excluding former USSR

Figure 1.13 World population

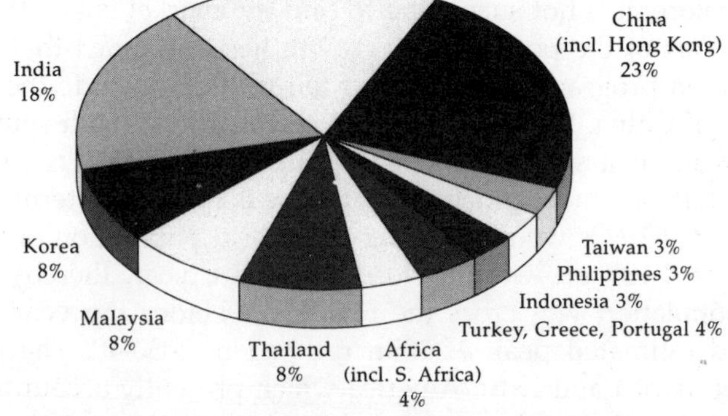

Figure 1.14 Model emerging markets portfolio
Source: Lloyd George Management

lation, over 60 per cent, is still in Asia and will remain in Asia for the next fifty years, even if Asia's population growth rate slows. Infant mortality rates and life expectancy have improved greatly (see Figures 1.1 and 1.2, earlier in this chapter).

Coupled with other factors such as political stability and low inflation, the potential for this large part of the planet's population to become consumers and savers is the most compelling argument for emerging market investors to overweight Asia.

The model emerging market portfolio shown in Figure 1.14 reflects much of this thinking in that China and India are the two prominent segments, followed by Latin America. By contrast, Southern Europe and Africa are given less weight. A diversification among the other Asian markets—Thailand, Malaysia, Korea, Indonesia, the Philippines and Taiwan—provides a broad exposure to growth and stability.

Privatization

Privatization is an important trend. From China to Peru, the developing world is following in the footsteps of the pioneer—in this case, Britain under Margaret Thatcher—who first had the vision to see that public services, such as airlines and telecommunications, would be better managed in a private shareholder-owned form than as public corporations. This achieves several objectives at once:

- It reduces the government deficit. This is is an attractive option to nearly all developing countries.
- It creates a new and large class of first-time share owners who tend to vote for pro-business and conservative policies. Owning shares is like running one's own house. It gives the individual a feeling of having a stake in his or her country's best and largest enterprises.
- It diminishes the power of trade unions.

A further incidental advantage to the international investment community is that (apart from giving large fees to the investment banks who underwrite the issues) it enables pension funds, for example, to buy large and liquid listed shares in new countries: Britain, France, Spain, Portugal, Mexico, Argentina, Chile, Malaysia, Singapore, Japan, the Philippines, to name only the best-known examples where the telecommunications industry has been listed, obviously a sector with great growth possibilities when one considers the small number of telephones per capita installed in various developing countries (see Figure 1.3, earlier in this chapter).

Timing	**Country**	**Likely approach**	**Access lines (000s)**
1993-4	Europe, Mid-East, Africa		
	Denmark	Equity offering	2792
	Greece	Equity offering/strategic sale	4800
	Hungary	Strategic sale	916
	Israel	Equity offering	1534
	Kenya	Strategic sale	157
	Netherlands	Equity offering	6466
	Nigeria	Strategic sale	250
	Portugal	Equity offering/strategic sale	1110
	Saudi Arabia	Strategic sale	1210
	South Africa	Equity offering	2866
	Americas		
	Colombia	Strategic sale	2268
	Costa Rica	Strategic sale	276
	Panama	Strategic sale/equity offering	197
	Peru	Strategic sale	501
	Puerto Rico	Strategic sale	872
	Pacific		
	Australia	Equity offering	7604
	Indonesia	Strategic sale	1169
	Singapore	Equity offering	982
	South Korea	Equity offering	10,486
1995-6	Europe & Mid-East		
	Czech Republic/Slovakia	Strategic sale	2125
	Belgium	Equity offering	3913
	France	Equity offering	29,100
	Germany	Equity offering	35,085
	Ireland	Equity offering	834
	Poland	Strategic sale	2953
	Sweden	Equity offering	5710
	Turkey	Equity offering	5877
	Americas		
	Uruguay	Strategic sale	376

Figure 1.15 Potential telecom privatizations world-wide, 1993-1996

Looking at potential telecommunications privatizations world-wide (see Figure 1.15), one can visualize the dramatic impact of national authorities relinquishing their control over this key strategic sector. As the drive towards profit and efficiency improves, so the speed with which telephones are installed also shows a remarkable improvement. This is common not only in Western Europe, but also in Asia and in the newly-democratized countries such as the Czech Republic and Hungary, and also in South America.

Second only to telephone privatizations which involve very large capital amounts and, therefore, have a great influence on the capitalization of individual emerging markets, there is the boom in world-wide air transport which, in Asia, for example, means that, among the billions of dollars spent on infrastructure projects, airport projects figure at the head of the list (see Figure 1.16). This is, therefore, an important trend even though it is not always apparent in the listed vehicles on stock markets.

The airline business is a great deal more problematic as it is much more prone to fierce international competition. It is now said that whereas twenty years ago every developing country had to have its own airline, today the symbol of national pride is to have its own stock exchange. Many of the small national airlines have had to be amalgamated into larger, regional carriers. This is particularly the case in Europe. This, therefore, may be a less attractive industry to invest in—although there are exceptions, such as the case of China where passenger traffic is growing at 30 per cent per annum. The national carrier, CAAC, has now split into more than twenty different provincial carriers, led by China Southern in Canton and China Eastern in Shanghai. The success of Dragonair, a Cathay Pacific subsidiary, as one of the few airlines having a wide range of permitted routes into various Chinese provincial cities, indicates the enormous demand for a still small number of flights. This then may be an area of investment interest in the future. (See Figure 1.17).

In Asia we see the enormous need for capital in the next ten years stemming from the ambitious infrastructure plans of every Asian country, to build roads, ports, airports and electrical power stations. The growth of industry, again in China, has gone far ahead of the electricity supply. One answer to this problem is to accelerate the construction of new power stations with private capital through means of the 'build, operate, transfer' (BOT) formula which may also include listing the completed power facility on a stock exchange. A pioneer of this has been Gordon Wu of Hopewell Holdings in Hong Kong, who has stolen a march on his competitors by building the six-lane highway linking Hong Kong and Canton. He has also shown others the way to achieve profits in this sector by building power stations in Southern China.

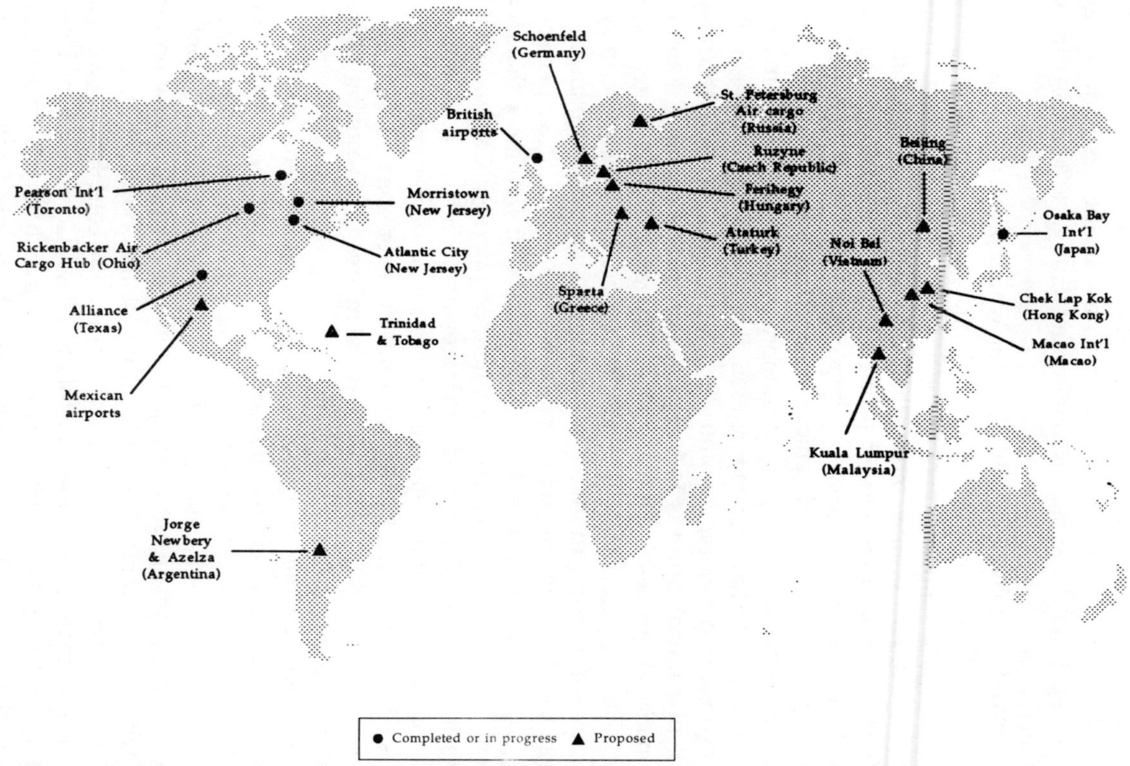

Figure 1.16 **Major world-wide private sector airport capital projects**
Source: Morgan Stanley from Public Works Financing International, October 1992, Lockheed Air Terminal Inc., January 1993

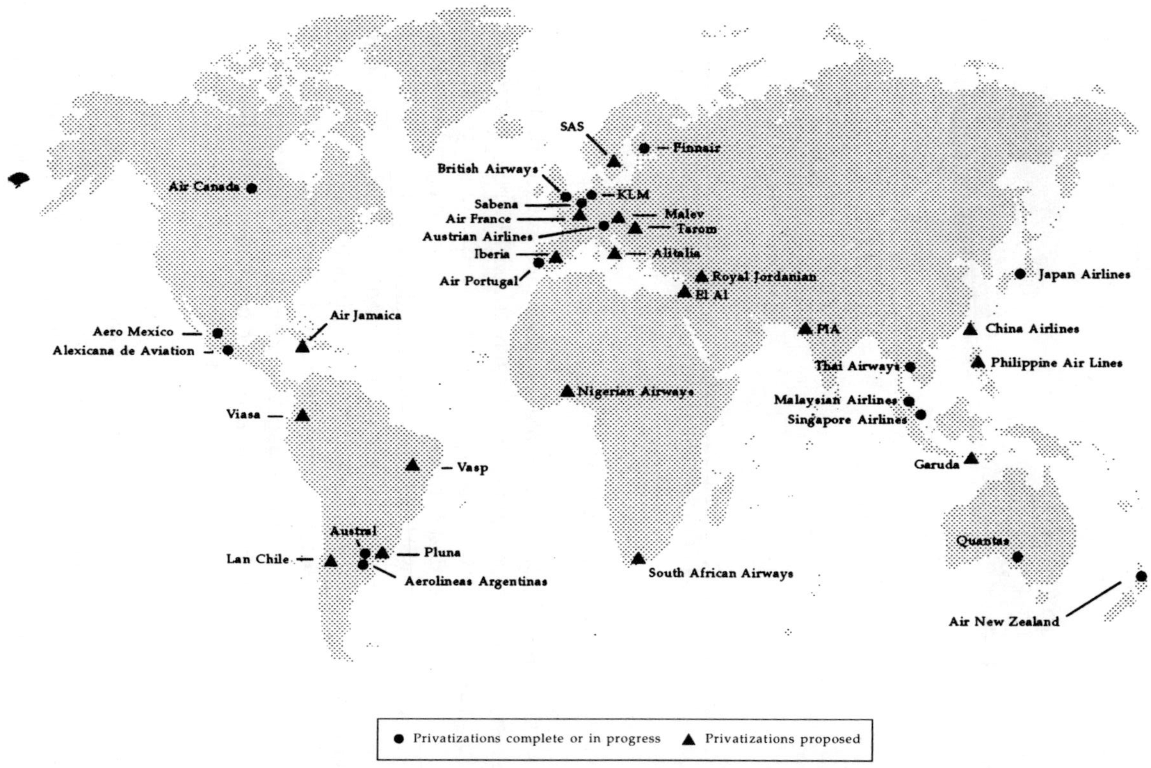

Figure 1.17 Airline privatizations around the world

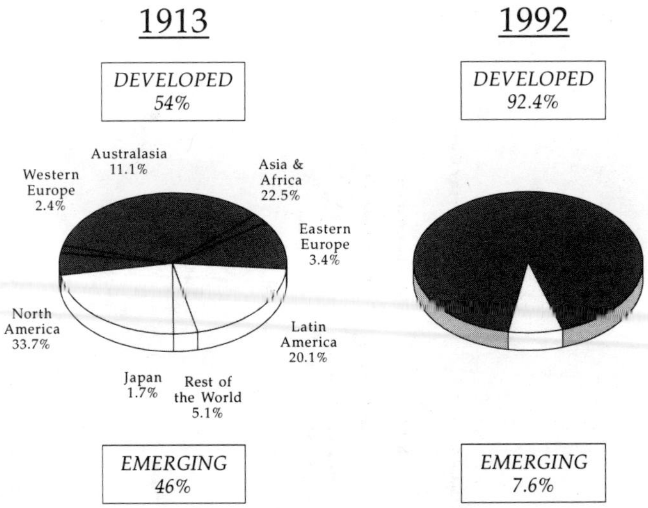

Figure 1.18 Comparison of UK portfolios in 1913 and 1993
Source: Baring Securities

Investing in the emerging markets

As this book is written, it is possible to envisage—for the first time in eighty years—a world of free capital flows such as existed before the First World War. Figure 1.18 portrays a typical British institutional portfolio of 1913. Latin America accounted for over 20 per cent, due mainly to investments in Argentine railways and land, Brazilian utilities and bonds and Mexican oil and railroads. There was also heavy investment in Russia, Poland and Eastern Europe, again principally represented by bonds and railways. Asia and Africa accounted for nearly one quarter of the total portfolio. India was obviously a major area of British investment, but this segment may also have typically included Malaysian rubber plantations and tin mines, South African gold mines and investments in primary commodities in both East and West Africa.

What we now call emerging markets accounted for nearly 50 per cent of the total overseas portfolio of a British investment trust. Compare the present situation, where emerging markets represent a mere 7.6 per cent. The imbalance is even more remarkable when one considers that the share of the world economy represented by these developing countries is over one-third, is growing fast, and is considerably larger than in 1913!

The trend in the 1990s towards investing in emerging markets is a reflection of the shift from bank finance, eurobonds and international borrowing towards development financing by means of equity issues, initial public offerings (IPOs) and privatizations. It also reflects the emphasis of the International Finance Corporation (IFC) whose job is to help private sector financial markets develop—in contrast to its big brother, the World Bank, whose job is to make international aid and loans to developing nations. Although the credit and risk analysis involved in both activities is similar, investment in the long term has a very different complexion compared to bank lending. The IFC has certainly been one of the architects of the rapid development of emerging markets.

Why invest in the emerging markets?

The most compelling argument for investing in the new emerging markets around the world today is that they have shown a consistently good performance over the past few years (see Figure 1.19). There is now plenty of

	1yr *31 Dec 92 - 93*	**5yr** *31 Dec 88 - 93*	**10yr** *31 Dec 83 - 93*
Argentina	57.84	792.8	1191.77
Brazil	108.27	105.72	172.92
Chile	28.49	391.19	1566.53
China* (CLSA All China)	(19.14)	-	-
Colombia	39.33	542.22	-
Greece	10.83	97.26	155.64
Hong Kong*	115.67	342.39	1258.76
India	16.92	98.18	278.98
Indonesia	109.84	56.96	-
Jordan	24.96	46.23	31.73
Korea	18.92	(17.58)	447.61
Malaysia	96.81	232.10	-
Mexico	46.14	644.53	2545.03
Nigeria	(16.67)	(10.41)	-
Pakistan	81.13	226.71	-
Philippines	128.76	203.83	-
Portugal	28.93	(5.56)	-
Singapore*	59.12	133.55	142.08
Taiwan	83.4	29.94	-
Thailand	101.88	364.23	956.45
Turkey	212.52	286.43	-
Venezuela	(10.03)	230.11	-
Zimbabwe	(57.17)	(10.28)	237.12
IFC Asia	67.75	61.92	-
IFC Latin America	53.03	350.06	-
IFC Composite	63.14	98.38	-

Figure 1.19 IFC market performances

**Local index used in US$ terms, IFC US$ Weekly Indices used for the remainder*

evidence to show that this is not a short-term trend but reflects some very important underlying economic changes in the world. Perhaps the best way of understanding this is if we put it in the context of history and consider what happened to Britain during the industrial revolution, between 1780 and 1840, when the first textile factories were established in Lancashire and the first railways were built across the country. Similarly in America, in the following generation, from 1840 to 1886, there was a great geographical expansion of canals, railroads and a westward move of population which led in turn to a great expansion of the banking system, of commerce and a dramatic growth in the overall economy. Japan's turn came first after the Meiji restoration in 1866 when its export industry underwent its first boom before and after the First World War. The real Japanese economic miracle, of course, occurred between 1955 and 1975.

If we compare the time taken to double per capita output (see Figure 1.20) between these classic Western and Japanese industrial revolutions with what is happening today in China or India, we can begin to appreciate the speed of change in these ancient civilizations as they industrialize. The result of this rapid industrialization in the most populous countries of the world is two-fold. First, it increases the economic growth rate of those countries, both in terms of their exports and also in terms of the improvement of their domestic living standards. Second, it tends to depress the growth rate in the old developed world, i.e. the US and the European Community, since manufacturing production moves away from the high cost areas to the low cost areas. We may, therefore, confidently predict that out of the 4.5 billion people in the Third World, 3 billion are likely to experience economic growth over the next ten years at an average of at least 7 per cent annually. By contrast, the growth rate in the so called 'First' world is not likely to exceed 2.5 per cent.

It is not fanciful to suggest that the capitalization of these emerging markets which today stands at about US$1100bn, will grow faster than any other asset class over the next ten years and will probably be second in size only to the United States stock market by the year 2000 (see Figure 1.21).

Emerging markets account for nearly 80 per cent of the world's population and 40 per cent of its total GNP, but only 6 per cent of its total market capitalization. If we take the period from 1965 to 1990, the annual GDP growth in the industrialized economies of the North averaged 3.1 per cent. The emerging markets of the South averaged 4.7 per cent. If anything, this discrepancy has widened during the 1990s, with the acceleration of growth in Asia and the slowdown in Europe. Thinking about the potential for emerging markets it is worth remembering that the average US pension fund still is less than 1 per cent invested in Asia. During 1993 alone, net equity flows into Latin America and the Pacific Rim have grown from US$20bn to nearly US$40bn, mainly as a result of a small shift in the total

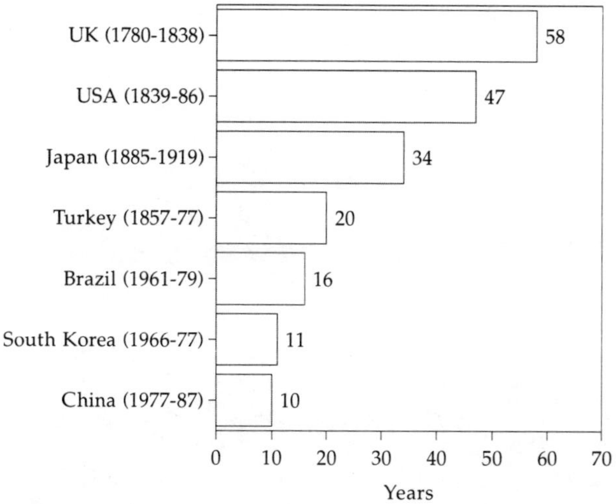

Figure 1.20 Productivity growth (time taken to double per capita output)

weightings of US institutions. Such is the enormous size of the capital available. The clearest evidence of the potential for an emerging market which reflects a truly dynamic economy is shown by the growth of Hong Kong as the main play on China. In 1983, Hong Kong's market capitalization was US$17bn. By the end of 1993, it had grown to well over US$300bn. During the next ten years, we may see similar growth in countries such as India or Brazil or even in unexpected places like Africa and Russia.

Investment methodology

In Asia, at least, the job of an investment manager has quickly moved beyond picking countries and launching country funds, as was the case between 1985-1990, to picking stocks within those countries. The Indonesian market, for example, moved from having just seven listed shares open to foreign investors in 1989 to having over 150 two years later. It was no longer a question of 'buying' Indonesia, but rather of buying a small selection of quality shares in a large and fast developing market. Knowledgeable investment managers are now focusing on small capitalization shares with good management and high growth potential.

This is the opposite approach to those who believe that they can 'index' their global portfolios. Although the indexing approach has many supporters, especially in the United States, it has shown its limitations in recent

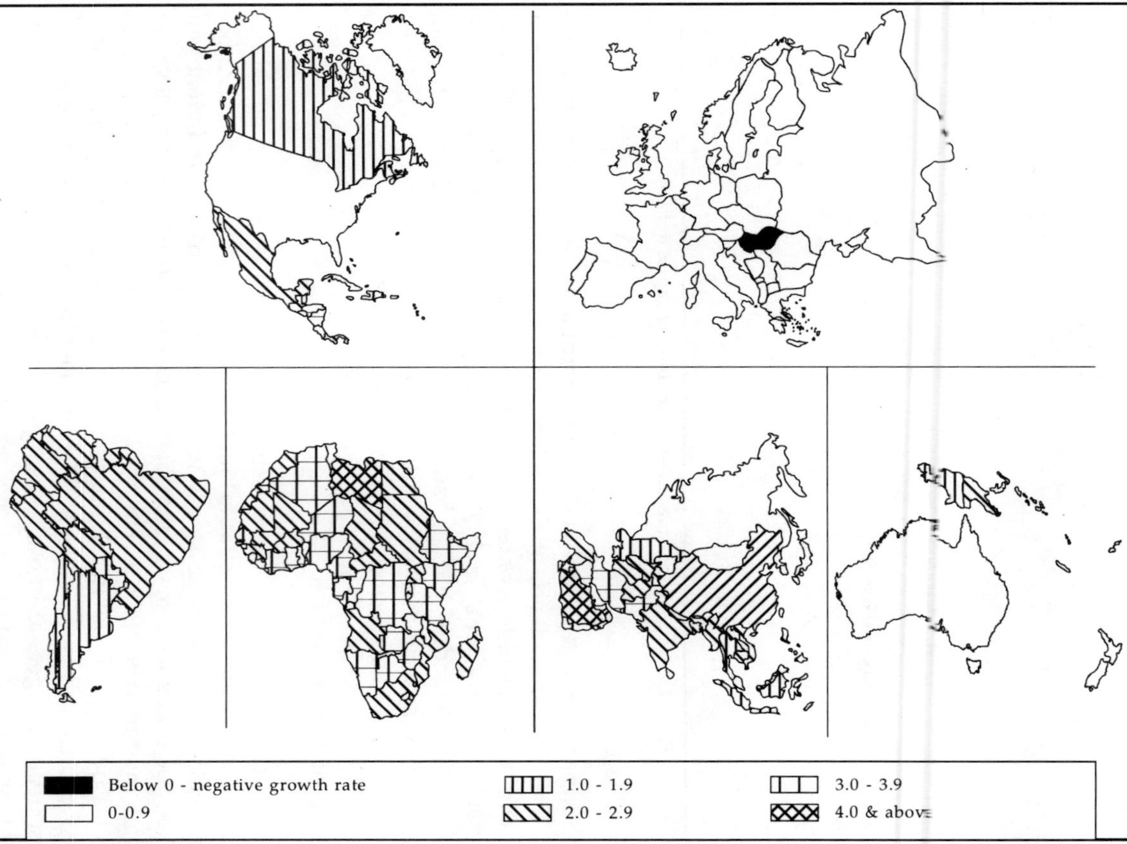

Figure 1.21 World growth rates

years. If we take the EAFE (Europe, Africa, Far East) Index, the great problem facing institutional investors in 1990-93 was the very high weighting given to Japan. As the Japanese market halved in value during these three years, those who took an indexing approach found themselves under-performing the world index significantly. Similarly with the emerging markets, it is dangerous to buy those which already have a large market capitalization—examples may include Taiwan in recent years, or perhaps Malaysia and Mexico, which have also performed very well in the past two years. Malaysia's market is now nearly 170 per cent of GNP, a dangerous ratio if one recalls that Japan's market was 150 per cent of GNP in 1989 and subsequently fell to half that level. One must, therefore, look at the size of economies, the growth of exports, the size of population and the overall growth rate and stability of each country before making a decision about an appropriate weighting in a global emerging market fund.

The best-performing emerging market funds have been prepared to make reasonably large bets on individual markets, for example Hong Kong as a way into China, Mexico with the Nafta[1] Agreement and Thailand with its strong economic growth and political stability. By contrast, some London-based managers have been tempted, for reasons of both proximity and cultural affinity, to invest heavily in markets like Portugal whose economic growth rate has disappointed owing to the overall recession in Europe. Economic growth must be the first criterion of capital market performance. Asia has been the living proof of this thesis over the past twenty years. Flexibility to move within the major regions is also a key to performance. Very few managers have first-hand knowledge of both Asia and Latin America, or indeed of other areas such as Africa and Eastern Europe. Regional funds are sometimes preferred for this reason. The best advice to give to an investor may be to take a five- to ten-year view and be patient for the best returns.

Managing a global emerging market portfolio

Experienced fund managers try to avoid fashionable trends and concentrate on long-term value. Ideally, the approach to identifying attractive companies in developing economies (or emerging markets) is no different from finding such companies in Europe, Japan or the United States—that is, in established stock markets. In practice, however, the amount of information available on companies in India, Brazil or in China, is often far less and an

[1] *North American Free Trade Area.*

Argentina	0.03
Brazil	0.14
Chile	0.15
Colombia	0.07
Greece	0.01
India	-0.16
Indonesia	0.16
Jordan	0.24
Korea	0.20
Malaysia	0.53
Mexico	0.31
Nigeria	-0.04
Pakistan	0.05
Philippines	0.40
Portugal	0.29
Taiwan	0.12
Thailand	0.41
Turkey	-0.13
Venezuela	-0.06
Zimbabwe	0.03

Figure 1.22 Emerging market correlations with US (US$)
Source: IFC

emerging market manager has to balance the 'top-down' approach with the detailed business of stock selection or 'bottom-up' approach.

One of the factors in balancing a global portfolio will be the correlation or non-correlation with the US market (typically) and the beta to each market compared with the US market. Figure 1.22, taken from IFC statistics, illustrates that the countries with the lowest beta are India, Turkey and Venezuela and those with the closest correlation with the US market are, not surprisingly, Mexico, but more unexpectedly, Thailand and the Philippines. Some Asian markets correlate very closely with the US market for a number of reasons. Firstly, because their currencies and, therefore, their interest rates cycle are closely linked to the US dollar and, secondly, because US investors tend to influence prices very strongly, for example, in leading Philippine companies which have ADRs listed in New York.

If we take the twelve largest emerging markets only we shall find an index portfolio will look approximately as shown in Figure 1.23. Hong Kong, as the stock market for China, occupies nearly 22 per cent of the emerging market universe. Other major East Asian markets, Korea, Taiwan, Malaysia and Thailand, occupy another 37 per cent whereas India surprisingly is only 5 per cent of the world total. Latin America, including Chile, is nearly 17 per cent. From the African continent only one stock market alone, that of South Africa (which might be described as a re-emerging market in 1994) is \$216bn in size or 15 per cent of the world total of \$1590bn. The

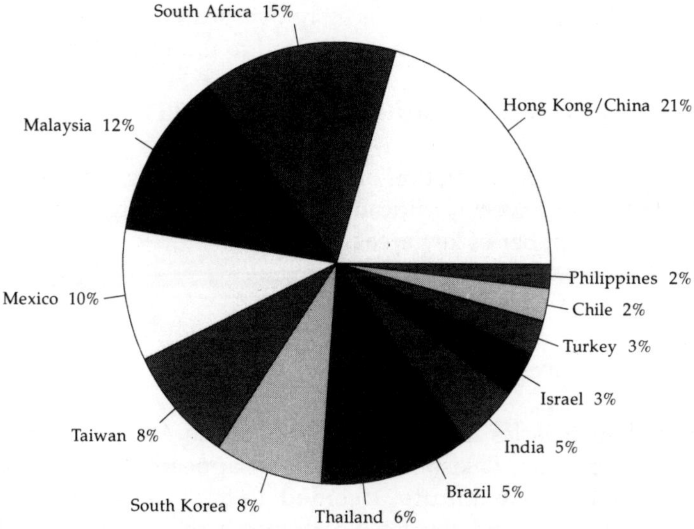

Figure 1.23 Index portfolio of the twelve largest emerging markets

remaining markets such as Israel and Turkey, Portugal and Greece, occupy less than 7 per cent of the world total.

If we then bring into consideration the growth rates of each country and the relative valuation or P/E multiple of different markets, we shall try to rebalance this into a portfolio based on growth and value. Our model portfolio will continue to put a large weight on Asia, but India, for example, would be increased to nearly 20 per cent and thus South Asia would balance East Asia and China with 25 per cent going to Latin America. Individual bets may be made on other countries such as South Africa or Turkey or even in Eastern Europe and Russia, but the broad weightings would reflect the potential that we see in 1994 to 2010. The growth of industrialization will be most rapid in China, in India and in Latin America, with the growth of the free trade zone from Mexico southward.

Many other factors such as political risk, inflation and currency volatility may play a part in altering these weightings in each quarter and each year ahead but these may be guidelines which will give young investment managers the best idea of where to spend their time and research effort in the emerging markets in different parts of the world.

Indexing, which has become so fashionable in the US as a passive approach to making investments, is unlikely catch on in the emerging market area. If it does it is likely to include other factors such as population and economic size, growth of exports and political stability. But the lesson of

Japan in 1989 to 1993 points clearly to the fact that unless market relative valuation is taken into account, a grossly overheated market may account for far too much in the overall index and lead to under-performance.

The General Agreement on Tariffs and Trade (GATT)

The 15 December 1993 completion of the seven year long Uruguay round of the GATT talks will have a significant impact on all emerging markets. This will be seen in a number of key areas:

- Textiles
- Agriculture
- Financial Services

The main beneficiaries in the textile area are the Asian countries including China/Hong Kong, Pakistan and India. It appears that the US and Europe have, at the last minute, decided to maintain the Multi Fibre Agreement (MFA) beyond the ten years in which it was originally scheduled to be phased out. If this is the case, the benefits to the Asian exporters will not be so immediate. However, there is no doubt that the cost differentials between Asia and the West in this key industry, which employs many millions of people in the developing world, mean that over the longer term the major production of clothing will shift East (see Figure 1.24).

Among the other large exporters of the emerging economies it is important to cite Thailand and Indonesia which are still major exporters of rice and agricultural products as well as cheap manufactures. The decision by both Japan and Korea to open their rice market to imports is of historic significance. Thailand in particular will feel an immediate benefit, although it is worth pointing out that Vietnam has moved up into the ranks of the top three rice exporters in only two years so competition on price may be intense but quality is also important.

The other main beneficiaries of the gradual dismantling of agricultural subsidies will be the countries of the pact, including Australia, New Zealand, Argentina, Brazil as well as Thailand. The most efficient, low-cost producers of wheat, corn, soya beans and livestock will see an improvement in their terms of trade as heavily-subsidized agricultural producers in Japan, Europe and the US are forced to reduce their costs.

The final impact of GATT will be felt in the financial services area. This is of key importance to the development of emerging stock markets since it will allow US investment banks, for example, to play a much more active role in the new capital markets in China, in India and in Latin America. Access to the banking sector will also be very significant. The ability to sell

Country	Exports as a % of GDP
China	35.0
Thailand	31.6
Chile	29.6
Venezuela	28.0
Portugal	27.9
Indonesia	26.3
Korea	26.2
Jordan	22.6
Colombia	17.6
Pakistan	14.1
Turkey	13.3
Greece	13.2
Argentina	13.1
Mexico	10.7
Brazil	7.1
India	6.2

Figure 1.24 The impact of GATT

insurance products in all these countries will contribute to the further development of their savings and capital markets as the middle-class population grows more numerous and more prosperous. The victory for free trade, although of great immediate significance, will in practice only be felt by exporters over a number of years. The ability of the developing countries to sell their products more freely to Europe, the US and Japan will be the test of whether they can continue to exhibit fast economic growth and rising living standards. This was the way in which the Asian tigers—Korea, Taiwan, Hong Kong and Singapore—followed in the footsteps of Japan, and produced their economic miracles by breaking into the large US consumer market with cheap and attractive products.

All change in the future?

What might we expect the world to look like in 2010? Clearly the present breakdown of world industrial production (30 per cent in the USA, 30 per cent in Europe, 20 per cent in Japan and 20 per cent in the rest of the world) will shift, so that China and India, for example, will become major industrial nations. In Latin America, too, we may expect Brazil—which already has a large base of industrial production around São Paolo—and Mexico, to become significant competitors. In the world car industry, which perhaps best reflects the overall trend of industry, these will be the main growth areas. South East Asia also will become a growing area. Perhaps the biggest question mark is what will happen to Russia, which has been contracting as a major economy for the past five years? If it has a turnaround and recovery it, too, will become a major destination for investment.

There are now 32,000 listed shares world-wide. Of these, 10,000 are in Asia outside Japan, a large proportion being accounted for by the Indian stock market. The Asian emerging markets' capitalization exceeds US$700bn, or 6 per cent of the total world stock market. The demands for capital from the emerging markets over the next five years are estimated to exceed US$600bn but, in Asia, there has been a surplus of US$100bn of savings available for investment over the past five years and there will be a larger amount available in the future, greatly facilitating the financing of large infrastructure projects. On the other hand, institutional investors world-wide, including the United States, Europe and Japanese pension funds, now control assets of over US$32 trillion and it is likely to double over the next ten years. This is the pool of capital which currently has the most impact on the growing capital markets of Asia, Latin America and the developing world.

The Chief Executive of General Electric (USA), John F Welch, sees the future of his company as being concentrated on three developing giants: China, India and Mexico, with South East Asia close behind. Their total population is roughly 2.5bn, some ten times that of the USA. In all four markets, political and economic risks are higher than in the US but General Electric believes that placing many small bets of US$20-50m each will cushion that risk. 'If the strategy is wrong, it is $1bn,' says Welch. 'If it is right, it is the future of the next century for this company.'

The impact on US employment is profound. Jobs will be shifting to the Pacific Rim, India and Mexico. The demand for capital goods in those areas is enormous. China, for example, will buy 100 wide-bodied aircraft each year for the next ten years. It will add US$100bn in power generating equipment by 2000. It has only 1300 CT scanners for its 62,000 hospitals and 200,00 clinics. Large US and European companies like this have to move to where the growth is, that involves investing today. Portfolio investors will follow where direct investment leads.

One forecast for the world's major economies in the next thirty years is for China, growing at over 10 per cent per annum, to overtake the US in the year 2016 and to have the largest economy in the world in the period 2020-2025 (see Figure 1.25). By contrast, the US and Japan would continue to grow at a moderate 3 per cent pace. Germany would stagnate along with the rest of Europe with its economy being less than half the size of that of Japan and quarter that of China. The most striking forecast is that, by the

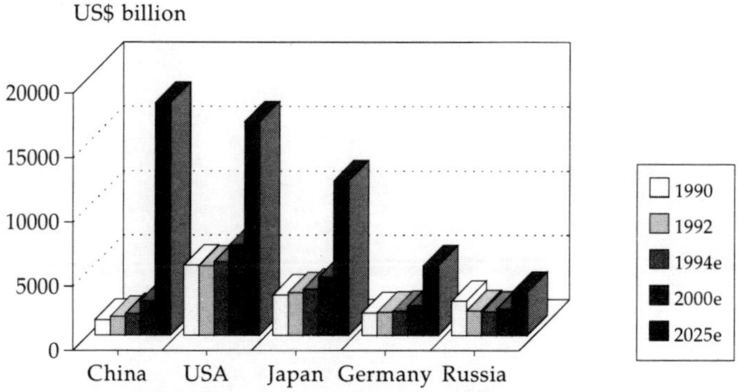

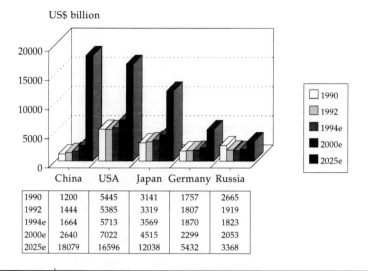

	China	USA	Japan	Germany	Russia
1990	1200	5445	3141	1757	2665
1992	1444	5385	3319	1807	1919
1994e	1664	5713	3569	1870	1823
2000e	2640	7022	4515	2299	2053
2025e	18079	16596	12038	5432	3368

Figure 1.25 Major world economies GDP

end of the century, the Russian economy would barely regain the GNP size that it had in 1990 and that it is likely to lag far behind by 2025. Despite its obvious wealth of raw materials, both political uncertainty and a lack of confidence by international investors, will hold back its growth.

Many questions can be raised about this forecast which basically extrapolates trends in the past three to five years. China will certainly grow more prosperous. It is also certain that it will have a major hiccup which will affect its economy at some point in the next decade. But the vision of General Electric's chairman is based on some very real numbers and reliable forecasts. World automobile production, for example—the industry which above all led to the industrialization of Germany and of the USA and, more recently, of Japan—is shifting dramatically away from the West to the Pacific Rim and to Latin America. In the next three years, the combined production of Korea, China and the other Asian producers will double. Latin America's vehicle production will grow by 30 per cent, whereas few forecasters are expecting more than a 10 per cent growth before 1996 in Germany, France or the United States.

The conclusion is that industrial production, economic growth and jobs are moving not only from West to East but from North to South.

PART II

East Asia

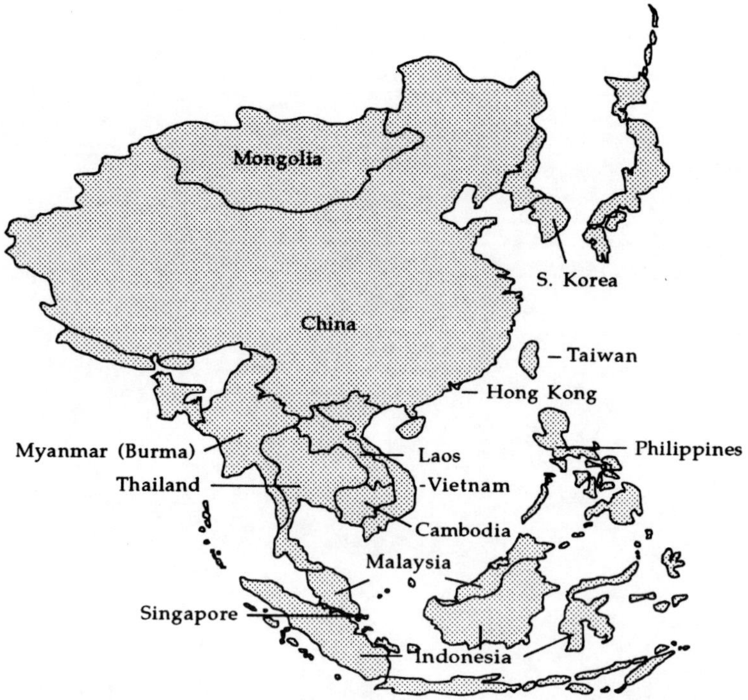

THE EMERGING MARKETS OF EAST ASIA

Chapter 2

East Asia - Introduction

The idea that the 21st century will be the Asia Pacific century has been widely discussed. It may be useful to examine the foundations of this prophecy. East Asia is overall an area of widely different cultures and traditions. For the investor it is also a region combining highly-advanced technological nations, such as Japan, with impoverished and backward nations, such as those of Indo-China and even the interior of China itself. On the whole, however, it appears to be an area of great promise with one-third of the world's population, considerable natural resources and a unique combination of high energy and what is often described as a 'Confucian' work ethic which radically distinguishes these Asian nations from, say, India or Latin America.

Nobody who visits Hong Kong, Shanghai, Seoul or Taipei can doubt that, with the speed and efficiency of business life, the confidence and optimism which are reflected in large-scale construction activity and the discipline and stability of the political structures, this region will be the locomotive of the world economy in the next fifteen years. Much of this visible success is based on years of building up, of saving and indeed of privation only a generation ago. It is vital to realize that Hong Kong only recently was a city of refugees. Seoul and Taipei have lived under authoritarian regimes with the threat of a large and aggressive communist neighbour. Bangkok was at the front line of the communist advance which, after 1975, reached its borders with the fall of Saigon and of Cambodia. Singapore has raised itself by its own exertions and the inspired leadership of Lee Kwan Yew from being a small backwater treaty port to an impressive modern financial centre.

Therefore, what is visible today is not the whole story. Much of the miracle of East Asia lies in the roots of the culture. While Japan's culture is based on the corporation, the secret of China's economic success lies in the family. Everywhere that an investor travels in Asia—in Taipei, in Hong Kong, in Malaysia, Jakarta, Kuala Lumpur and Singapore—the leading listed companies will be almost entirely those run by Chinese families. Many of them have made their fortunes in real estate. Much of the wealth which is now visibly listed in new stock markets such as Jakarta has, for thirty years previously, been private and hidden from public view. The

	Taiwan	S. Korea	Hong Kong	Malaysia	Thailand	Philippines	China
Population (m)	20.9	44.8	5.96	18.9	58.7	65.7	1210
GNP (US$bn)	220.8	321.5	109.7	63.4	118.1	55.1	478.6
Real GNP growth (%)							
1992	6.8	4.7	5	8	7.5	0	11.5
1993	6.3	6.2	5.4	8.6	7.5	2.4	10
1994[f]	6.8	6.5	4.5	8	7.9	4.1	7
Per capita income (US$)	10,565	7176	18,406	3337	2012	839	395
Exports (US$bn)	86.6	82.4	140	48.7	37.8	11	78
Imports (US$bn)	81	85.9	145.6	39	48.1	15.8	75.6
Foreign direct investment (US$m)	1183	900	3300	4615	2300	364	72,300
Inflation	3.9	5	9.4	3.9	5	7.3	17
Interest rates	8.3	8.5	6.8	8.5	10	16.2	28.2
Market capitalization (US$bn)	124	119	300.5	175	92.2	26.4	1.4
No. listed companies	280	693	465	420	220	174	34
Index performance in '93 (%) in US$	71.7	24.6	115.7	102.9	88.5	152.8	(19.1)
Price/earnings (P/E) ratios							
1993[e]	30.5	19.7	16.4	27.3	22.7	28.8	15.9
1994[f]	23.1	16.9	14.1	18	19.1	21.2	14.5
Earnings per share (EPS) growth							
1993[e]	4.3	9	25.8	14.8	12	14.3	6.2
1994[f]	13	22	16.2	16	12	26.2	24
Average daily turnover (US$m)	638	430	575	130	256	10	2.7
Dividend yield	1.8	1.9	3.8	1.9	2.9	1	1
Stock market performance, '88-'93 (%)	176.2	62.3	416.1	375.0	484.5	387.0	n/a
Currency to US$ perf., '88-'93 (%)	6.5	(1.6)	1.1	0.6	(1.2)	(30.4)	n/a

Figure 2.1 **East Asia: country statistics (31 December 1993)**

	Indonesia	Vietnam	Papua New Guinea	Mongolia	Laos	Burma (Myanamar)	Cambodia
Population (m)	187	70.4	3.91	2.3	4.3	44.5	8.7
GNP (US$bn)	124.8	10,500	4800	231	989	11,125	1740
Real GNP growth (%)							
1992	6	8.3	5.6	-9.6	7.3	1.2	7
1993	6.2	7.5	10.3	0	7.1	2.3	7.3
1994[f]	6.5	8.2	7.5	2.1	6.9	3.5	7
Per capita income (US$)	667	149	1228	100	230	250	200
Exports (US$bn)	39.3	2829	2200	285	200	600	300
Imports (US$bn)	30.2	2975	990	316	160	500	270
Foreign direct investment (US$m)	6000	2377	n/a	n/a			
Inflation	8.5	15	5	321 ('92)	9.8 ('92)	21.9	75 ('92)
Interest rates	20	26.4	11.1				
Market capitalization (US$bn)	25						
No. listed companies	170						
Index performance in '93 (%) in US$	109.8						
Price/earnings (P/E) ratios							
1993[e]	20.4						
1994[f]	17.5						
Earnings per share (EPS) growth							
1993[e]	6.5						
1994[f]	17						
Average daily turnover (US$m)	20						
Dividend yield	2.1						
Stock market performance, '88-'93 (%)	312.1						
Currency to US$ perf., '88-'93 (%)	(21.9)						

Figure 2.2 **East Asia: country statistics (31 December 1993)**

stock markets, therefore, of the East Asian region are only now beginning to catch up with the tremendous economic growth which has characterized the region for more than twenty years. The insecurity which characterized refugee communities of the 1960s is being replaced by a new-found self confidence. Money is readily available for many projects, especially those undertaken by overseas Chinese in China itself.

It cannot be over-emphasized just what an important role China is playing and will play, in the life of the East Asian area as a whole, not only as an economic influence but also as a cultural and potential military power with a growing impact on all its neighbours. Stability and continued economic growth in China are necessary for the continued growth of the investment markets in the whole 'Greater China' region which we may take to be defined from the borders of Korea to the islands of the Indonesian archipelago and the Southern Philippines. The peaceful resolution of China's relations with Taiwan, for example, will have an enormous impact on both economies and also on Hong Kong and those countries which have close relations with Taiwan, such as the Philippines, Korea and Singapore. Vietnam, although not yet an investable market, is a country of 70m people and has the potential to be a large and vital economy competing not only with China but also with its Asean neighbours such as Thailand and Indonesia.

Japan's role in this whole East Asian boom is also very important. Although Japan has not been included in this survey of emerging markets, it is the major source of capital, of lending and of aid for its Asian neighbours. The rise or fall of the yen has an immediate impact on trade in Korea, in Taiwan and even in Thailand. Japan is by far the largest direct investor in both Indonesia and in Thailand. It is estimated that there are well over five hundred Japanese companies with wholly-owned assembly plants and factories mainly around the Bangkok region. Japan is the leader of the Asian region in technology, in management, in retailing and in living standards. However, it is not—and it never will be—the political leader of the region and the reasons are quite clear: The 1941-45 war during which Japan occupied and overran large parts of China, Hong Kong, Singapore, Malaya and Indonesia, has left deep scars. The two former Japanese colonies of Korea and Taiwan have also been deeply influenced by the more than fifty years of Japanese occupation. The enmity between the Chinese and Japanese will not disappear in one or even two generations. This is perhaps the main reason why Japanese investment in China has lagged not only far behind that of the overseas Chinese, but also behind the American and European companies which have committed capital to manufacturing in China. The Japanese have taken a more cautious approach and while hundreds of salesmen have been posted around China, there has been no long-term capital commitment. But Japan undoubtedly has a positive role to play. It will import a growing volume of goods manufactured in South East Asia. It is the principal buyer of raw materials and commodities such as rice. The recent opening up of the rice market of Japan and also Korea is, therefore, of great significance to Thailand and to Vietnam among others. Japan may play a major role in the reconstruction of countries such as Burma, Laos and indeed Vietnam itself.

But while there is no doubt that, in the mid-1990s, the pendulum of world wealth and economic activity is swinging strongly towards South East Asia, we must not overlook the risks for investors in this region. Those risks are mainly associated with the volatility of young capital markets and also of political events and surprises in a region which is, broadly-speaking, not yet democratic. The succession in China must be a key issue. The absorption of Hong Kong into China after 1997 will have a great impact on investor confidence throughout the area. The looming question of North Korea has been preoccupying US strategic thinkers in recent months. There is little doubt that the North Korean economy is close to collapse but that it still has the ability and the willingness to use military power. However, many of the risks which were sufficient to deter long-term investors in countries like Malaysia ten or twenty years ago—the ethnic tensions and inequalities between Malays and Chinese—have now been largely resolved by the growing prosperity of these nations. Economic growth, therefore, should produce greater political stability. The rise in living standards in Korea and in Taiwan has led directly to the end of martial law and the introduction of a proper working democracy with opposition parties and a free press.

In conclusion, the East Asian area must be the major region for a emerging market fund. It contains the greatest population, its markets have larger and faster growing capitalizations and the growth rates of its economies are superior to both India and South America. Its currencies are closely linked to the US dollar, while the underlying cultural factors—education, literacy, the work ethic, savings, the family—are still strong and underpin future decades of growth. The major weighting in a global portfolio should, therefore, remain in this dynamic region of the world.

Chapter 3

Cambodia, Laos & Burma

Population (C,L,B):	8.7m, 4.3m, 44.5m
GNP per capita (C,L,B):	c. $150, c. $200, c. $200

Although none of these three smaller Asian countries yet has a stock exchange, they are all turning towards a more free market economy and slowly, over the next few years, may evolve towards a situation rather more encouraging to foreign investment.

As can be seen from the figures shown above, these three countries are easily the poorest and most backward in Asia. In the case of Laos and Cambodia, this is owing to a generation of communism and civil war which cost Cambodia, for example, the lives of over one million of its people. Laos is a poor, agriculturally-rich, country which used to be known as the 'Land of a Million Elephants'. Cambodia has finally emerged from its suffering, with Prince Sianouk returned as head of state after twenty years' exile and the help of a UN-sponsored peace plan and the slow reconstruction of the economy. However, like Laos, Cambodia may become an economic province of Thailand, rather than its previous status as a military province of Vietnam.

The history of Indo-China over the centuries reflected the swing of power between these two nations, although the Khmer empire in the 13th century dominated its neighbours. Today it is Thailand which is the leading economic power in the peninsula.

The author visited Myanmar in September 1992 at the invitation of the government who wish to establish a stock exchange. After spending several days there, seeing the economy first hand, it was apparent that however much Burma would like to have more foreign investment, it will not come until there is a change in the political situation. The rule of General Ne Win since 1962 has been an unmitigated disaster for Burma's once rich and prosperous economy. Natural resources include petroleum, gems, diamonds, rice, teak, mahogany and, most of all, a well educated and literate population. The country was once one of the jewels of the British empire. Today, it is a sadly isolated and impoverished country. Nevertheless, the free market is slowly returning to Burma. Trade with China is booming in the north. Some foreign banks are looking to re-establish their branches in Rangoon

(Yangon). International oil companies have been prospecting. Burma is inviting foreign investment and the probability is that a political change, if it occurs in the next few years, will bring an opening up and rapid restructuring of the Burmese economy.

Chapter 4

China

Population:	1210m
Gross national product:	$478.6bn
Market capitalization:	$25bn
Currency/US$:	8.70 yuan

Introduction

China is the biggest of all emerging markets potentially as it has the world's largest, and fastest growing, developing economy. It is quite clearly the nation with the potential to have the most impact on the world's affairs in the next fifty years. This is not only because of its vast population—now believed to be over 1200m, or about 25 per cent of the world total—but also because, as the Chinese economy continues to grow at 10 per cent per annum, the demand for every possible kind of raw material and manufactured product by the newly-wealthy Chinese people grows at an exponential rate. We can measure this in the immediate proximity of China, in the British colony of Hong Kong in the demand for Hong Kong property, Hong Kong shares, for hotel rooms and airline reservations, for gold and ginseng. Further afield, we can see the impact on university places in the USA and Canada, on many commodity prices including timber, copper, oil, aluminium, cotton and wool. The plans for expansion in infrastructure, transport and telecommunications in China in the next ten years have great implications for every Western company, especially such major manufacturers as Boeing, General Electric, Caterpillar, Bechtel, GEC (UK), Alcatel (France) and the great Japanese trading houses such as Mitsubishi and Mitsui.

The investment opportunities in China today are broad and varied, but the risks are also considerable. China has had no tradition of law and still has no proper legal system today. The currency market has been stabilized, but is still subject to volatility and the country lacks a proper central bank or, indeed, an overall modern banking system. International patent law and copyright law is not fully enforced. In many ways, China today is the Wild West and the character of its recently-established stock exchanges in Shanghai and Shenzhen fully reflect this culture. Yet a knowledgeable and long-term investor should not be deterred by this observation. Anyone buying shares in London or New York fifty or one hundred years ago, in Tokyo,

	1988	1989	1990	1991	1992	1993
Population (m)	1106	1122	1139	1156	1178	1210
GNP (US$bn)	376.5	422.7	369.8	371.2	411.7	478.6
Real GNP growth (%)	10.9	3.9	5.2	7.1	12.8	11.5
Per capita income (US$)	340	377	325	321	350	395
Exports (US$bn)	41.1	43.2	51.5	58.9	69.7	78
Imports (US$bn)	46.4	48.8	42.4	50.2	63.6	75.6
Foreign direct investment (US$bn)	8.4	6.1	7.3	12.1	58.2	72.3
Inflation	20.7	16.3	3.1	3.6	6.2	17
Interest rates (lending)	21.2	35.9	48.8	28.6	23.9	28.2
International reserves (US$bn)	18.5	18	29.6	43.7	46.7	32
Market capitalization (U$bn)	n/a	n/a	n/a	n/a	18.3	40.6
No. of listed companies	n/a	n/a	n/a	n/a	183	52
'B' share index performance in US$	n/a	n/a	n/a	n/a	n/a	-19.1
Price/earnings ratios (P/E)	n/a	n/a	n/a	n/a	21	15.9
Earnings per share (EPS) growth	n/a	n/a	n/a	84	28	6.2
Average daily turnover (US$m)	n/a	n/a	n/a	n/a	3	17
Dividend yield	n/a	n/a	n/a	n/a	1	1
Currency to US$ (yuan)	3.7221	4.7221	5.2221	5.4342	5.7518	5.7612

Figure 4.1 China: key statistics

Taipei or Seoul fifteen years ago, would have experienced many of the same uncertainties: lack of regulation, volatility and risk.

The most remarkable thing is how much progress China has made in the past decade towards becoming a modern economy and how quickly it has established modern financial markets. It requires no apology, therefore, to spend the most time and research effort on China above all other emerging markets.

China as a manufacturing nation

The major impact of China on the world will be to reduce labour rates and to open up to increased trade one of the world's biggest and most dynamic markets. In the simplest terms, if we compare Volkswagen in Shanghai with Volkswagen in Germany, the cost of labour for a German car worker is over one hundred times that of a China car worker, doing the same job. (see Figure 4.2) Always assuming that free trade prevails in the world in the next ten years, there is little doubt that industrial production of cars and many other items will shift at an accelerating rate towards China.

	1993 forecast costs ($)	Ranking	1991 cost ($)	Ranking
Germany (West)	24.87	1	22.49	1
Norway	21.90	2	22.20	2
Switzerland	21.64	3	21.38	4
Belgium	21.00	4	19.50	6
Netherlands	19.83	5	18.47	7
Austria	19.26	6	17.61	9
Denmark	19.21	7	17.98	8
Sweden	18.30	8	21.45	3
Former DDR	17.30	9	14.56	13
Japan	16.91	10	13.23	16
USA	16.40	11	15.27	12
France	16.26	12	15.34	11
Finland	15.36	13	20.84	5
Italy	14.82	14	17.42	10
Australia	12.91	15	13.63	14
UK	12.37	16	13.41	15
Ireland	11.88	17	12.04	18
Spain	11.73	18	12.36	17
New Zealand	8.19	19	8.26	19
Taiwan	5.46	20	4.35	21
Singapore	5.12	21	4.39	20
S. Korea	4.93	22	4.13	23
Portugal	4.63	23	4.20	22
Hong Kong	4.21	24	3.47	24
Brazil	2.68	25	2.51	25
Mexico	2.41	26	1.97	26
Hungary	1.82	27	1.38	28
Malaysia	1.80	28	1.69	27
Poland	1.40	29	1.00	31
Former Czechoslovakia	1.14	30	0.70	32
Thailand	0.71	31	0.60	34
Romania	0.68	32	1.06	30
Philippines	0.68	33	0.64	33
Bulgaria	0.63	34	0.28	35
CHINA	**0.57**	**35**	**0.27**	**36**
Yugoslavia/Serbia	0.40	36	1.14	29
Indonesia	0.28	37	0.22	37
Russia	0.02	38	0.03	38

Figure 4.2 World labour costs in US$ per hour (manufacturing sector)
Source: Morgan Stanley Research, DRI McGraw-Hill

It is important to emphasize that this trend does not have negative implications for the West, it is not a zero-sum game. China will be very different from Japan and will not run large trade surpluses. It will be a major importer. Chinese consumers want to own brand-name luxury goods. They want to acquire motor cycles and cars. They want to dress well. Chinese women have already become avid consumers of cosmetic products. There is a tendency for the sophisticated Chinese consumer to go straight for the most expensive and sophisticated product available. Nationally, too, China will be a major purchaser of computers, telecommunications and transport equipment. Over the last decade, the Western world has begun to benefit from this. Sales to emerging economies, led by China, accounted for 25 per cent of the growth in the developed world of the USA, Europe and Japan.

Japan will become increasingly involved with China's modernization. China is already Japan's second largest trading partner. With the Japanese labour force confronting a demographic squeeze over the next twenty years, the only outlet for Japanese industry is to use China's large, trainable, efficient and cheap labour force.

By various means we can analyse the situation of China's economy today. Industry is growing fast and is nearly 50 per cent of GNP. Agriculture has fallen from nearly 80 per cent to 30 per cent. Foreign trade is now over one-third of GNP and growing fast. In addition, it is worth emphasizing that although the coastal provinces of Guangdong, centred on Canton (and with a close relation to Hong Kong) and of Jiangsu, centred on Shanghai, each account for nearly 10 per cent of national income. that the economic miracle in China is increasingly diversified across the whole country including the interior provinces. Indeed, one leading commentator at the Centre for East Asian Studies at the University of Hong Kong, Professor Edward Chen, has commented that the focus of China's economic development in the next ten years will shift from the Pearl River in the South to the Yangtse River in the centre of China, with the city of Wuhan (formerly known as Hankow) becoming one of the leading centres of growth.

If we analyse China's foreign trade, we can see that Hong Kong still represents 45 per cent of demand for Chinese exports. This figure alone underlines the enormous strategic importance of Hong Kong to China. It continues to be China's principal source of foreign exchange. On the import side, Hong Kong is slightly less important but still accounts for nearly 26 per cent, followed by Japan at 17 per cent. It is noticeable also that Russia, with 2.7 per cent of exports and 4.4 per cent of imports, although small, is growing as a trading partner. One economist remarked that 'Siberia is full of natural resources and empty of people. China is, in some respects, the opposite'.

Foreign investment in China

China's secret advantage is the overseas Chinese. There are 50m ethnic Chinese living in the countries of Asia and the West Coast of the United States, Australia and Canada. Although Hong Kong accounts for the largest part of the foreign investment in China, it is noticeable that wealthy Chinese from Indonesia, Thailand, Malaysia and elsewhere have recently been undertaking very large projects, very often in their home towns in China. The amount of foreign investment in China has shot up in 1993 and indeed it is of some concern to other developing countries that capital has been diverted away from Thailand, Indonesia and other low-cost Asian producers towards China. It is also true to say that many US and other multinationals have woken up to the challenge and promise of China in the past two years and have begun, for the first time, to invest for the long-term by building manufacturing plants, marketing networks and creating subsidiary companies in China.

There is a striking contrast between China and Russia today. Many commentators think that China might break up into several nations just as the Soviet Union has done. However, a closer look at the composition and character of the Chinese population reveals that 90 per cent are Han Chinese, whereas the Russians accounted for only half of the population in their own empire. The culture is more homogenous, too, and there is a common acceptance today that Deng Xiaoping's economic reforms are here to stay and that there is a consensus about improving living standards and modernizing the economy, rather than political democracy as has been Russia's main preoccupation under Yeltsin. In Figures 4.3 & 4.4, we have compared (with the help of Morgan Stanley) the global restructuring which is being undertaken in these two former communist giants.

It emphasizes the need to analyse the cultural factors in making investment decisions in the emerging markets. Do the people have the capacity and the commitment to build free markets? Even after fifteen years of economic reform, the battle to overcome collective state planning and communist ideology is not yet over in China. State enterprises still account for 50 per cent of industrial output and employ hundreds of millions of people. The need to preserve jobs has led to the slow pace of reform of the state sector. By contrast, the 'town and village enterprises' which have sprung up all over China have been the main source of the increased output and growth of exports. The problem of inflation is still the main one plaguing China's economic technocrats. Money supply has grown nearly 50 per cent in 1992-3 and the government seems powerless to control it. On the other hand, the government is no longer able to collect taxes from the provinces particularly the booming southern provinces which have a great deal of economic independence.

	China	Russia
RESULTS		
GDP growth	+12% per annum	-17% per annum
Budget deficit as % of GNP	2-4%	15%
Subsidies as % of GNP	4%	8-10%
Money supply growth %	50% year-on-year	30% month-on-month
Foreign direct investment	$15-20 billion per annum	$1 billion total
Capital net inflow/outflow (+/-)	+$10-12 billion per annum	-$10-20 billion per annum
Inflation	12-30% year-on-year	880% year-on-year
CHARACTERISTICS		
Population	Homogeneous	Anything but homogeneous
Social culture	Consenus on attaining wealth	Conflicting social goals
Income distribution	Worsening: regional and city/country gaps	Very bad in regional and social group disparities
Corruption	Increasing	Very high
Privatization	Leasing only (50 years)	Rapid corporate, dwelling and small business privatization; very slow for agriculture
Agriculture	Huge (600-800m) peasant class	Agricultural workers—not peasants
Structure of economy	People-intensive; capital equipment and infrastructure shortage	Capital intensive—mainly outdated capital
Protectionist impact	High	Fairly low
Commercial legal system	Primitive	Primitive but improving
Culture	Pro-business	Pro-political power
Political system	Autocratic	Democratic
Openness to world economy	Fairly high in manufacturing, which accounts for two-thirds of exports. 18% of GDP is in exports	Very low and dominated by energy and materials, which account for two-thirds of exports
Savings rate	High—probably equal to 30-40% of GNP	Low—flight from money due to inflation
Capital flows	Big inward flow—key role played by overseas Chinese	Big capital outflows
MAJOR RISKS TO REFORM		
	• Rising income differentials • Regionalism • Economic hard landing • Global protectionism • Arms expenditure	• Military • Break-up of federation • Loss of economic control • Lack of economic direction

Figure 4.3 Global restructuring: success vs. failure

Source: Morgan Stanley

	Former Soviet Union	Eastern Europe	Middle East	China	South-East Asia	Latin America
A. CULTURAL FACTORS						
1. Entrepreneurship and individual responsibility as a culture	4	4	4	1	1	1
2. Education orientated toward economic needs	4	3	4	3	1	2
3. Economic growth-orientated government which acknowledges its limits	4	3	4	2	1	2
4. Sound public administration (with relevant skill, experience and outlook)	4	2	1	2	1	3
5. Existence of private property etc., adequacy of legal structure, private property safeguards, currency convertibility	4	2	1	3	1	1
B ECONOMIC & FINANCIAL FACTORS						
6. Financial structure (adequacy of banking systems)	4	3	2	4	1	3
7. Adequate domestically-generated wealth, capital and savings to provide basis for economic take-off or external availability of capital on free market basis	4	4	2	1	1	2
8. Stock of relevant social capital (infrastructure)	4	4	1	3	1	3
9. Fiscal imbalance/excessive concentration of resources on military sector	4	3	3	2	1	2
C. ADAPTABILITY OF ECONOMY TO INTERNATIONAL MARKET						
10. Suitability of country's existing product range to international markets	1	4	1	3	1	1
11. Degree of openness to and integration of economy into international markets	4	3	2	2	1	3
12. Long-term comparative advantage of area in terms of labour costs	1	1	4	1	3	1
D. SOCIAL & POLITICAL FACTORS						
13. Political risk (as hindrance to foreign investment)	4	3	3	3	1	3
14. Narrow income distribution	4	1	4	4	1	3
Average score:	**3.6**	**2.9**	**2.6**	**2.4**	**1.1**	**2.1**

Notes: 1 = Generally adequate; 2 = Varied with positive bias; 3 = Varied with negative bias; 4 = Generally inadequate
This table assesses the probability of the major areas of the world undergoing restructuring achieving self-generated prosperity or becoming increasingly dependent on foreign (particularly, foreign state-sponsored) capital inflows. the higher the score, the less likely spontaneous development)

Figure 4.4 Global restructuring: regional capacity for self-energizing wealth creation
Source: Morgan Stanley

What are the major investment opportunities in China today?

- 1. Capital goods:
  - *a. telecommunications*
  - *b. transport*
  - *c. electricity power generation*
- 2. Consumer goods:
  - *a. retailing*
  - *b. cosmetics and pharmaceuticals*

During the initial stages of the reform programme which started in 1979 under Deng Xiaoping's leadership and inspiration, the vast majority of foreign investors in China—probably over 80 per cent—were overseas Chinese investors coming through Hong Kong. Naturally the Hong Kong investors concentrated on the areas where they felt most comfortable and familiar, that is the neighbouring province of Guangdong, from which many of them had originated a generation before. Even within Guangdong Province, most of the investment projects were small, were in light manufacturing and were concentrated around Guangzhou itself and one or two other towns, such as Dongguan, which was particularly favoured by Hong Kong businessmen.

In addition, the extraordinary success enjoyed by the Special Economic Zones which started in 1980, focused, above all, on Shenzhen which started with a population of 50,000 people and, by the end of the decade, had reach 2.5m and was a thriving metropolis and a 'buffer zone' between Hong Kong and Guangdong Province. Much of the real estate development, stock market and property speculation and other activities which were not allowed in China itself became rampant in Shenzhen.

As time went by, however, the focus and source of foreign investment in China gradually changed. The sources began to diversify to include not only the overseas Chinese (although they still dominated the picture) but also US, European and Japanese companies which saw the need to be present in what is clearly the world's largest new market-place. In addition, the location of factories began to spread much more widely than the southern provinces, towards Shanghai, Beijing and Tianjin, the North and even the central provinces of China with their large populations. In 1993, for example, it was estimated that over US$100bn of foreign direct investment in China was announced, with about 30 per cent actually contracted and remitted into the country. Among the large number of projects included in this figure were such well known names as Chrysler, Volkswagen, Pilkington Glass, Peugeot, Coca Cola, IBM, American International Group (for life insurance products) and various international banks and brokers which began to see China's financial system opening up for the first time.

China responded to the thirst of foreign investors by making all the right announcements on economic reform, market opening, tax, currency and other issues of concern.

Capital markets in China

The Shanghai stock market re-opened in December 1990 and has made remarkable progress in the three and a half years since. It has today a market capitalization of over US$17bn with over one hundred companies listed and many more waiting to be issued. There is little doubt that the Chinese authorities have placed the development of Shanghai as the new financial centre of China. The massive construction taking place on the south bank of the Huangpu River, in the area known as Pudong, is the key to this development. Not only will the stock exchange move to Pudong in 1995, but Pudong itself will be a Special Economic Zone, with significant tax and regulatory advantages to foreign investors, with a free trade zone designed to encourage the development of light manufacturing, industry and a container port, which may be linked to a new deep-water port on the Yangtze River estuary. Shanghai's position at the centre of China and the move of the Yangtze River makes it critically important for the modernization of the country as a whole. Over 30 foreign banks now have offices in Shanghai. It has the largest foreign exchange market in China. The stock market is an integral part of this whole development and will become the national stock exchange of China, with companies drawn from all over the country being listed and traded through a centrally-computerized exchange in Shanghai.

History

The first stock market in China was recorded as early as 1914, with the development of a securities market in Shanghai, when a set of regulations governing the trading of securities was enacted by the old government of Shanghai. In 1920, China's first securities exchange was opened in Shanghai, primarily to trade government bonds. Other exchanges later opened in Beijing and Tianjin. Securities trading was abolished when the Chinese communists took over China from the Kuomintang in 1949. The Beijing and Tianjin securities exchanges were reopened in 1949 and 1950 respectively, but were again closed in 1952. After Deng Xiaoping came to power in 1978 and the implementation of widespread economic reforms, fledgling securities markets started to re-emerge in various major cities around the country, summarized as follows.

- 1984 Public issue of shares in Shanghai for Fielo Acoustics Company, the first public issue of securities in China since 1949.

■ 1986 The creation of over-the-counter (OTC) or secondary market in Shanghai. The first share trading counter was set up by the Shanghai branch of the Industrial and Commercial Bank of China.

■ 1988 Shenzhen starts to issue public shares with the listing of the Shenzhen Development Bank on the Shenzhen OTC market.

■ 1990 The establishment of the first centralized stock exchange in China in Shenzhen on 1 December. Official opening of the Shanghai Stock Exchange on 19 December.

■ 1991 Official opening of the Shenzhen Stock Exchange on 3 July. The stock market opens its doors to foreign investors with the issue rules governing B shares in Shanghai and Shenzhen set by local governments and respective local branches of the People's Bank of China (PBOC). First international offering of B shares on the Shenzhen Stock Exchange — Shenzhen Southern Glass Joint Stock Co Ltd.

■ 1992 First international offering of B shares on the SSE — Shanghai Vacuum Electron Device Co Ltd. First B shares listed on the SSE — Shanghai Vacuum Co Ltd., 21 February. First B shares listed on the Shenzhen Stock Exchange — Shenzhen Southern Glass Joint Stock Co Ltd on 28 February.

Different types of share in China

There are three types of shares presently listed by Chinese companies:

- 1. **'A' shares** which are shares held by the state, Chinese corporations and individual domestic Chinese residents, and traded both in Shanghai and Shenzhen.

- 2. **'B' shares** which are reserved for foreigners, traded by Hong Kong brokers, but listed in Shanghai and Shenzhen, in US dollars and Hong Kong dollars respectively.
- 3. **'H' shares** which are issued by mainland Chinese corporations, and listed on the Hong Kong Stock Exchange.

'A' shares have tended to trade at a premium to 'B' shares due to the huge demand by Chinese investors for any kind of share. Personal savings in China have grown very rapidly over the past few years and although real estate markets are beginning to develop there are still few outlets for Chinese investors. 'B' shares, on the other hand, although they were greeted with great excitement by the international investment community in the spring of 1992, have subsequently been rather a disappointment since they are illiquid and difficult to trade. There is not a very large choice of companies in the list of 'B' shares (see Figure 4.5).

Shanghai 'B' shares

China Textile Machinery	Sh Haixin	Sh Rubber Belt
Sh Chlor Alkali	Sh Hero	Sh Sanmao Textile
Sh Dajiang Group	Sh Jin Jiang Tower	Sh Industrial Sewing Machine
Sh Dazhong Taxi	Sh Jinqiao Export	China Sh Shang-Ling Refrigerators
Sh Diesel Engine	Sh Lian Hua Fibre	Sh Tyre & Rubber
Sh Erfangji	Sh Outer Gaoqiao	Sh Vacuum & Electric
China First Pencil	Sh Phoenix Bicycle	Sh Wingsung Stationery
Sh Forever Bicycle	Sh Yaohua Pilkington Glass	
Sh Friendship Store	Sh Refrigerator Compressor	

Shenzhen 'B' Shares

Sz China Bicycles	Zhuhai Lizhu Pharm	Sz Tellus Machinery
Chiwan Wharf	Sz Real Estate Group	Sz Tsann Kuen (China) Enterprise
Sz Fiyta Holdings	Sz China Merchants Shekou Port Service	Sz Vanke
Sz Gintian Industry	Sz Shenbao	Sz Victor Onward
Sz Huafa Electronics	China Southern Glass	Sz Yili Mineral Water
Sz Konka Electronics	Sz Petrochem	Sz Zhongchu
Sz Lionda	Sz Properties	

Figure 4.5 China: list of 'B' shares

Internationalization of China's securities markets

With the growing international demand for Chinese instruments and Chinese shares of any kind, some Chinese companies have gone straight to the largest international stock exchange—that is, in New York—to raise capital. The first one was Brilliance China, listed in New York in October 1992, although the company was Brilliance Incorporated. Brilliance is, in fact, China's largest manufacturer of minivans from the knock-down kits from Toyota. This example will undoubtedly inspire other companies in China to list overseas although the authorities are trying to control the flow. Two Shanghai companies are currently listing their ADRs in New York in the spring of 1994. Further listings are expected in London, Vancouver and

Singapore, among other places, in 1994-5. However, it is certainly true that the Chinese authorities, together with the Hong Kong stock exchange, have planned that Hong Kong will be the principal location for raising capital by Chinese companies in the next few years, both before and after 1997. There are, in addition, a great number of China plays listed in Hong Kong and other Asian markets and available for international investors.

How to invest in China

If the prospect of direct investment in Chinese factories or Chinese businesses were to appear daunting to the average investor and if, in addition, the risks and the difficulties of buying Shanghai and Shenzhen listed shares were a disincentive, Hong Kong provides several attractive options. The advantage of the Hong Kong market is that it is large, well-established and easy to trade in. The laws are British laws. The currency is the Hong Kong dollar which has been, for more than ten years, at a fixed-exchange rate to the US dollar and there is no problem about moving capital in and out. There is an increasingly large number of China funds listed not only in Hong Kong but also in London and New York. The following closed-end funds may be of interest.

- BOC China Fund (Bank of China)
- Cathay Clemente
- China & Eastern (Barings)
- China Assets
- China Fund (Morgan Grenfell)
- China Investment & Development (Kleinwort Benson)
- China Investment Co (Crosby)
- China Investment Trust (Jupiter Tyndall)
- Chine Investissement 2000 (Banque Worms)
- Fleming Chinese (Jardine Fleming)
- Greater China Fund Inc (Barings)
- JF China Investment Company (Jardine Fleming)
- JF China Region Fund Inc (Jardine Fleming)
- JF Chian Region Ltd (Jardine Fleming)
- KWR China Fund (Rothschild & Ka Wah Bank)
- Lloyd George Standard Chartered China Fund
- Shanghai Growth
- SHK Pearl River Delta Investment (SHK)
- The China Fund Inc (Wardley)
- Wardley China Fund

In addition, there are some open-ended funds which are available to US and European investors.

- Indosuez Asia Shanghai Fund
- Jupiter Tyndall GF China
- SHK China Fund
- Barclays China (PRC) Fund
- GT Shenzhen & China Fund

The Eaton Vance Greater China Growth Fund was launched in December 1992 and has grown rapidly in its first year showing a performance of 80 per cent. There are also the following SEC-registered funds.

- Greater China Fund Inc — Barings
- JF China Region Fund Inc — Jardine Fleming
- The China Fund Inc — Wardley
- Templeton China World Inc — Templeton

In terms of shares which may be seen to be good China plays there is, in addition to the B shares and H shares listed (see Figure 4.6), an interesting selection of so called 'red chips,' which are listed in Hong Kong (see Figure 4.7) but are generally owned or controlled by Chinese corporations, which have achieved a listing in Hong Kong either by acquisition or by a 'back door' listing. The largest by far is CITIC Hong Kong which is the subsidiary of the China International Trust and Investment Corporation and which has broad holdings in industry, aviation, property and infrastructure development. In addition, major Chinese corporations such as China Resources, China Travel and China Merchant Steamship have listed subsidiaries in Hong Kong. The large provincial organizations such as Guangdong Enterprises have also listed some of their attractive franchises in the fast-growing province adjacent to Hong Kong.

Altogether these may be among the most attractive shares for the long-term investor to consider as a way into China using Hong Kong as an avenue. These red chips have strong parent support from their PRC parent companies. They make asset injections at a considerable discount to avoid dilution of earnings and they provide investment opportunities in industries which are not currently available in the form of B and H shares. Information can be difficult to obtain and, therefore, a firsthand visit and careful analysis is necessary to evaluate the company fundamentals.

The Chinese index has been quite volatile in its first two years, 1992-3, and the Chinese currency, the yuan, has dropped quite dramatically against the US dollar. These are among some of the risks which investors in China must consider.

Current 'H' shares
Beiren Printing
Guangzhou Shipyard
Kunming Machine Tool
Maanshan Iron & Steel
Shanghai Petrochemical
Tsingtao Brewery
Yizheng Chemical

List of additional companies expected in 1994

Company	*Business*
Changchun First Automobile Works	Transport
Chengdu Cable	Cable mfg.
Dongbei Electricity Transmission	Electricity
Foshan Ceramics	Ceramics mfg
Guangdong-Shenzhen Railway	Transport
Harbin Electricity	Power supply
Hubei Second Automobile Works	Transport
Luoyang Glassworks	Float-glass mfg.
Panda Electronics	TV & video mfg.
Qingling Automobiles	Transport
Shanxi Jingwei Textile	Textiles
Shandong Zhouxian Power	Power supply
Xian Aircraft Manufacturing	Aviation
Wuhan Iron & Steel	Steel-making
Jilin Petrochemical	Petrochemicals
China Eastern Airlines	Aviation
China Southern Airlines	Aviation
Huanen Int'l Power Development	Power supply
Huanen Electricity	Power supply
Legend Holdings	Computers
Shenye	Investment
Shanghai Hualian Shipbuilding	Shipbuilding
Shijiazhuang First Pharmaceutical	Pharmaceuticals

Figure 4.6 China: list of 'H' shares

Settlement procedures

- Shanghai — T + 3. Trades are quoted and settled in US dollars. All transactions are settled via book entries at the clearing house, Securities Central Clearing & Registration Corporation (SCCRC).

- Shenzhen — T + 3. Trades are quoted and settled in Hong Kong dollars. Each 'B' share issuing company has a foreign bank branch as its clearing bank which serves as the registration agent for the issue. There are three foreign clearing banks: Citibank, HSBC and Standard Chartered Bank. All transactions are settled via book entries at the clearing banks.

	Market capitalization (HK$m)
Citic Pacific	40,160
China Overseas	7445
Guangdong Investment	7087
Shougang Concord Int.	5203
Guangzhou Investment	5115
China Travel	5020
China Resources	4611
World Trade Centre Group	3926
Kader Investment	3496
Ka Wah Bank	3418
Denway	2890
China Aerospace	2783
Union Bank	2016
First Shanghai	1828
Continental Mariner	1554
Lolliman	1359
Paragon	1307
Santai	1202
Ong Holdings	1133
ONFEM (Laws Property)	1050
Hoi Shing	638
Chee Shing	559
Hai Hong	502
Fu Hui	497
Min Xin Holdings	488
Paladin	463
Everbright (Newfoundland) Int.	390
International Industries	382
Seabase International	83

Figure 4.7 Red chip companies listed in Hong Kong

	Market capitalization (HK$ million)
CITIC Pacific	40,160
China Overseas Land	7445
Guangdong Inv	7087
Magang	6455
Guangzhou Inv	5115
Shougang Int'l	5203
Shanghai Petrochemical	6434
China Travel HK	5020
China Resources Ent	4611
Ka Wah Bank	3418
World Trade	3926
Tsingtao Brewery	3538
Denway Inv	2890
Union Bank	2016
China Aerospace	2783
Shougang Grand	2690
Stone Electronic	2040
Continental Mariner	1554
Paragon	1307
Wing Shan	1240

Figure 4.8 China: 20 largest stocks by market capitalization

Company	**Market cap. (US$m)**	*Company*	**Volume (US$ '000s)**
Shanghai Tyre & Rubber	194.5	Shanghai Tyre & Rubber	723
Shenzhen China Bicycle	174.8	Shenzhen China Bicycle	552
Shenzhen Tsann Kuenn	104.4	Shanghai Jinquiao Export	506
Shanghai Erfangi	97.7	Shanghai Erfangi	431
Shenzhen Southern Glass	80.0	Shanghai Outer Gaoqiao	409
Shanhai Jinqiao Export	75.9	Shanghai Chlor Alkali	342
Shenzhen Zhao Shang	75.4	Shenzhen Southern Glass	276
Shenzhen Konka	72.4	Shenzhen Zhao Shang	235
Shanghai Outer Gaoqiao	58.7	Shanghai Dazhong Taxi	185
Shanghai Dazhong Taxi	57.1	Shenzhen Vanke Co.	169
Shenzhen Vanke Co.	53.6	Shenzhen Tsann Kuen	125
Shenzhen Gintian	43.3	Shanghai China Textile	87
Shenzhen Huafa	35.4	Shenzhen Chiwan Wharf	87
Shenzhen Property	35.3	Shanghai Refra	72
Shenzhen Zhuhai Spec	29.8	Shanghai Wing Song	53
Shanghai Vacuum	28.0	Shenzhen Yili Mineral	52
Shenzhen Chiwan Wharf	25.4	Shenzhen Gintian	51
Shenzhen Victor Onward	21.9	Shanghai Vacuum	49
Shanghai Refra	20.3	Shenzhen Tellus	45
Shanghai Wing Song	15.0	Shenzhen Petrochemical	34

Figure 4.9 China: 20 largest companies by market capitalization and average daily volume

Chapter 5

Hong Kong

Population:	5.8m
Gross national product:	US$109.7bn
Market capitalization:	US$235bn
Currency/US$:	7.80 HK dollars

Is Hong Kong an emerging market? This debate among investment managers has been somewhat muted in 1993. With the listing on the Hong Kong Stock Exchange of six major Chinese mainland companies—Tsingtao Beer, Shanghai Petrochemical, Beiren Printing, Guangzhou Shipyard, Maanshan Iron and Steel, and Kunming Machine Tool—there can no longer be any question that Hong Kong is a major stock market for China, which is itself the largest developing economy in the world. The characteristic of the companies listed above also clearly manifests a bias towards heavy industry and areas of basic technology which will logically change the make up of the Hong Kong Stock Exchange over the next few years, from its traditional characteristic of a market of trading companies, property companies, utilities and a handful of manufacturers to a market which more fully reflects the industrial weight of China and the large Chinese corporations, such as CITIC and China Resources among others. So, although Hong Kong, with a per capita income of nearly US$20,000 or well in excess of many European countries, is far above the defined level of emerging market categories, it must be included because of its being the main entry point into China.

Looking at the history of Hong Kong it is apparent that it has always been China's window on the world. Even during the 1950-78 period of hardline Maoist totalitarianism, when China was economically isolated from the rest of the world, the only source of foreign exchange for the People's Republic was through selling water and basic foodstuffs to Hong Kong. Western businessmen flocked during those years to the annual Canton trade fair where it was already apparent that China had the capability of competing in such basic products as toys, silk garments and electrical products. Since 1978, the latent dynamism and energy of China's entrepreneurs and workers has been released so that China has become what it was always

	1988	1989	1990	1991	1992	1993
Population (m)	5.67	5.73	5.79	5.85	5.9	5.96
GNP (US$bn)	55.6	64	71.3	81.2	94.9	109.7
Real GNP growth (%)	8.3	2.8	3.2	4.2	5	5.4
Per capita income (US$)	9806	11169	12314	13880	16085	18406
Exports (US$bn)	63.2	73.1	82	98.2	118.6	140
Imports (US$bn)	64.3	72.2	82.7	100.3	122.9	145.6
Foreign direct investment (US$m)	3355	1900	2200	2600	3000	3300
Inflation	7.5	10.1	9.8	12	9.4	9.4
Interest rates (lending)	10	10	10	8.5	6.5	6.8
International reserves (US$bn)	6.9	7.5	8.3	10.7	12.8	13.8
Market capitalization (US$bn)	74.4	77.6	83.3	121.7	170.8	300.5
No. of listed companies	304	294	295	357	413	465
Index performance in US$	16.7	5.5	6.6	42.1	28.3	115.7
Price/earnings ratios (P/E)	12.5	11.8	10.1	13.1	20.6	16.4
Earnings per share (EPS) growth	31	13	3	24	28	25.8
Average daily turnover (US$m)	103	160	149	173	359	575
Dividend yield	4.5	5.5	5.8	4.7	4.3	3.8
Currency to US$ (HK dollar)	7.8	7.81	7.8	7.78	7.74	7.8

Figure 5.1 Hong Kong: key statistics

destined to be, a trading giant with US$150bn of trade with the western world, growing at nearly 30 per cent per annum.

The extraordinary recovery in confidence since 4 June 1989 has directly impacted the Hong Kong stock market which has grown by nearly five times in four years. The number of listed companies in Hong Kong has nearly doubled, with one new issue virtually every week, often over-subscribed by 50 or 100 times. More and more small Chinese family businesses with sales or assets in mainland China have sought a listing in Hong Kong. More and more international investors have seen clearly that Hong Kong, with its sound British legal and commercial system, its Hong Kong dollar firmly pegged to the US dollar and its international accounting standards, represents the best possible avenue for investing in China.

It is also true to say that in only three years' time, on 1 July 1997, Hong Kong will be re-incorporated into China as a Special Administrative Region. One of the many valuable legacies which China will inherit from Britain is a long-established and smooth-running stock exchange, internationally-recognized as having the highest standards of investor protection and corporate disclosure. With a market capitalization of over US$300bn and nearly 500 listed companies, it is far too large for any US pension fund or Japanese insurance company to ignore any longer. Since the 1987 stock market crash Hong Kong has greatly improved its listing procedures and, as a consequence, has greatly increased the flow of international investment into this

	Market capitalization (US$m)
HSBC	31,095.9
HK Telecom	22,793.1
Hutchison	17,399.9
Hang Seng Bank	16,013.0
SHK Prop.	15,208.2
China Light	13,177.3
Swire Pacific	12,447.0
Cheung Kong	11,651.8
Wharf Holdings	8414.0
Henderson Land	7795.4
HK Land	7528.3
HK Electric	7271.1
New World Dev.	6732.4
Jardine Matheson	6604.9
Citic Pacific	5161.0
Wheelock	4980.2
Hopewell Hldgs	4842.8
Cathay Pacific	4676.0
World International	4396.5
HK & China Gas	4250.8

Figure 5.2 Hong Kong: 20 largest companies by market capitalization (as at 31 Dec. 1993)

market. As a fund management centre it has grown enormously in the past ten years. According to some estimates there is nearly US$500bn of assets held in the territory. The great British journalist, William Rees-Mogg, has described Hong Kong as the most dynamic city in the world and the prototype of 21st century capitalism with its entrepreneurial dynamism and free-wheeling capitalist energy.

Although China clearly intends to develop its own stock exchanges, led by Shanghai but followed not only by Shenzhen (a special zone adjacent to Hong Kong) but by other cities such as Shenyang in the North East, Shengdu in Sichuan province, Wuhan in central China, Tianjin and many others, it will be, even by the most optimistic forecasts, at least 5-10 years before Shanghai can begin to rival Hong Kong as a financial centre. In the meantime, the flood of mainland investment into property and shares in Hong Kong in 1990-94 has been extraordinary, with an estimated US$20bn flowing into Hong Kong assets. The Bank of China has built a towering new headquarters. China Resources has expanded and has dozens of subsidiaries in the territory. CITIC has become the leading Chinese conglomerate, with a US$2.5bn capitalization and major stakes in the airline, Cathay Pacific, in Hong Kong Telecom and in the airport handling company, HACTL.

Even though foreign investors are astonished by the rapidly-changing skylines and extraordinarily speedy modernization of Hong Kong, the less

Rank	**Company**	**% of HSI**
1	HSBC	11.5
2	HK Telecom	8.5
3	Hutchison	6.5
4	Hang Seng Bank	5.9
5	SHK Properties	5.6
6	China Light	4.9
7	Swire Pacific	4.6
8	Cheung Kong	4.3
9	Wharf Holdings	3.1
10	Henderson Land	2.9
11	HK Land	2.8
12	HK Electric	2.7
13	New World Development	2.5
14	Jardine Matheson	2.4
15	Citic Pacific	1.9
		70.1
	Total HSI market capitalization = US$269,522.7	

Figure 5.3 Hong Kong: The Hang Seng Index 15 largest stocks (as at 31 December 1993)

visible fact is that it has taken decades to build up the infrastructure and, even more important, to build up the confidence which is the most basic foundation of a successful business centre. That fragile legacy may survive the handover to Chinese rule but the first decade of the 21st century will be the testing time for Hong Kong to answer the question whether it can maintain its extraordinary role which, in 1994, appears to be China's financial centre and the most dynamic city on the planet.

Exchange address

The Stock Exchange of Hong Kong Ltd.
Main Floor
One and Two Exchange Square
8 Connaught Place
Central
Hong Kong

Tel: 522 1122 / Fax: 810 4475

Chapter 6

Indonesia

Population:	187m
Gross national product:	$124.8bn
Market capitalization:	$25bn
Currency:	2102 rupiah

Indonesia's coming of age as an emerging market occurred rapidly in the early 1990s. Compared with the former British colonies of Singapore, Malaysia and India, Indonesia had, during the Dutch colonial period which ended in 1949, little tradition of an established capital market. The first international fund to invest in the Indonesian market only appeared in 1989. Since then the growth of the Jakarta Stock Exchange has been extraordinary, with market capitalization growing by a factor of 100 times in five years, up to US$25bn, in late 1993 and the number of listed companies open to foreign investors increasing from 7 to over 170.

Over this five-year period, however, there has been a boom and bust cycle in Jakarta—characteristic of a newly-open stock market—which attracted a sudden flood of foreign capital, with which it was unable to cope in terms of market regulations, dealing and listing procedures or accounting standards. Many foreign investors were bitterly disappointed by the poor quality of Indonesian corporate earnings announcements and a sudden bear market ensued. The market, which had traded as high as a P/E of 30 times, fell to a far more reasonable 10 times. Subsequently, the fundamental virtues of Indonesia's political stability and steady economic growth came back into focus and the market started gradually to recover in 1992-3.

Standards have improved and the number of international brokerage companies participating in Jakarta increased. There can be no doubt to a dispassionate observer of the potential of this enormous country which will have a population of 200m before the end of the century. Indonesia is also a large oil producer and exporter, has substantial reserves of gold and many other minerals and has rivalled Malaysia in plantation resources, with a growing acreage of palm oil planted and available tropical timber forests. Along with Brazil, Indonesia is considered by ecologists to have one of the richest and most varied flora and fauna in the tropics.

	1988	1989	1990	1991	1992	1993
Population (m)	173	176	179	182	184	187
GNP (US$bn)	90.6	93	104	110.9	117.6	124.8
Real GNP growth (%)	5.7	7.4	7.4	6.6	6	6.2
Per capita income (US$)	524	528	581	609	639	667
Exports (US$bn)	19.5	22.1	25.7	29.1	33.9	39.3
Imports (US$bn)	14.6	16.3	21.8	25.6	27	30.2
Foreign direct investment (US$m)	3090	3303	5206	5250	6120	6000
Inflation	7.4	6.1	9.5	9.5	7.6	8.5
Interest rates (prime)	22.5	21.5	26	28	24	20
International reserves (US$bn)	5	5.4	7.5	9.3	10.4	11.2
Market capitalization (US$bn)	0.25	2.4	6.2	8.1	12.1	25
No. of listed companies	24	76	123	98	158	170
Index performance in US$ (%)	n/a	25.3	1.3	43.7	7.7	109.8
Price/earnings (P/E) ratios	5	9.6	17.6	17.1	16	20.4
Earnings per share (EPS growth)	19	41	50	8	0	6.5
Average daily turnover (US$m)	0.07	4.4	13.5	12	13	20
Dividend yield	2.2	1.5	2.8	2.9	2.8	2.1
Currency to US$ (rupiah)	1735	1784	1889	1984	2064	2098

Figure 6.1 Indonesia: key statistics

However, the real transformation of Indonesia, since the collapse of the oil price in 1986, has been achieved by the group of pragmatic economists in the ministries of trade and finance in the Suharto administration. This meant that oil exports have fallen from being 95 per cent of Indonesia's foreign exchange earnings, to less than 40 per cent. Taking their place has been a rapid growth in manufactured exports in such areas as textiles and garments, shoes and electronics. A combination of the long-established Chinese business community, in Jakarta and Surabaya, with a population of over 6m and a steady inflow of Japanese corporate capital, with the large indigenous labour force, has meant that Indonesia is one of the few countries able to rival India and China as a long-term competitor of the newly-industrialized countries. Whilst it is smaller in population than the other two Asian giants, it is richer in resources. It is the least known because it is the most varied of all the Asian nations and, as a consequence, it has often proved a difficult and testing place for foreign direct investors. It requires patience and application to succeed in a foreign joint venture with Indonesian partners and it is still only possible to own 49 per cent of an Indonesian business.

The Chinese, whilst small in number—less than 3 per cent of the population—command nearly 80 per cent of the commercial life of the country. Much of their wealth has been siphoned away to Singapore, Hong Kong

Company	**Market cap. (US$m)**	*Company*	**Volume (US$m)**
Barito Pacific Timber	4348	Barito Pacific Timber	6.93
Indocement	3521	Bank Inter. Indonesia	3.62
Astra International	2102	Astra International	3.39
Gudang Garam	1574	Indocement	1.70
Unilever Indonesia	1153	Semen Gresik	1.56
Indah Kiat Paper & Pulp	1088	Japfa	1.35
Bank Inter. Indonesia	1062	Charoen Pokphand	1.25
Inti Indorayon Utama	888	Indah Kiat Paper & Pulp	1.18
Jakarta Int'l Hotel	842	Kalbe Farma	1.18
Kalbe Farma	794	Duta Aggada R.	1.13
H.M. Sampoerna	717	Semen Cibinong	1.03
Bank Bali	574	Polysindo	1.02
Duta Anggada R.	571	Smart	0.88
Lippo Bank	569	H.M. Sampoerna	0.82
Polysindo	545	Argha Karya	0.62
Bank Dagang Nas. Ind.	537	Bank Niaga	0.54
Semen Gresik	527	Indorayon	0.50
Bank Danamon	494	Modernland	0.48
Branta Mulia	474	Lippo Bank	0.47
Modern Photo	471	Gadha Tunggal	0.35

Figure 6.2 Indonesia: 20 largest companies by market capitalization and average daily volume

and other overseas destinations. There have been some complaints in recent years that they have redirected vast amounts of their Indonesian-earned capital towards investment in China. A long-term observer must, therefore, conclude that there is a political risk, that ethnic tension and disparities of wealth could give rise to a further confidence crisis in Indonesia when Suharto goes. Political risk factors must be balanced, therefore, against the great economic potential of the country but will probably mean that Indonesia commands a slightly lower multiple than Singapore, Malaysia or Thailand.

Exchange address

Capital Market Executive Agency (Indonesia Stock Exchange)
Jalan Medan Merdeka Selatan 13/14
PO Box 439, Jakarta
Indonesia

Tel: 6221 361 460 or 6221 365 509

Chapter 7

South Korea

Population:	45m
Gross national product:	$321.5bn
Market capitalization:	$119bn
Currency:	810 won

The South Korean market in the 1980s was the perfect example of an emerging market which rapidly came of age and began to display the dynamic growth which had been characteristic of the national economy in the preceding decade. The number of Korean companies listed doubled over the 1985-90 period to nearly 700 listed stocks. During the same period, the amount of capitalization grew from US$7bn to U$110bn, at which level it was equivalent to 46 per cent of GNP. For the past two years, however, the Korean economy has been in a period of relatively slow growth and the market has also marked time with fewer new listings and sluggish earnings per share growth.

Looking at the political and economic background in Korea, it is apparent to many foreign observers that, having been the most successful of all the newly-industrialized countries in the 1970s and 1980s, South Korea appears to be going through a period of fundamental structural change. On the one hand the military authoritarian government, which ruled from 1962 until 1987, has given way to a fully-liberalized democracy; a new government under Kim Yung Sam took office in 1993 with a determined policy to stamp out corruption and institute political reforms. At the same time, the Korean export machine, which powered the 9 per cent average economic growth of the country's economy over the past twenty years, has sputtered to a halt as costs have risen and as consumer demand in major western economies has slowed down, Korea has been increasingly squeezed by low-cost competitors such as China.

Many of the industries which gave Korea such an enviable growth rate—shoes, textiles and consumer electronics, for example—are no longer appropriate for a middle-class economy with a per capita income of over US$7000 and an increasingly restive and demanding labour force. Many big US multinationals which had used Korea for twenty years as a cheap produc-

	1988	1989	1990	1991	1992	1993
Population (m)	42	42.4	43.5	43.9	44.4	44.8
GNP (US$bn)	172.8	211.2	242.2	281.7	294.5	321.5
Real GNP growth (%)	12.4	6.8	9.3	8.4	4.7	6.2
Per capita income (US$)	4114	4981	5568	6417	6633	7176
Exports (US$bn)	60.7	62.4	65	71.9	76.6	82.4
Imports (US$bn)	51.8	61.5	69.8	81.5	81.8	85.9
Foreign direct investment (US$m)	894	812	895	1175	803	900
Inflation	7.1	5.7	8.6	9.3	6.2	5
Interest rates (lending)	10.1	11.3	10	10	10	8.5
International reserves (US$bn)	12.4	15.2	14.8	13.7	17.1	18.8
Market capitalization (US$bn)	94.3	140.5	110.3	96.1	107.4	119
No. of listed companies	502	626	669	686	687	693
Index performance in US$ (%)	100.6	1.4	-27.5	-17.4	6.9	24.6
Price/earnings (P/E) ratios	23	23.2	18.8	15	21.6	19.7
Earnings per share (EPS growth)	31	10	21	6	4	9
Average daily turnover (US$m)	281	420	264	288	397	430
Dividend yield	1.1	1.2	1.7	1.9	2.1	1.9
Currency to US$ (won)	684	680	716	761	788	810

Figure 7.1 South Korea: key statistics

tion source have now turned to new areas such as China, Indonesia and even Vietnam. However, any long-term observer of the Korean people is bound to take the view that they are flexible, determined and extremely hardworking. (Their average working week is the longest in the world at over fifty hours.) The instance of their boldness and flexibility is the enthusiasm with which Korean businessmen have grasped the new opportunities in Eastern Europe and especially in Russia. Korean consumer products have certainly made considerable headway in these new markets, compared with their competitors in Japan. However, the profitability of pioneering into new areas, where payment in hard currency is often uncertain and difficult, is not always assured.

Such, too, has been the experience of many large Korean corporations which took advantage of the re-establishment of diplomatic relations with China in August 1992 to accelerate rapidly their direct investment in manufacturing plants and joint ventures, mainly in the Chinese peninsular province of Shandong which faces Korea across the Yellow Sea. This experience, too, has not been an entirely happy one for Korean investors and there have already been reports of labour problems and misunderstandings between the Korean and Chinese partners in such joint ventures.

The real challenge, however, for South Korea in the 1990s is the inevitable economic integration with North Korea, which must occur, although the timing is impossible to guess. Most international observers looking at North Korea in early 1994 would give the survival of the country and its isolated, hardline communist regime only months at most. There are reports of starvation. The country is surviving on small remittances from the immigrant Korean community in Japan. There is virtually no hard currency. Kim Il Sung and his son, Kim Jong Il, have successfully isolated the country from nearly all outside influences but the disappearance of its two major backers, the Soviet Union and China, has left the country economically and militarily isolated and vulnerable. In the 1950-53 war, North Korea only survived with China's backing and support. Now that South Korea has successfully completed the diplomatic encirclement of their Northern neighbour it appears to be only a matter of time before the last piece of the jigsaw puzzle of North Asia falls into place and Korea becomes an open country. When this happens, the 20m people of North Korea will join their 40m compatriots in the South to form an economic dynamo which will challenge Japan in many key industrial sectors. (The coal resources and the industrial base built by the Japanese prior to 1945 were all in the northern half of the peninsula.)

Korea will not make the same mistakes as Germany. There will be no costly reunification programme. The currency will not be maintained at an artificially high level. Wage rates in the North will be cheap and competitive with China. The border is likely to be maintained to prevent massive flows of refugees from North to South. South Korea will have an immediate benefit in being able to cut its very heavy defence spending, currently about 6 per cent of GNP, which is the highest in the world apart from Israel. The political risk factor affecting the valuation of South Korean asset prices will be improved overnight. The South Korean market was standing in late 1993 on a P/E of ten times prospective earnings. With falling interest rates and improving exports, there is every possibility that the South Korean market, which has lagged behind the rest of Asia in 1993, will enjoy an excellent performance in 1994 which would be further enhanced by political developments of the nature outlined above.

The Korean Stock Exchange

The Korean Stock Exchange was set up in 1956 with the Securities and Exchange Law being passed in 1962. Regulation is carried out by the Ministry of Finance with the Securities and Exchange Commission, the Securities Supervisory Board and the Korean Stock Exchange acting as the daily regulators.

Company	Market cap. (US$bn)	Company	Volume (US$m)
KEPCO	14.68	Hyundai Motor Co.	10.57
POSCO	3.07	Goldstar	9.74
Samsung Electronics	2.89	Ssangyong Cement	9.19
Goldstar	2.12	Samsung Display Devices	8.61
Hyundai Motor Co.	2.08	KoreaExpress	8.58
Hanil Bank	1.63	Hyundai Eng. & Const.	8.28
Korea First Bank	1.62	Daewoo Corp	7.66
Cho Heung Bank	1.61	Daewoo Electronics	6.39
Shinhan Bank	1.60	Dae Han Jung Suok	6.27
Kia Motor Corp	1.59	Dong Ah Construction	5.46
Daewoo Corp	1.59	Korea Long Term Credit Bank	5.41
Daewoo Securities	1.48	Choong Nam Spinning	5.22
Commercial Bank of Korea	1.46	Hyundai Motor Service	5.18
Bank of Seoul	1.46	Keumkang	5.00
Yukong	1.44	Kolong Industries	4.63
Lucky Ltd.	1.42	Shinsegae	4.56
Daewoo Heavy Industries	1.38	Cheil Foods & Chemicals	4.47
Lucky Securities	1.24	Pang Lim	4.39
Dong Suh Securities	1.22	Daewoo Heavy Industries	4.37
Daewoo Electronics	1.20	The Commercial Bank of Korea	4.29

Figure 7.2 South Korea: 20 largest companies by market capitalization and average daily volume

The market is divided into two sections, with new issues initially going on the second section. Each year, the exchange decides whether a company ought to move up or down. All listed companies are included in the Korean Composite Stock Price Index (KOSPI) which is the only official index, although it has various sub-indices. It is important to note that individuals still make up over 40 per cent of investment in the stock market and they tend to look at the absolute price rather than at appropriate valuations. This has been changing slowly but it makes bonus issues—usually a distribution of the revaluation reserve—popular.

Foreign investment has been possible on a direct basis since 1 January 1993. However, individuals are limited to 3 per cent of a company and total foreign holdings may not exceed 10 per cent. There are certain limited exceptions to this and companies may impose lower limits if they wish.

Much of the Korean economy is dominated by 'Chaebols'. These are family-owned and managed companies with assets of more than 400bn won (US$150m) which feature a complex system of cross-ownership with their subsidiary and affiliated companies. They are extremely powerful: in 1990, the top ten accounted for 77.3 per cent of GNP and the top fifty, 97.4 per cent. This dominance makes their relationship with the government complex. In weak economic circumstances the politicians look to them to rescue the situation but, in prosperous times, the authorities try to reduce their power. This is the current situation. The Fair Trade Commission has talked about lowering the limit on equity investment in subsidiaries, encouraging private companies to list and limiting the voting rights held by tax-sheltering non-profit organizations. Cross-payment guarantees between subsidiaries have already been limited. In the past, the Chaebols have been adept at getting around new regulations and the government is naturally cautious because of its unwillingness to harm the economy.

Technical notes

- Settlement is two working days after trading. 40 per cent of the order value is required as a deposit. Institutions used to be wholly exempted from this requirement but now have to provide a 20 per cent deposit.

- The Korean Securities Settlement Corporation (KSSC) operates a book-entry system.

- Foreign shareholders must appoint a recognized institution which may be among others the Korean branch of a foreign bank or securities house.

- Commissions are negligible but are usually:

up to 200m won	0.4 per cent
200m to 500m won	0.3 per cent + 200,000 won
over 500m won	0.2 per cent + 700,000 won.

- Listing criteria: The time lapse since incorporation must been at least five years without any suspension of business. Minimum amount of capital stock and shareholders' equity must be 2bn won and 3bn won respectively. The number of outstanding shares must be at least 200,000 won. A public offering for the subscription or sale of shares must have been made within 6 months preceding the date of application; the number of shares offered to the public must be at least 30 per cent of the total number of outstanding shares as of the application date; and the number of voting shares offered to the public must be a minimum of 30 per cent of the total outstanding voting shares. The debt ratio as of the end of the last business year must be less than 15 times the average debt ratio of listed corporations in the same industry (not applicable to banking, insurance and leasing corporations). Normal profit and net profit must have been reported for each of the last three business years and the ratios of net profit to capital stock for 2 of the last 3 years must have been at least 150 per cent of the maximum interest rate on one year time deposits or at least 150 per cent for the last business year and at least 75 per cent for each of the two remaining years. There must have been no impairment of capital stock at the end of the last business year. The asset and earning value per share must exceed par value. In cases where a rights offering was made within one year preceding the application date, the total amount of the offerings must not have been more than 50 per cent of the capital stock as of the end of the business year 2 years before the application date. The ratio of shares held by each shareholder must have remained unchanged for one year preceding the date of application, excluding changes resulting from public offerings, etc. The issuer must have a contract with a transfer agent to provide clerical services related to share transfer. Stock certificates must be uniform stock certificates in accordance with the Securities Certificate Handling Regulation. There shall be no other condition counter to the best interests of investors or the public.

- Direct investment in equities has been allowed since January 1992. However, there is a 10 per cent foreign ownership limit and companies may decide to have a lower level. The introduction and repatriation of funds will be freely allowed—in exceptional circumstances—as long as a foreign exchange bank has confirmed their use for equity investment. Dividends are taxed at a rate that varies according to the relevant tax treaty. Capital gains are not taxed except on residents of countries without a tax treaty with South Korea. They face a rate of 10.75 per cent of the sum realized or 26.875 per cent of the profit, whichever is lower.

Exchange address

Korean Stock Exchange
33 Yoido-dong
Youngdeungpo-gu
Seoul 150-010
Korea

Tel: 822 780 2271. Fax: 822 786 0263

Chapter 8

Malaysia

Population:	18.9m
Gross national product:	\$63.4bn
Market capitalization:	\$175bn
Currency/US\$:	2.6 ringgit

Malaysia has been one of the great successes of the past twenty years, overcoming many obstacles and, among many doubters in the international investment community, to become today perhaps the most stable and rapidly growing of the developing economies of South East Asia. Following the secession of Singapore from the Federation of Malaysia in 1965, Malaysia immediately faced the problem of its mixed population which is 58 per cent Malay, 31 per cent Chinese and 11 per cent Indian (with a total today of 19m). In 1969, there were fierce anti-Chinese riots in the peninsula and the government reacted by enacting the new economic policy which, over the 1970-90 period, successfully redistributed the wealth of the country and particularly the share ownership structure from the dominant Chinese and British business elite to the Bumiputra or Malay population.

The fact that this was achieved peacefully was in no small part due to the fact that Malaysia's GNP has grown at a steady annual rate of over 7 per cent (and, in fact, over the past five years by 9 per cent per annum). Per capita income has grown by 50 per cent since 1988 and this has done a great deal to defuse the inter-ethnic jealousies which plagued its early years as an independent country. Like other Asian nations, Malaysia is also undergoing a transition of power from one generation to another. This is symbolized by Dr Mahathir Mohammed, who has been prime minister since 1980, and his designated successor, the young, 43-year old finance minister, Anwar Ibraham, who is now deputy prime minister. Anwar, who started his career as a fundamentalist Muslim firebrand also symbolizes the taming of the extremist elements in the ruling party, the UMNO, and their adoption of a pragmatic economic policy, which is far more welcoming to foreign investment, than in the immediately post colonial decades.

Malaysia has also transformed itself in the 1980s from being a predominantly plantation based economy dependent on rubber, tin and palm oil, to

	1988	1989	1990	1991	1992	1993
Population (m)	16.9	17.4	17.8	18.3	18.6	18.9
GNP (US$bn)	34.7	38	42.7	47.6	56	63.4
Real GNP growth (%)	8.9	9.2	9.8	8.8	8	8.6
Per capita income (US$)	2053	2184	2399	2601	3011	3337
Exports (US$bn)	20.9	24.8	28.9	34.3	38.6	48.7
Imports (US$bn)	15.3	20.9	27.1	34.4	35.9	39
Foreign direct investment (US$bn)	818	1863	3196	6519	6765	4615
Inflation	2.5	2.8	3.1	4.3	4.7	3.9
Interest rates (lending)	7	7	7.5	8.5	9.2	8.5
International reserves (US$bn)	6.5	7.8	9.7	10.9	18.1	22.5
Market capitalization (US$bn)	29	50.1	54	58	92.2	175
No. of listed companies	295	307	282	324	370	420
IFC index performance in US$	27.7	44	-11.2	12.1	27.9	102.9
Price/earnings ratios (P/E)	n/a	23.3	19	21	23.5	27.3
Earnings per share (EPS) growth	29	29.2	8.2	15.1	8	14.8
Average daily turnover (US$m)	10.4	28.3	61	43.2	81.5	130
Dividend yield	1.2	1.3	1.5	1.7	1.9	1.8
Currency to US$ (ringgit)	2.71	2.7	2.7	2.72	2.62	2.6

Figure 8.1 Malaysia: key statistics

being a dynamic exporter of manufactured goods which has established its own car industry and has attracted a large share of foreign direct investment from Japan, from Singapore and from other leading industrial nations. Foreign direct investment overall has risen from US$800m in 1988, to over US$6bn in 1992. Political stability has also led to a stable currency in the Malaysian ringgit, which has varied very little against the US dollar in the past five years, with a low inflation rate averaging 3 per cent per annum. Malaysia's international reserves have also tripled in the past four years to nearly US$25bn. All this economic good news has been reflected in the strong performance of the Malaysian stock market.

At the end of 1989, Kuala Lumpur took decisive action to end its dependence on Singapore where most Malaysian shares predominantly traded both before and after the joint federation prior to 1965. At one stroke, Singapore lost nearly half of its trading volume and Kuala Lumpur gained an increased international stature and a vastly improved daily turnover, which went from US$10m in 1988 to US$130m in 1993. Also, in the past three years, there has been active IPO activity with the number of Malaysian listed companies rising by 50 per cent between 1991 and 1994. Both the corporate finance underwriting the stockbroking sectors of the Malaysian

Company	**Market cap. (US$m)**	*Company*	**Volume (US$ '000s)**
Tenaga Nasional	15,963	Idris Hydraulic (Malaysia)	52,252
Telekom Malaysia	15,103	Landmarks	31,575
Resorts World	6300	Promet	24,105
Malayan Banking	5650	Diversified Resources	19,267
Genting	4941	Bedford	17,893
Sime Darby	3657	Faber Group	15,435
Technology Resources Ind.	2852	Multi-Purpose Holdings	12,161
United Engineers	2827	Malayan United Industries	12,025
Tanjon Public Limited Co.	2529	Asia Pacific Land	10,841
Magnum Corporation	2420	Renong	10,443
Perusahaan Otomobil Nasional	2349	Advance Synergy	9993
Malaysian Int'l Shipping Co.	2027	Pan Global Equities	9742
Rothmans of Pall Mall	2027	Olympia Industries	9623
Renong	2019	Granite Industries	9597
Malaysian Airline System	1894	Palmco Holdings	9013
Multi-Purpose Holdings	1635	Ganda Holdings	9000
Hong Leong Credit	1573	Technology Resources Inc.	8591
Public Bank	1472	Industrial Oxygen Inc.	8504
AMMB Holdings	1434	Pegkalen Holdings	8403
Development & Com Bank	1433	Sri Hartamas Corporation	8395

Figure 8.2 Malaysia: 20 largest stocks by market capitalization and average daily volume

financial scene have dramatically expanded their activities and improved their standards.

Although there is little doubt that the speculative element in the Malaysian stock market continues to be very important (and many shares are regularly traded by the political parties, with periods leading up to elections exhibiting particularly active trading), there is no doubt that this broadening of the Malaysian market shows a healthy growth, and makes the task of stock selection, for an international investment manager far more challenging. Malaysia's ambitious infrastructure development plans, for example, have led to a large increase in listed construction and engineering companies and, on the other hand, the ambitious privatization programme has done much to increase the market capitalization with such important listings as Telekom Malaysia which accounts for 12 per cent of market capitalization.

In one respect, Malaysia defies conventional analysis since its market capitalization is now nearly three times as large as its economy. On a price earnings ratio basis, as well, Malaysia appears to be rather expensive since it sells between 25 and 30 times projected earnings. Nevertheless, its image among international investors and its consistent growth rate of 9 per cent will undoubtedly maintain it among the leading countries to be included in emerging market funds in years to come. Compared with its neighbour, Indonesia, which has a population ten times greater, its growth potential may not be as great but its long-term stability and well established market must be considered very attractive arguments for investors.

Recent developments

Although the Malaysian market fell 25 per cent in the first quarter of 1994, this followed a 100 per cent rise in 1993 and may be considered a normal and healthy correction. The underlying growth rate of the Malaysian economy and the healthy earnings growth of many listed Malaysian companies will continue to attract a lot of international capital. The number of listed companies has grown by 50 per cent in the last three years and this reflects the rapid diversification which the Malaysian economy has been undergoing. Notwithstanding its volatility, the Malaysian stock market retains its position as one of the most attractive emerging markets, fully open to foreign investors in the fast growing South East Asian region.

Exchange address

The Kuala Lumpur Stock Exchange
3rd & 4th Floors, Exchange Square
Off Jalan Semantan
50490 Kuala Lumpur
PO Box 11023
50732 Kuala Lumpur

Tel: 603 254 6433 / Fax: 603 255 7463

Chapter 9

Mongolia

Population:	2.3m
Gross national product:	$231m
Currency/US$:	400 tugrik

For over a century the Mongol horde, under Genghis Khan and his successors, conquered and dominated a large part of the Eurasian land mass including China. Then, in the succeeding centuries, Mongolia returned to being a peaceful and pastoral nation with a small population, which became a buffer state between Russia and China. From 1921 to 1990, Outer Mongolia was a staunch Soviet ally, entirely dependent on Moscow for economic aid. With the collapse of the Soviet Union, Mongolia, like some of the Eastern European countries, lost the lifeline that for seventy years had provided everything in terms of its daily trade and imports. In 1992, the gross national product fell by 10 per cent, foreign trade fell by 60 per cent and Mongolia bravely decided to follow the path of economic reform, establish a stock exchange and invite foreign investments.

With two million people spread over a large land area of 1.5m square kilometres, Mongolia's main resources lie in its estimated reserves of 3000 tons of gold and its enormous copper resources, (almost five billion tons), which is its sole major export. Living standards are low. Agriculture is the mainstay of the population with large herds of cattle, sheep, horses and camels. The capital, Ulan Bator, has half a million people. Mongolia is regarded as politically stable. Elections in 1992 saw former communists win seventy-one of the seventy-six new parliamentary seats. President Ochirbat was elected in June 1993. A foreign investment law has been enacted which is quite favourable to mining and exploration. However, infrastructure is woefully lacking and the difficulty with the stock exchange, which started with a burst of enthusiasm in 1991-2, based on the Russian model of issuing vouchers to the whole population, is that there are few major companies listed and little economic foundation for a thriving capital market. Mongolia's strategic position is also somewhat vulnerable.

	1988	1989	1990	1991	1992	1993
Population (m)	2.05	2.1	2.15	2.2	2.25	2.3
GNP (US$m)	863	945	692	242	225	231
Real GNP growth (%)	5.1	4.2	2.5	16.2	9.6	0
Per capita income (US$)	421	450	322	110	100	100
Exports (US$m)	816	796	679	421	297	285
Imports (US$bn)	1779	1912	786	514	359	316
Inflation	-	-	-	120	320	-
Interest rates (prime)	-	-	-	-	-	-
International reserves(US$m)	-	-	28.8	33.1	10	-
Currency to US$ (tugrik)	3.35	3.35	5.62	50	200	400

Figure 9.1 Mongolia: key statistics

Chapter 10

The Philippines

Population:	65.7m
Gross national product:	\$55.1bn
Market capitalization:	\$26.4bn
Currency/US\$:	28.1 pesos

Thirty years ago, Manila had the second most active stock exchange in Asia, after Tokyo, and US investors actively traded shares in leading Philippine companies. It is indeed testament to the need for an investor to make long-term strategic judgements in picking 'winners' among the emerging markets to see exactly what went wrong. Ferdinand Marcos took power in 1965 and virtually proclaimed himself dictator when martial law was declared in 1972. Then began a long period of economic and political decline for the Philippines and confidence among international investors gradually deteriorated with inevitable consequences for the stock market. Corruption became endemic in the Philippine ruling class and the costs of doing business in the country escalated accordingly. Inflation, which stemmed from the inability of the central bank to control money supply and, therefore, prices, averaged nearly 15 per cent p.a. compared with a third of that level in the other Asian countries.

It is often said by foreign observers that the work ethic in the Philippines is markedly inferior to that of the so called 'Confucian' countries such as Korea, Japan, China or Taiwan. But no-one who has experienced the devoted industry of Filipino workers overseas would accept such a generalization easily. The evidence that the Filipino people would respond to strong and honest government has been manifested by the steady improvement in the Philippine economy in the past two years since Fidel Ramos succeeded Mrs Corazon Aquino in May 1992. Exports during the past two years have jumped 50 per cent and foreign direct investment has begun to improve. Inflation has also halved from 17 per cent in 1991 to less than 7 per cent by the end of 1993. This in turn has led to a sharp fall in the very high interest rates which had prevailed at the beginning of the decade. Slowly but surely, the Philippines' international position improved, with

	1988	1989	1990	1991	1992	1993
Population (m)	58.7	60.1	61.5	62.9	64.3	65.7
GNP (US$bn)	38.1	42.4	44	45.3	52.5	55.1
Real GNP growth (%)	6.3	5.9	2.1	0.7	0.6	2.4
Per capita income (US$)	650	705	715	720	816	839
Exports (US$bn)	7.1	7.8	8.2	8.8	9.8	11
Imports (US$bn)	8.2	10.4	12.2	12	14.5	15.8
Foreign direct investment (US$m)	156	219	245	257	260	364
Inflation	8.8	10.6	12.7	17.7	8.9	7.3
Interest rates (lending)	16.6	23.8	26.8	23.8	17.9	16.2
International reserves (US$bn)	1	1.4	0.9	3.2	4.4	4.7
Market capitalization (US$bn)	4.3	12.0	5.8	10.1	14.1	38.8
No. of listed companies	141	144	153	161	170	180
Index performance in US$ (%)	26.8	58.7	-56.1	102.6	7.6	152.8
Price/earnings (P/E) ratios	12.6	14.1	11.3	11.3	14.1	38.8
Earnings per share (EPS) growth	22	9	18	28	4	14.3
Average daily turnover (US$m)	3.5	9.6	4.9	6.0	12.4	27.1
Dividend yield	1	2.8	4	1.2	1.3	1
Currency to US$ (pesos)	20.5	21.8	27.2	26.2	23.6	26.8

Figure 10.1 The Philippines: key statistics

foreign exchange reserves rising to nearly $5bn and the currency, the peso, which had suffered constant devaluation during the Marcos period, at last beginning to stabilize around 26 pesos to the US dollar.

There is no question that the Philippines has attractive features for international investors. With a well-educated population of 66m people and a large archipelago of tropical islands, with substantial natural resources, the Philippines has long been a favoured tourist destination, although the growth of the travel business was severely held back by political instability and fears of visitors about their personal security. Even today, Manila is not as safe a city as Hong Kong or Singapore. However, things are improving rapidly. One indicator of international investor interest has been the moderate success enjoyed by the Subic Bay development in the two years since it was handed back to the Philippine government by the departing US forces. (They also evacuated the large and important Clark Air Force Base. This was due to the runway being covered in volcanic ash from Mount Pinatubo, rather than from any political pressure.)

Outlook

With the US having departed from its military bases in the Philippines in 1991 and voters having successfully transferred political authority in a free election last year, the economic destiny of the Philippines is in the hands of the people more than at any other point in the island's history. Given the country's abundant resources and its young and well educated population, the preconditions for economic growth and prosperity are in place and the outlook for economic growth is positive.

Recent economic performance

From its recent peak of 6.3 per cent in 1988, annual GDP growth slowed for each of the next three years. Although Corazon Aquino's installation as president in 1986 was greeted with widespread enthusiasm both in the Philippines and abroad, political events and natural disasters conspired to make her term in office a trying period for the country. Six attempted *coups d'état* against Aquino's government and the eruption of a major volcano at Mt. Pinatubo made any long-term economic agenda difficult to fulfill. Matters were aggravated further during this period by the Gulf War as it resulted in the return to the Philippines of over one million guest workers in the Middle East. This in turn led to a reduction in much-needed foreign exchange remittances and higher unemployment domestically.

One senses, in visiting the Philippines, that the peaceful election of Fidel Ramos in June 1992 represents a significant turning point and that economic prospects and, perhaps more importantly, national pride, have taken a turn for the better. This renewed public spirit is probably best exemplified by the outpouring of volunteers for the ambitious redevelopment project at the former US Naval Base at Subic Bay. Under the able leadership of Richard Gordon, some 2500 full time employees and 6000 volunteers are attempting to create a free trade zone for tourist and light manufacturing related industries.

One of the first major measures introduced by the Ramos government initiated to restore the economy to long-term stability include tax increases to narrow the government's budget deficit. Revenue raising measures include an expanded value added tax, a stock transaction levy, and increased excises duties on tobacco and alcohol. Increased taxes are intended to raise an additional 7bn pesos in 1993/94. The greatest accomplishment of the Ramos administration has been in formulating a coherent energy strategy. A reorganization of the National Power Corporation and an opening of the power sector to encourage the establishment of independent power generation facilities should largely remedy the country's electricity shortage by 1996. Other major accomplishments include the liberalization of foreign ex-

	1990	1991	1992	1993[f]	1994[f]	1995[f]
Real GNP growth	2.1	0.7	0.6	2.4	2.6	5.1
Peso/US dollar (yr-end)	27.2	26.2	23.2	26.8	30.5	34.5
Inflation (av. %)	12.7	17.7	8.9	7.3	6.5	6.1
Av. lending rate (yr-end %)	26.8	23.8	17.9	16.2	11.2	10.8

Figure 10.2 The economic outlook for the Philippines

Year-end	1986	1989	1992	1993
Manila Commercial/Industrial Index	548.0	1584.9	1784.0	4756.0
Market price/earnings P/E (X)	5.8	14.1	14.1	38.8
Earnings growth (%)	(102.8)	2.3	12.3	12.5
Dividend yield (%)	1.5	3.6	1.0	0.3
Market capitalization (US$bn)	2.0	12.0	13.8	40.3
Monthly turnover (US$m)	34.0	108.0	220.0	1495.0*

**as of December 1993*

Figure 10.3 Philippines stock market indicators

change markets and foreign investment regulations. Following the introduction of a new act allowing 100 per cent foreign ownership of business assets, foreign direct investment grew by 150 per cent to US$800m in the first 7 months of 1993. As in other South East Asian economies, the ability of the Philippines to attract foreign investment on a large scale is critical to its economic takeoff.

There remain, however, areas of continued concern over the outlook for macroeconomic stability. While external debt has fallen from 97 per cent of GNP in 1986 to 60 per cent in 1992, debt rescheduling with the IMF remains an area of uncertainty and the Philippine government continues to operate at a deficit of US$ 4bn per annum.

The stock exchanges

Established in 1927, the Manila Stock Exchange was the Philippines' sole stock exchange until the opening of the Makati Stock Exchange in 1965. The growth of the Makati Stock Exchange has reflected the growth of Makati as the Philippines pre-eminent business center over the past 20 years and, in 1988, Makati overtook Manila as the country's leading stock exchange.

There are currently 98 members of the Manila Stock Exchange and 110 members of the Makati Stock Exchange, although 70 per cent of turnover in value terms takes place in Manila. There are plans currently underway to connect the two exchanges by computer link-up to ensure uniform prices and to promote more efficient trading. Both the Manila and Makati Stock Exchanges are self-regulated bodies. The Manila Stock Exchange is governed by a board of governors with 11 members elected annually and the operations of the exchange are overseen by seven standing committees. The Makati Stock Exchange operates under a similar structure with a 13 member board of governors and eight standing committees. Although the government has long supported the merger of the two exchanges, this seems unlikely because of the large vested interests in each exchange.

Recent stock market performance

Despite the Philippines weak economy over the past five years, the Philippines stock market has been among the best performing stock market of South East Asia during that period. In 1993, the Manila Stock Exchange Commercial and Industrial Index appreciated by 153 per cent. While blue chip stocks have performed well, the most noteworthy feature of the market has been the increased activity in smaller capitalization stocks (there are now over 180 listed stocks) and the active new issues market. Public offerings of securities have increased sharply in recent years, rising from 7.4bn pesos in 1991 to 12.7bn pesos in 1992. In the first 10 months of 1993, a total of 12.6bn pesos has been raised in offerings. The largest of the recent public issues have been Ayala Land (P 2.5bn) and Meralco (P2.6bn) in 1991, Philippine National Bank (P2.9bn) and Philippine Long Distance Telephone in 1992, and JG Summit (P2.8bn), and Benpress (3.8bn) in 1993. The over-subscription of these issues both domestically and overseas is an indication of the increase in interest in the Philippine stock market in recent years.

Summary of key points

Major political and economic developments since 1991

- Evacuation of Subic Bay and Clark Airforce Base by US;
- Peaceful election of Fidel Ramos in June 1992 for 6-year term;
- Chronic energy shortages between 1991 and 1993, averaging 5 hours per day.

Company	**Market cap. (US$m)**	*Company*	**Volume (US$m)**
San Miguel	3482	Meralco B	1125
PLDT	3277	PLDT	1125
Ayala Corp	2655	PNB	615
Ayala Land	2603	Globe Telecom GMCR, Inc. A	602
Meralco	1989	Int'l Cont Terminal Services	362
JG Summit	1925	Meralco A	392
PNB	1335	Engineering Equipment Inc.	361
PCI Bank	746	Phil Orion Properties A	347
Metro Bank	652	San Miguel B	345
Bank of Philippine Islands	493	Phil Telegraph & Tel A	339
ABS-CBN	467	San Miguel A	317
Far East Bank	452	Ayala Land Inc B	293
Filinvest Land	396	First Philippine Hldg B	234
International Container	375	Kuok Phil Properties A	191
City Trust Bank	309	Phil Telegraph & Tel B	175
Manila Mining	274	Ayala Corporation A	173
Jollibee Food Corp	262	Robinson's Land	162
Metro Pacific Corp	239	First Philippine Hldg	160
Union Bank	220	Manila Mining Corporation	155
First Phil Holdings	215	Abacus Cons. Res & Holding A	151

Figure 10.4 The Philippines: 20 largest companies by market capitalization and average daily volume

Major cultural forces

- US colonization from 1898;
- Collaboration of elite with Japanese during WWII and lack of reprisals post war. No tradition of land reform which served as successful form of economic democratization in Korea, Taiwan, and Japan;
- US legal and political institutions and educational system and indeed same chronic over-supply of lawyers;
- 80 per cent of population Roman Catholic without strong Confucian or protestant work ethic;
- Rich natural resources in agriculture, copper, and newly discovered oil fields.

Exchange addresses

Manila Stock Exchange
Prensa St Cor Muelle de la Industria
Binondo, Manila

Tel: 632 471125 or 632 408860

Makati Stock Exchange
Ayala Building, Ayala Avenue
Metro Manila

Tel: 632 887871 or 632 886411

Chapter 11

Taiwan

Population:	20.9m
Gross national product:	US$220.8bn
Market capitalization:	US$124bn
Currency/US$:	26.10 New Taiwan dollars

Taiwan, like South Korea, was one of the great success stories of the 1980s with the Taipei market rising by a factor of twelve in the period 1987 to 1989. At one point, the capitalization of the small number of Taiwanese-listed companies was nearly US$250bn, with individual banking shares selling at many times their book value and more highly valued than Citibank. Taiwan has also had the influence of the bear market prevailing in Japan since 1989. There seems no rational explanation why Taiwan should have underperformed so drastically compared with Hong Kong in the past three years. Clearly the market was very over-valued in 1989 and the economy of Taiwan has also had a sluggish period with exports growing barely 10 per cent per annum. However, exports are no longer the whole story of Taiwan, as they were in the 1960-85 period.

The tremendous success of Taiwan's exporters has led to an enormous concentration of wealth in this small island of Formosa which has possibly the largest black economy in the world in proportion to its reported statistics. Taiwan has regularly recorded a trade surplus of between US$10-15bn per annum and the official foreign exchange reserves of the Central Bank of China in Taipei are over US$85bn—a remarkable figure for such a small country. However, the unofficial estimate of privately held foreign currency wealth is nearly US$400bn or double the official estimate of GNP. There has been a shift from export-led growth to a new boom in domestic consumption (just as in Japan).

With the new consumer wealth of the urban middle-class population in Taipei and Kiaohsiung has come simultaneously a period of political liberalization. With the end of martial law in 1987, and the end of the Chiang dynasty with the death of his son, Chiang Ching Kuo in 1988, there have emerged opposition parties—such as the New Democratic Party—challenging the political monopoly of the KMT and also the ascendancy of Tai-

	1988	1989	1990	1991	1992	1993
Population (m)	19.9	20.1	20.4	20.6	20.7	20.9
GNP (US$bn)	125.3	150.3	160.9	180.2	210.9	220.8
Real GNP growth (%)	7.8	7.3	5	7.3	6.1	6.3
Per capita income (US$)	6296	7478	7887	8748	10188	10565
Exports (US$bn)	60.7	66.3	67.2	73.2	81.5	86.6
Imports (US$bn)	49.7	52.3	54.7	62	72	81
Foreign direct investment (US$m)	1183	2418	2302	1778	1461	1183
Inflation	1.3	4.4	4.1	3.6	4.7	3.9
Interest rates (prime)	7	10.5	10	8.6	8.3	8.3
International reserves (US$bn)	73.9	73.2	72.4	82.4	82.3	80.6
Market capitalization (US$bn)	120.1	240	112.4	123.7	103	124
No. of listed companies	163	181	198	221	256	280
Index performance in US$ (%)	122.4	100.4	-54.6	7	-25.7	71.7
Price/earnings (P/E) ratios	68.9	92	33	38	30.1	30.5
Earnings per share (EPS growth)	8	13	23	20	2.3	4.3
Average daily turnover (US$m)	959	3385	2873	1315	817	638
Dividend yield	0.7	1.7	1.4	1.6	2.4	1.8
Currency to US$ (NT$)	28.2	26.05	26.63	25.5	25.2	26.4

Figure 11.1 Taiwan: key statistics

wanese politicians such as President Lee (rather than the KMT group which came from the mainland in 1949).

The combination of all these factors means that political priorities are changing. Led by economic forces, a very gradual rapprochement with mainland China is also occurring. The need for Taiwan to compete in basic industries which, with the rise of the New Taiwan dollar and the considerable increase in labour costs in a country with per capita income now well over US$10,000, means that many of the traditional areas of growth—textiles, plastics, boatbuilding, steel, cement—are clearly industrial activities which mainland China, with its labour costs of less than 5 per cent of those of Taiwan, will be much better positioned to succeed. Taiwanese businessmen have been able to bring their marketing knowledge, as well as technology and their large capital resources, to make this magic combination of land, labour and capital, work to form a very effective and competitive formula in world export markets, such as we have seen in the Special Economic Zones of China in Shenzhen and Xiamen in the coastal province of Fujian, where most of the US$5bn of Taiwanese direct investment in China is concentrated.

One of the predictable developments in 1994-5 will be the commencement of direct flights from Taipei to mainland cities such as Shanghai and Xiamen. This will have a dramatic effect on the economy of Taiwan and the international investor perception of the Taiwanese share market as a China play. (It will also have an immediate and negative impact on Hong Kong which has depended heavily on the need for Taiwanese businessmen and tourists to use the British colony as a neutral entry point between the two major Chinese communities. Hong Kong hotels, retail outlets, airlines and travel services will all suffer from this change, although some might argue that the overcrowding of Hong Kong's Kai Tak airport has reached such a point that a cooling down of the Taiwan/China air traffic can only be beneficial.) It is in this light, therefore, that investors should look at the presently unfashionable Taiwanese market—the potential of Taiwan to become a major regional hub for China travel and investments.

Against this positive interpretation there are, of course, still some rigidities in the rules allowing foreign investors to enter and exit from Taiwanese shares. At present fund managers have to use a 'facility' of a stated amount of US$20m, for example, which must be committed to Taiwan, at least in bank deposits if not in shares, for a minimum period of twelve months. Compared with the ease and flexible movement of capital in other Asian markets such as Hong Kong, Singapore, Malaysia, this constitutes a definitely negative characteristic. However, an easing of political tensions with the mainland will undoubtedly lead to a gradual easing of the regulations for foreign investors, just as we expect the same trend to appear in South Korea during the 1990s.

Although, in some respects, Taiwan is no longer an emerging market but a country which has achieved a high standard of living, its inclusion in this survey has been justified, just as in the case of Hong Kong, by its characteristic as a China-related market in which investors may seek to find China investments in Taipei-listed shares.

Taiwan's political scene

The KMT

Last year legislative elections saw many younger, locally-born politicians elected, ousting old guard mainland Chinese representatives. Although KMT regained power, the internal party structure was altered and the opposition party (DPP) was able to capitalize on growing discontent to increase its numbers in the legislature.

The resignation of Hau-Pei-Tsan in February resulted in high tension, especially when KMT legislators, against party wishes, sided with the opposition on such issues as the passage of the Sunshine Bill and denying funding for the high-speed railway.

The non-mainstream New Alliance faction left the KMT and formed the Chinese New Party (CNP). The CNP states that its main objective is 'first breaking down the KMT and then building it back up again'. This put considerable pressure on the mainstream party because, if the question of party vice-chairman were not addressed, there could have been a party split. This resulted in four vice-chairmen being elected, two from each side of he party.

The citizens of Taiwan value political and economic stability and the DPP has yet to come forth with a comprehensive plan. However, it is evident that KMT's absolute power is slowly weakening and the result will be a more democratic and well-balanced political arena.

Cross-Strait talks

The talks between China and Taiwan broke down with nothing being achieved. However, Taiwanese look upon the question of China and possible unification or independence in a calm manner and are simply getting on with business as though nothing will happen over the next few years.

Beijing has released a white paper outlining its policy towards Taiwan. Of Taiwan's interest in joining the UN it says, 'There is only one China and Taiwan is a part of it. So there is no such thing as having two seats under one country.'

Economics

The country is facing a temporary slow down as GNP growth for 1993 is set at 6.1 per cent, down from 7 per cent at the start of the year. The new government is, therefore, resetting priorities (e.g. a scaling down and stretching of the six-year National Development Plan and a slowdown in government borrowing) and the central bank is now firmly engaged in a monetary policy of reduction in interest rates in order to accommodate and stimulate the economy.

The stock market

After reaching an historical high of 12,682 points on 12 February 1990 Taiwan began a long-term bear market. Early in 1992, the Tarex rebounded from 4640 points to the year's high of 5459 points but performed poorly for the rest of the year. In the first quarter of 1993, the index enjoyed a 2000 point boost, mainly due to calm in the political arena. However, relations between China and Taiwan have been strained by the former's release of a

Company	Market cap. (US$m)	Company	Volume (US$m)
China Steel	5070	Hualon-Teijran	686
First Commercial Bank	4853	Shinkong Spinning	591
Hua Nan Bank	4711	Kwong Fong Industries	542
Chang Hwa Bank	4350	ADI	429
ICBC	2940	Taiwan Agriculture & Forestry	410
Nan Ya Plastics	2873	United Microelectronics	370
Cathay Life Insurance	2626	Pao Shiang Industrial	363
Formosa Plastics	2184	Imperial Hotel	338
Asia Cement	2099	Hwang Dihlon Lon Textile	339
Taiwan Cement	2073	Min Hsing Cotton Mill	289
MBB Taipei	1876	Liton Electronic	263
China Airline	1716	Hone Yi Fiber Industrial	195
China Trust	1653	Shin Shin Supermarket	164
Evergreen Marine	1602	Tey Feng Tire	161
Formosa Chemicals & Fibre	1526	Taiwan Sakura	156
Tatung	1403	Formosan Rubber Group	145
MBB Hsin Chu	1385	MBB Kaohsiung	137
Cathay Construction	1376	China Development Corp	134
China Development Corp	1359	United Ceramics	132
MBB Taichung	1301	Cathay Life Insurance	100

Figure 11.2 Taiwan: 20 largest companies by market capitalization and average daily volume

white paper reasserting its claim over the island and the break up of Cross-Strait negotiations between the semi-official Strait's Exchange Foundation of Taiwan and Association of Relations Across the Taiwan Strait of China, which have affected investor confidence in the stock market.

Technical notes

- Transaction tax is 0.1425 per cent. The stock exchange trading hours are 09.00 to 12.00, Monday to Friday, and 09.00 to 11.00 on Saturdays.
- Computer Aided Trading System (CATS)
  - June 1990: Convertible bonds were included in CATS
  - November 1991: Computerized bond trading began
  - October 1992: Improvement of the trading system of add-lot transactions into the book-entry system
  - August 1992: Fully-automated trading system launched

Rules for foreign investors

In August 1993, the central bank raised the ceiling for total foreign investment in the Taiwan stock market from $2.5bn to $5bn. At the end of January 1993, the SEC approved a total of 39 foreign institutional investors to invest in the securities market. The approved investment amount is US$1750m.

As from 2 February 1993, the government lowered the qualifications for foreign institutional investors and raised the investment ceiling from US$50m to US$100m for each foreign institutional investor. Approved foreign banks, trust companies and foreign subsidiaries which are part of a joint venture with a local security firm can now invest directly.

Note that foreign currency reserves amount to $85bn; 58 per cent is in US dollars, while 33 per cent in European currencies.

Exchange address

Taiwan Stock Exchange
City Building
85 Yen Ping South Road
Taipei

Tel: 02 311 4020 or 02 396 9270 / Fax: 02 311 4004 or 02 375 3669

Chapter 12

Thailand

Population:	58.7m
Gross national product:	$118.1bn
Market capitalization:	$92.2bn
Currency/US$:	25.5 baht

Thailand, which until 1938 was known as the Kingdom of Siam, is not only one of the most attractive countries for a visitor to Asia in which to arrive; it also has a fast growing modern economy in and around Bangkok and an exciting and rewarding stock exchange. With a population which will reach 60m in 1995, of whom the vast majority follow the teachings of Buddha, Thailand's wealth was based until ten years ago on its rich soil and favourable climate which has enabled it to become the world's foremost exporter of rice and, in addition, a major producer of tapioca, maize and rubber. It has large tropical timber resources and is a major producer and trader of gems which sometimes originate from neighbouring countries in the Indo-China peninsula such as Burma.

By means of an astute monarchy and subtle diplomacy during the long colonial period from 1880 to 1950, Thailand was able to resist the pressure of the British Empire in the West and the French colonialists in the East. Wedged between Burma and Vietnam, Thailand became a buffer kingdom between these two colonial powers. Even during the Second World War Thailand managed to preserve its neutrality, although Japanese troops crossed over the country to invade Malaya and Singapore.

Despite its independence, Siam was not immune to foreign influences and the wary but benevolent acceptance of foreign investors today reflects the 19th century openness to foreign traders and ideas, led by the great King Mongkut who began the tradition of Western education among the nobility. A large and prosperous Chinese community has been absorbed over the past 200 years into the general population—especially in the capital city, Bangkok. Most Chinese have taken Thai names and are now indistinguishable from the general population, except that, as elsewhere in South East Asia, they play a dominant role in business and most of the companies

	1988	1989	1990	1991	1992	1993
Population (m)	54.3	55.2	56.1	56.9	57.8	58.7
GNP (US$bn)	59.5	69.4	81.5	93.6	104.9	118.1
Real GNP growth (%)	13.2	12.3	10	8.2	7.5	7.5
Per capita income (US$)	1096	125.7	1453	1645	1815	2012
Exports (US$bn)	15.8	19.9	22.8	28.3	32.8	37.8
Imports (US$bn)	19.7	25.3	32.7	37.9	41.3	48.1
Foreign direct investment (US$m)	1102	1728	2303	2001	2116	2300
Inflation	3.8	5.4	6	5.7	4.1	5
Interest rates (prime)	12	13	16.3	14	11.5	10
International reserves (US$bn)	6.1	9.5	13.3	17.5	20.4	23.1
Market capitalization (US$bn)	8.8	25.7	23.9	35.2	58.2	92.2
No. of listed companies	122	145	159	170	192	220
Index performance in US$ (%)	35.7	123.6	-29.4	17.3	23.4	88.5
Price/earnings (P/E) ratios	14.3	26.4	23.5	25.7	22.1	22.7
Earnings per share (EPS) growth	32	31	3.5	6	26	12
Average daily turnover (US$m)	25	59.4	101.2	128.5	295.3	256
Dividend yield	3.8	2.1	3.9	3.6	3	2.9
Currency to US$ (baht)	25.2	25.6	25.3	25.1	25.5	25.5

Figure 12.1 Thailand: key statistics

in which foreign investors take an interest are owned and managed by Chinese families.

The most striking pattern of Thailand's history is its stability and resilience in the face of crises and conflicts in the surrounding region. During the last 40 years, Thailand's position seemed extremely vulnerable in the face of the communist tide which came south from China through Vietnam, Laos and Cambodia. Popular among Pentagon strategists was the 'domino theory'. Under this scenario, Thailand would inevitably succumb to the combination of military strength and fifth-column undermining of the local populace.

However, history has proved the pessimists wrong and the reasons are clear.

From an early period, Thailand's peasant population had a stake in the land, as well as a sturdy independence. They also exhibited a consistent and profound reverence for their monarch, symbolized today by King Bhumibol Adulyadej, who has reigned since 1946. Just as Thailand resisted communism, so too it has resisted the destruction of the ancient Asian monarchies which engulfed Burma, Laos and Vietnam. There have been numerous *coups d'état* led by Thailand's strong military class, but none have ventured to attack the sacred throne itself or to propose a republic. Since 1932, a constitutional monarchy with strong powers of consultation and influence has been in place. As recently as 1991, there was further military activity and popular unrest, after which the king was forced to intervene and appoint an interim government.

This long-term historic perspective is, therefore, of value in assessing political risk today for an investor in Thailand. Coupled with the confident sense of identity and destiny of the Thai people and the Buddhist approach to life, which is generally tolerant and easygoing, there has been a capable group of economists and technocrats which has managed Thailand's long-term development plan along similar lines to those of the MITI in Tokyo. It is no coincidence, in fact, that Japanese corporations have been the largest and most numerous investors in Thailand over the last 20 years.

Stability is also apparent in the long-term behaviour of the currency, the baht, which has held its value compared to the US dollar with extraordinary consistency over the past few years. One of Thailand's principal foreign exchange earners is, of course, tourism. Over 5m visitors a year come to the country. If we consider the abundance of natural resources, the attractive climate and well-trained labour force and excellent service sector, it is, therefore, not surprising that Thailand has enjoyed one of the world's highest rates of economic growth.

During the past 7 years the average annual growth has been nearly 9 per cent which means that per capita income has risen from $900 in 1987 to over $2000 in 1993. Exports have nearly tripled during the same period. However, within that growth there has been a significant shift away from agriculture, traditionally the backbone of the Thai economy, to manufactured products. Agriculture today accounts for only 14 per cent of GNP (See Figure 12.2). As can be seen from Figure 12.3, manufactured goods now account for 3/4 of Thailand's exports and within this sector we find garments, electrical parts and integrated circuits, shoes, canned food and gemstones, although it is true that rice, tapioca and rubber are still important in the overall picture. This has led to a steady and growing annual inflow of foreign direct investment.

Since 1986, the year from which the Japanese yen effectively doubled in value against the US dollar, there has been a particular inflow of Japanese manufacturers. Taiwan has been the second major source of foreign investment, mainly in textiles, garments, shoes, electronics and other like industries.

The stock market

The Securities Exchange of Thailand was set up in 1974 and started operating in 1976 with 14 companies listed. The first speculative boom occurred

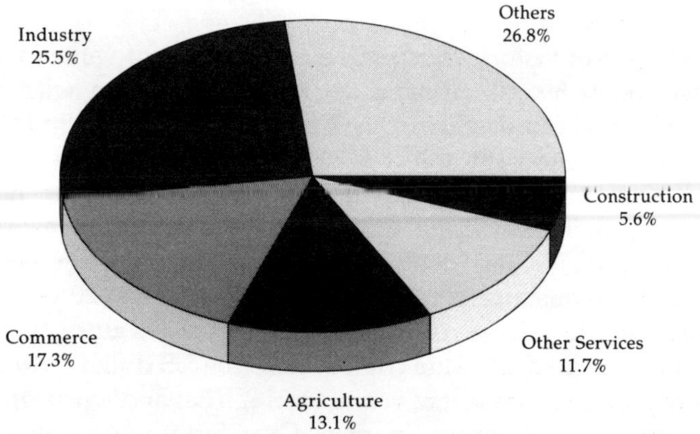

Figure 12.2 Thailand: GDP by sector (1992)
Source: Baring Securities

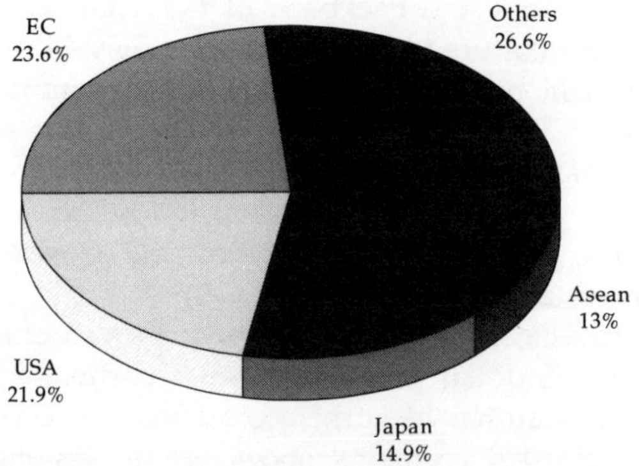

Figure 12.3 Thailand: Exports by country (1992)
Source: Baring Securities

in 1978 and was followed by the inevitable bust after the collapse of a finance company. During the next three years there was very little activity on the Bangkok Exchange, but local interest slowly began to recover from 1982 onwards and, by 1985, the first tentative international interest began with the launch of the Bangkok Fund. During the world stock market boom in 1987, Thailand began to be discovered more widely by fund managers around the world and, despite the crash in October 1987, the market showed a near 70 per cent gain. Prompted by this development, the SET set up a foreign board designed for foreigners wishing to trade foreign registered shares between themselves with premiums paid for scarce foreign shares.

The continuing boom in the Thai economy in 1988-89 caused interest rates to rise sharply and market capitalization grew steadily, reaching over US$30bn by the middle of 1990, when the balloon was abruptly punctured by Saddam Hussain's invasion of Kuwait. The Thai market fell by over 50 per cent in the next three months as foreign investors moved *en masse* to repatriate their gains. Despite a recovery in early 1991, with the victory of the allies in the Gulf, confidence did not really return to the Thai market until late in 1992 after the previous 12 months' political turmoil had subsided. In the final months of 1993, the market put on a strong showing, rising 40 per cent between September and December with market capitalization exceeding US$100bn for the first time and the number of listed companies rising to over 225. Thus, in less than five years, Thailand's stock exchange had dramatically reflected its underlying economic growth and, in fact, the market was equal in value to nearly 80 per cent of GNP. Domestic investors as well as foreign funds were active players in the market and the domestic broking and fund management sectors were large, active and profitable.

However, it remains to be seen whether Thailand in the 1990s will enjoy such favourable conditions as it did in the 1980s. One factor which is sure to affect its strategic position is the growing competition from Vietnam as it liberalizes its rules for foreign investors and builds up basic industries in areas where Thailand has been most competitive and successful—textiles, garments, shoes, canned foods and basic consumer electronics. With a population of over 70m industrious and hardworking people, Vietnam is possibly the only real competitor (apart from China) that can challenge Thailand in the export markets. Nevertheless, Thailand will probably continue to be a favourite destination for foreign funds and must be an important component of any global emerging market fund. Its growth rate, stability, sound financial position and pro-business government are all permanent features, and the resilience with which Thailand has weathered political and economic storms and crises is perhaps the most compelling argument for investors.

Company	**Market cap. (US$m)**	*Company*	**Volume (US$m)**
Bangkok Bank	7177	Bangkok Bank	10.9
Krung Thai Bank	3791	Krung Thai Bank	10.5
Bangkok Land	3691	Bangkok Bank of Commerce	7.0
Thai Farmers Bank	3691	Siam City Bank	6.2
Siam Cement	3572	PTT Exploration & Production	6.1
Thai Airways Int'l	3436	Thai Farmers Bank	5.8
Land & House	2922	Siam Panich Leasing	5.5
Shinawatra Computer	2749	Krisda Mahanakorn	5.2
Siam Commercial Bank	2727	First Bangkok City Bank	5.2
Advance Info Service	2522	Bangkok Metropolitan Bank	5.0
Siam City Cement	1646	Raimon Land	5.0
Thai Military Bank	1543	Thai Military Bank	4.8
First Bangkok City Bank	1461	Bangkok Land	4.7
Bank of Ayudhya	1459	IFCT	4.7
Finance One	1259	Rattana Real Estate	4.2
Phatra Thanakit	1238	Tanayong	3.4
Siam City Bank	1185	First City Investment	3.3
Tanayong	1088	Bank of Asia	3.0
MDX	1074	Wall Street Finance & Sec.	2.9
PTT Exploration & Prod	1046	Bank of Ayudha	2.7

Figure 12.4 Thailand: 20 largest companies by market capitalization and average daily volume

Exchange address

Securities Exchange of Thailand
2/F Sinthon Building
132 Wireless Road
Bangkok 10500
Thailand

Tel: 662 250 0001/8 or 662 250 0010/15; Fax: 662 254 3040

Chapter 13

Vietnam

Population:	70.4m
Gross national product:	$10.5bn
Currency/US$:	11,000 dong

Vietnam is often discussed among fund managers as the next tiger economy of South East Asia. With a population of about 70m, of whom half are under the age of twenty, it is large enough to challenge Thailand, Indonesia, the Philippines and even China as a low cost manufacturer. Its economic reform programme, known as Doi Moi, started only in 1986, or nearly ten years after China's reforms, and has proceeded more slowly. Nevertheless, foreign direct investment has built up in the past three years (See Figure 13.2). The large offshore oil reserves, so far untapped, are estimated to be 2-3bn barrels. On the other hand, no stock exchange has yet been established, although it is expected by the end of 1994, once privatization of state companies finally gets underway (see Figure 13.3).

Although it stands on the trading routes half way between India and China, Vietnam has always had a distinctive culture of its own and, in the last one hundred years, this has been reinforced by the French colonization which began in 1885 and continued until 1954 when the French surrendered North Vietnam after their defeat at Dienbien Phu. By 1955, all French forces had left Vietnam and the American involvement in South Vietnam built up from 1965 onwards. The communists finally completed their conquest of the country on 30 April 1975 with the taking of Saigon. It was thus barely ten years after the military triumph of communism that its state directed economy was tacitly admitted to be a failure and private enterprise began to be encouraged again. Obviously, the southern part of the country had the majority of entrepreneurs, a recent memory of Western culture and influence and a trading mentality which would enable markets to be reborn. It is, therefore, appropriate that, in April 1993, the governor the State Bank of Vietnam announced that the first securities exchange would be opened in Ho Chi Minh city, formerly known as Saigon.

On the whole, Vietnam appears to be a promising target for the emerging market fund manager and investor. Its economy has performed well, its

	1988	1989	1990	1991	1992	1993
Population (m)	63.7	64.8	66.2	67.7	69	70.4
GNP (US$bn)	6.8	7.6	8.4	9.1	9.9	10.5
Real GNP growth (%)	5.2	8	5.1	6	8.3	7.5
Per capita income (US$)	107	117	127	134	143	149
Exports (US$m)	1038	1946	2404	1970	2460	2829
Imports (US$bn)	2757	2566	2752	2239	2380	2975
Foreign direct investment (US$m)	360	512	589	1185	1981	2377
Inflation	394	35	68	68	18	15
Interest rates	n/a	n/a	n/a	n/a	48	26.4
International reserves(US$m)	8	34	111	94	91	165
Currency to US$ (dong)	900	4300	6800	11980	10550	11000

Figure 13.1 Vietnam: key statistics

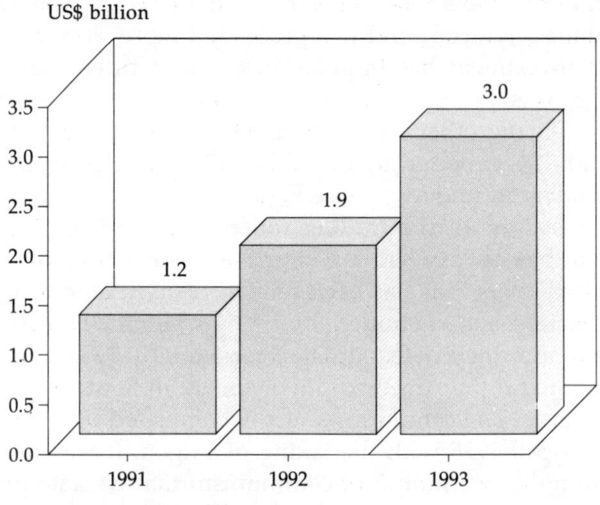

Figure 13.2 Vietnam: Foreign direct investment

Approved for privatization	Location
Legamex Garmet Factory	Ho Chi Minh City
Union of Transport Agents	Ho Chi Minh City
Appying for privatization	
Binh Minh Plastic Enterprise	Ho Chi Minh City
Bien Hoa Wool Factory	Ho Chi Minh City
Hiep An Shoe Factory	Ho Chi Minh City
Doi Tan Brick factory	Ho Chi Minh City
Company for Commercial Equipment, Restaurants & Services	Hanoi
Hoan Kiem Union for Production, Business & Export-Import	Hanoi
Thach Ban Brick factory	Hanoi
Long An Export Co	Long An Province
Hai Au Mechanical Engineering Workshop	Haiphong
Haiphong Bus Company	Haiphong

Figure 13.3 Vietnam: Privatization programme

Sources: Ministry of Finance, Far Eastern Economic Review (1 July 1993)

people are industrious and eager to improve their living standards and there is a sound rationale for following the flow of foreign direct investment into a country at this early stage of development. Vietnam has also a foreign debt of US$15.46bn which trades at considerable discounts. One factor which could propel economic growth in Vietnam is the estimated 2m Vietnamese people living in the United States, France and elsewhere who regularly remit funds home and could become investors in their mother country.

[illegible]

PART III

South Asia

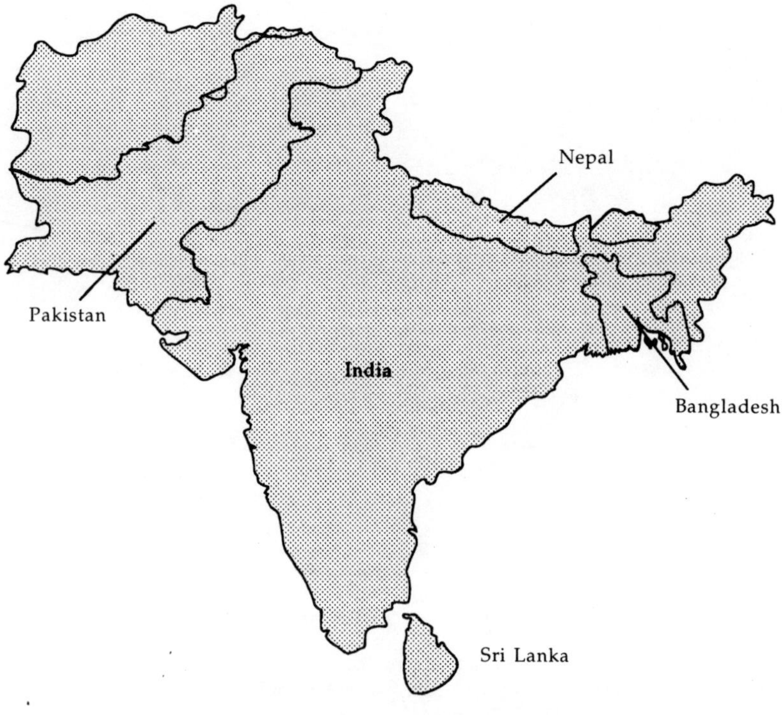

THE EMERGING MARKETS OF SOUTH ASIA

Chapter 14

South Asia - Introduction

The countries of the Indian sub-continent are like some of the former socialist countries, emerging from a generation in which government policy was directed towards equalizing incomes rather than creating wealth, in other words, positive discouragement of capital and free enterprise. Despite this, many companies in India, Pakistan and Sri Lanka today have remained in private hands and are extremely competitive. Even more important, the infrastructure is there for a real and immediate recovery in capital markets. The banking system, the legal and accounting system are well established and the English language is widely spoken. These are tremendous advantages in the competition for capital which characterizes the emerging markets of the 1990s.

During the past five years, the pace of reform in India and the surrounding countries has accelerated. For more than forty years before that it became extremely difficult for multi-national companies to establish a fully-owned subsidiary in India to manufacture and export freely. More importantly, imports were severely restricted as India, like other large developing countries such as Brazil, followed the policy of import substitution in order to build up its domestic industries. This not only resulted in a great deal of inefficiency but also caused many strategic industries such as cement, steel, energy and even food to be kept insulated from global competitors. The best known example was the exclusion of Coca Cola from India since the mid-1970s which led to a local substitute being produced under the name of Campa Cola. Now both Coke and Pepsi are back in India. IBM has returned after nearly fifteen years, during which time the US viewed India as a highly-suspect buyer of super computers which were destined for the important task of predicting and monitoring the monsoon season but were thought, by the Americans, to be used for defence purposes, and of which India, as a close ally of the Soviet Union, was deemed not to be a worthy recipient.

Now all this has changed. The collapse of the Soviet Union has had a dramatic effect not only on foreign policy, but on domestic economic policy-making in India and among its socialist neighbours such as Sri Lanka. The Nehru Fabian experiment of the 1950s greatly influenced Bandanaraike in Ceylon and, to a lesser extent, government planners in Karachi and Islama-

	India	Pakistan	Sri Lanka	Nepal	Bangladesh
Population (m)	895	120.8	17.86	19.9	114.3
GNP (US$bn)	264	52.2	9.99	3	25.1
Real GNP growth (%)					
1992	1.2	6.5	4.3	3.1	4
1993	3	3.2	5.6	2.5	5
1994[f]	4	4.5	6	2.8	5.5
Per capita income (US$)	295	432	510	170	220
Exports (US$bn)	21.6	6.6	2.56	0.48	2.5
Imports (US$bn)	21.4	9.8	3.45	0.99	4
Foreign direct investment (US$m)	389	450	174	n/a	n/a
Inflation	8	9.8	12	15	3
Interest rates	18	12.6	20.4	16	13
International reserves (US$m)	8000	1725	1262	556.7	2200
Market capitalization (US$bn)	70.1	8.1	1.9	0.083	0.4
No. listed companies	6500	645	198	59	144
Price/earnings (P/E) ratios					
1993[e]	31.7	17.5	15.2	24.5	13.9
1994[f]	27.3	14.6	11.3	17.5	10.7
Earnings per share (EPS) growth					
1993[e]	20	24	17	14	25
1994[f]	23	27	28	16	30
Average daily turnover (US$m)	54.5	9.5	1.8	0.005	0.04
Dividend yield	1.04	2.4	2.8	3.1	4.5
Stock market performance, '88-'93 (%)	131.7	230.6	n/a	n/a	n/a
Currency to US$ perf, '88-'93 (%)	(107.3)	(62.1)	(49.6)	n/a	n/a

Figure 14.1 **South Asia: country statistics (31 December 1993)**

bad. The failure of the Socialist model, therefore, had a deep impact on economists and civil servants in New Delhi. Simultaneously, the subcontinent has turned to the West, particularly to Britain and the US, for investment and closer co-operation in many fields. A fresh wind is blowing through the corridors of power in India. Like China, this also shows that a fast-growing economic strength will, over the next twenty years, enable it to become a regional military power. India has intervened in both Sri Lanka (in recent years) and in Bangladesh. The conflict in Kashmir, like that in Northern Ireland, goes on from year to year and appears no nearer to a resolution. For investors, however, the important development has been the recent reduction of tensions between Pakistan and India with the re-election of Benazir Bhutto and the diminishing influence of the Hindu extremists in India, led by Mr Advani of the BJP.

Culturally, too, South Asia offers many advantages to the Western investor. There are already a large number of listed companies, but they are little known and little researched. In India alone, there are over twenty stock exchanges and over seven thousand listed companies, most of them with an average market capitalization of less than US$50m. It offers a fertile field for both the investment manager and analyst and perhaps also for the purveyors of corporate finance, mergers and acquisitions specialists and underwriters. The opening up, therefore, of the Indian capital market to foreign investors and to foreign brokers and banks will begin to demonstrate results in the very near future. In 1993, we have already seen about twelve Indian companies issuing global depository receipts which have been quickly taken up by investment managers in London, Hong Kong and New York. Indian convertible bonds will no doubt become as fashionable for Swiss banks to add to their portfolios as Japanese convertible bonds were in the early 1980s. The new-found stability of the rupee must be a very important factor in building up this investor confidence. So, too, has been the widely-applauded decision to ease exchange controls and move towards a full convertibility of the currency. Far from inducing a flight of capital, this has resulted in much of the money which was parked offshore by wealthy Indians coming home to be used for attractive investments. The 11m overseas Indians, scattered as they are not only in the Gulf, in Singapore and Hong Kong, but also in the UK and the US, can, like the overseas Chinese, play a vital role in bringing capital, technology and an effective marketing network to the home country as it attempts to move up the industrial and technological ladder.

At present, the listed investment opportunities in India and Pakistan and Sri Lanka are mainly in the basic industry sectors such as textiles, cement, shipping and steel. A closer look, however, at what is happening in the real business world—Bombay, Karachi and Madras—would reveal that the combination of fluent English, highly-trained graduate scientists and engineers and comparatively low labour costs is producing a boom in such areas as software engineering, which means that many multi-national companies, such as Swissair among others, are now using India as a global computer base in which to process information on a 24-hour daily basis. This is undoubtedly a trend which will grow in the coming decades. India will move up-market but it will enter the fields of biotechnology as well as semi-conductors and software.

There are, of course, two faces to the Indian economy. There is still a vast percentage of the population engaged in the simplest forms of agriculture. On the other hand, now, after a generation of driving old English automobiles such as Ambassadors, the automobile industry in India is poised for a take off with the re-entry of the Japanese among others. India could well become a significant exporter of automobiles in the next ten years.

There can be no doubt of the enormous wealth and the enormous potential of South Asia in the next twenty years if peace and stability are maintained. The wealth of this region historically is well documented. That wealth is based not only on natural resources, but also on the vast populations and the ingenuity and creative resources of the people. Pakistan has been a good example of a country with few natural resources which has overcome many obstacles to modernize and build an industrial base in the past twenty years. Since it is the least known of the major emerging regions in the world, the Indian sub-continent probably has the greatest potential for investors.

Chapter 15

Bangladesh

Population:	114.3m
Gross national product:	US$25.1bn
Market capitalization:	US$400m
Currency/US$:	39.8 taka

Although it achieved independence little more than 20 years ago, Bangladesh has had a tumultuous political history with successive periods of democracy, dictatorship and, most recently, a Westminster-derived parliamentary system. Although Bangladesh remains poor and overcrowded, previously-unknown political stability and sustained economic progress has been achieved in the last several years.

Bangladesh's independence was sparked by the victory of the Awami League of East Pakistan in a 1970 election, with its major campaign platform being to seek regional autonomy for East Pakistan.

Following bitter opposition by West Pakistan and a series of fruitless negotiations, the Pakistani army overran East Pakistan yielding independence to Bangladesh only after India entered the war in December 1971. Sheik Mujibur Rahman, the leader of East Pakistan's Awami League, led Bangladesh's first elected government in 1973 in accordance with the country's newly-established Constitution. In 1975, Mujibur was assassinated and his government removed in a military coup by Khandker Mustaque Ahmed. The period between 1975 and 1981 was marked by successive coups and power struggles involving rival military figures. Army Chief of Staff Lieutenant Gen. H. M. Ershad became president in March 1982 through a bloodless coup and led Bangladesh until 1990 when he was deposed in the climax of anti-government protests in Dhaka and later jailed and tried for a long list of charges involving corruption and the usurpation of unauthorized powers. In a bitterly contested election with widespread voter participation, Khaleda Zia emerged as president.

The 12-year period of dictatorship offered little hope for the vast majority of Bangladeshis—either politically or economically—despite large amounts of foreign aid which was often poorly allocated and subject to

	1988	1989	1990	1991	1992	1993
Population (m)	102	104.4	106.6	109	111.6	114.3
GNP (US$bn)	20.3	20.8	22.2	23	23.9	25.1
Real GNP growth (%)	2.9	2.5	6.6	3.6	4	5
Per capita income (US$)	199	199.7	208.5	211	214	220
Exports (US$bn)	1	1	1	2	2	2.5
Imports (US$bn)	3	3	3	3.8	4	4
Foreign direct investment (US$bn)	2.6	2	3	2	10	
Inflation	9.4	10	8.5	7.2	4.3	3
Interest rates (prime)	16	16	18	16	14	13
International reserves (US$m)	890	960	590	960	1600	2200
Market capitalization (US$m)	434	478	349	291	330	400
No. of listed companies	111	116	134	138	142	144
Index performance in US$ (%)	3.2	14.8	32.5	21.6	23.4	33.7
Price/earnings (P/E) ratios	8	23.9	14.7	11.5	17.4	13.9
Earnings per share (EPS) growth					19	25
Av. daily turnover (US$ 000s)	15.7	19.5	21.7	11.7	25	38.1
Dividend yield	7	4.4	7.3	7.7	6.6	4.5
Currency to US$ (taka)	31.5	32.3	34.9	35.7	39	39.8

Figure 15.1 Bangladesh: key statistics

graft. In addition, numerous natural disasters have frustrated efforts at development.

The economy

The Bangladeshi economy remains largely dependent on agriculture which contributes nearly 40 per cent of output and employs nearly 70 per cent of the country's work-force. While the principal agricultural product is jute, Bangladesh also produces rice, tea, oil seeds, pulses and sugar cane. In the last several years, agricultural output has grown by an average of 4.5 per cent, aided by improved exports and favorable monsoon and weather conditions. The government has also withdrawn VAT taxes on fertilizer consumption, which has increased by 27 per cent in the last three years. Major industrial products include textiles, leather, and pharmaceuticals, while processed shrimp production is growing sharply. Over the past two years, industrial production has grown by an average of 8 per cent—fuelled by increased efficiency and output in the jute and fertilizer industries.

The focus of the government's economic policy is to increase export competitiveness through reduction in tariffs and import levies on production inputs in these products. Bangladesh is well positioned to export textiles, leather, and processed foods. In the last two years, Bangladesh's economy has improved significantly. Foreign exchange reserves have increased from below 2 months of imports in 1990 to nearly 7 in 1993. Inflationary pressures have eased considerably and CPI increases are expected to fall to below 5 per cent in 1993, from a recent high of 11 per cent in 1988. One area where the economy has seen little improvement in recent years has been in labour efficiency. Due to high levels of illiteracy, strong labour activism, and a recent 60 per cent rise in minimum wages, production output per worker has grown slower than wage increases.

Bangladesh's economic reform process has yet to show significant accomplishments beyond trade reform and the government has not yet been able to advance its privatization programme for state-owned enterprises.

The stock market

The Dhaka Stock Exchange was originally launched on 28 April 1954, under the name of the East Pakistan Stock Exchange Limited. Its name was

Company	**Market cap. (US$m)**	*Company*	**Volume (US$m)**
Bangladesh Tobacco	101.3	Bata Shoe Company	110.2
Bangladesh Oxygen	33.0	Beximco Pharmaceutical	96.7
Glaxo	30.7	Apex Footwear Ltd	70.4
Bata Shoe	18.8	Bangladesh Oxygen	54.3
Beximco Pharmacy	17.3	Apex Tannery	41.1
Padma Textiles	11.2	Chittagong Cement	24.2
City Bank	11.9	Ashraf Textile Mills	23.0
AB Bank	9.1	Padma Textile Mills	19.2
Reckitt & Colman	7.6	Eastern Cables	18.9
Monno Ceramic	7.5	6th ICB Mutual Fund	14.9
Apex Tannery	7.3	Bengal Food Ltd	14.5
IFIC	6.8	B General Insurance Co.	14.1
NBL	6.1	United Insurance Co.	10.2
Rupali Bank	5.9	Usmania Glass Sheet	8.8
Islami Bank	5.6	Monno Ceramic Industries	8.4
Tamijuddin Textiles	5.4	Tallu Spinning Mills Ltd.	8.3
ICB	5.1	Beximco Ltd.	7.5
Ashraf Textiles	4.6	Singer Bangladesh	7.2
Chittagong Cement	4.5	5th ICB Mutual Fund	7.1
Singer Bangladesh	3.9	Beximco Infusions	7.0

Figure 15.2 Bangladesh: 20 largest companies by market capitalization and average daily volume

amended to the Dhaka Stock Exchange Limited in 1964. During the tumultuous years following the establishment of Bangladesh's independence, trading on the Shaka Stock Exchange was suspended, only to resume in 1976 with nine companies listed. There are currently 144 companies listed on the Dhaka Stock Exchange and a total market capitalization of US$400m. Although the market is undemanding on a 1994 prospective P/E ratio of 8 times, liquidity continues to be a problem with average daily trading volume of the exchange at US$ 35,000.

Chapter 16

India

Population:	895m
Gross national product:	$264bn
Market capitalization:	$70.1bn
Currency/US$:	31.37 rupees

India is the other sleeping giant of Asia. There is little doubt that, along with China, it is the emerging market with the greatest potential. Although both its economic growth rate and its pace of reform have proceeded at a more sedate pace than in China, many observers have likened the two Asian giants to the tortoise and the hare. India possesses many inherited advantages which China lacks: the English language, a long-established legal and commercial system with good accounting standards, a good physical infrastructure and, most important, a class of experienced entrepreneurs and businessmen. The political stability, which comes from its democratic tradition of more than 45 years since independence, is also very important. It has survived a number of crises and changes with its stable national base intact. The economy and the stock exchange have continued to grow and develop steadily despite the assassination of Mrs Indira Ghandi and of her son, Rajiv; despite the Hindu/Muslim tension and killings which most recently resulted from the destruction of the Ayudhya mosque; despite the Bombay Stock Exchange scandal of 1992; and despite the loss of 30 per cent of India's exports which used to go to the former Soviet Union.

In 1993, India's exports were again growing by 20 per cent per annum, and the rupee was stable. The foreign exchange reserves had been restored to a healthy level and Prime Minister Rao appears to have weathered the political storms while the opposition BJP, or fundamental Hindu party, has lost a great deal of support and prestige in recent elections. Thus India appears set for a period of continued stability and steady economic reform with good prospects for investors. It could well account for 20 per cent of a global emerging market portfolio. To put this into perspective, India accounts for about half the total companies listed in the emerging markets,

	1988	1989	1990	1991	1992	1993
Population (m)	797	812	827	555	874	895
GNP (US$bn)	270.2	263.7	282.8	239	238.2	264
Real GNP growth (%)	7.3	10.4	5.8	1.2	3	4
Per capita income (US$)	339	325	342	280	272	295
Exports (US$bn)	13.5	16.6	18.9	18.6	21.2	21.6
Imports (US$bn)	20.1	22	26	21	24.7	21.4
Foreign direct investment (US$m)	218	159	230	154	192	389
Inflation	9.7	6.0	8.0	10.5	9.6	8
Interest rates (lending)	16.5	16.5	16.5	20	18	18
International reserves (US$bn)	4.9	3.9	1.5	3.6	5.4	8
Market capitalization (US$bn)	23.6	27.3	38.5	47.7	63.2	70.1
No. of listed companies	5841	5968	6100	6250	6400	6500
IFC Index performance in US$ (%)	37.6	4.5	18.7	18.15	22.9	17.0
Price/earnings (P/E) ratios	21.5	18.3	20.6	26.4	37.9	31.7
Earnings per share (EPS) growth	6	45	14	10	25	20
Average daily turnover (US$m)	n/a	40.1	48.2	56	47.1	54.5
Dividend yield	3.2	1.9	1.9	1.3	0.9	1.04
Currency to US$ (rupee)	13.89	16.14	17.43	22.57	27.5	31.4

Figure 16.1 India: key statistics

but only 8.4 per cent of their total market capitalization and only 3.5 per cent of the total value traded (US$) in these markets. Compared to other emerging markets, India has a large number of companies with medium to small market capitalization. This makes the task of researching all the companies in the Indian corporate sector extensive and cumbersome. Indian stocks appear to be thinly traded when compared to the US or even other emerging markets. The comparative trading value as a percentage of market capitalization are:

- US: 56 per cent
- Emerging markets: 77 per cent
- India: 31 per cent

History and outlook

India is a federal democratic republic comprising a union of 25 states and 7 centrally-administered territories. Consequent to its independence from the UK in 1947, a parliamentary form of government was established under the

Constitution of India (the Constitution) which came into force in 1950. The parliament, consisting of the Lower House (Lok Sabha) and the Upper House (Rajya Sabha), sits in New Delhi. The Lok Sabha is elected directly by universal suffrage for a period of 5 years, while the Rajya Sabha comprises members indirectly elected by the states and union territories for a 6-year term and members nominated by the president of India. Although there is never-ending political infighting and permanent crises in some or other part of the country, the Indian Constitution and democratic system have proved to be remarkably resilient. They are sustained by a free and multilingual press, with about 1300 daily newspapers published.

India is the seventh largest country in the world, covering an area of approximately 3.3m square kilometres. With a population currently estimated at 880m (1991 census), India has a wide diversity of languages, cultures, religions and social life, often giving the impression of being pulled apart. Yet, despite secessionist pressures in Punjab and the north-eastern region, the country has managed to soldier on. Its great strength has been the strong democratic tradition.

The country's economic history begins with the centrally-planned model initiated through the 5-year plans in 1950, with the primary focus being to control the direction of all investment and major economic decisions through the government. The Planning Commission set up in 1950 was required to assess the available resources and to identify growth areas. Such a structure provided an early boost to the industrialization of the economy which was predominantly agricultural when the British left. However, in due course, under the influence of an inward-looking policy and a vested bureaucracy, the centrally-planned model of growth became an effective stranglehold on industrial development. A gradual reversal of policy and the start of economic liberalization began in the early 1980s, first under the government of Mrs Indira Gandhi and then under that of Rajiv Gandhi. With the positive measures introduced in the 1985 budget, annual GDP growth rates rose from an average of 3 per cent since the 1940s, to an average of 5.4 per cent between 1986 and 1990. However, these growth rates were achieved at the cost of fiscal prudence and, coupled with a rising oil import bill, adverse balance of payments and a large foreign debt, caused a deepening crisis in the economy by 1991. Mid-term elections in July 1991 ushered in the new government under prime minister P V Narasimha Rao with Dr Manmohan Singh, an economist, as finance minister. The crisis was tackled with an emergency loan from the IMF. The IMF induced the government to embark on a series of radical reforms to liberalize the economy and encourage investment.

The major conditions imposed by the IMF were: a reduction in the government deficit; liberalization of industry and moves towards convertibility of the rupee. Initial reforms related to a new industrial policy and abolition of industrial licensing for most sectors of Indian industry. Other reforms announced so far have been:

- an increase in the permitted level of foreign ownership up to 51 per cent of equity in a wide range of industries;
- a reduction of tariff barriers and the abolition of import controls on a majority of items;
- renewed emphasis on and encouragement of exports;
- divestment by government of its holdings in public sector industrial undertakings;
- partial convertibility of the rupee on current account;
- opening of domestic stock markets to direct portfolio investment by approved foreign financial institutions;
- abolition of pricing controls for domestic capital issues;
- relaxation of foreign exchange controls;
- permission for Indian corporations to raise capital through GDRs/ADRs abroad;
- reduction of interest rates; and
- rationalization of tax structure.

As a result of the reform process which began in mid-1991, the economy has slowly recovered. In the two years since then, the mood has distinctly changed from one of despair and cynicism, towards optimism and hope. Foreign exchange reserves are now reasonably comfortable at US$8bn, thanks to capital inflows, and inflation has been kept under check. A 21 per cent growth in exports and an upsurge in investment plans in India are other positive outcomes. The GDP growth rate is projected at 4 per cent for 1993-94, with the actual thrust for a higher level of 6 per cent and above expected from 1995.

For years, analysts have spoken of the immense potential of India. For a long time this potential has remained unrealized. A caged tiger or a 'sleeping elephant' have also been used in the past to describe India, but it now does seem that the tiger is being uncaged. The follow-up budgets of February 1992 and February 1993, with further reforms, indicated the government's firm commitment to liberalization. The overwhelming changes that are taking place in the country are by no means the complete cure for all its problems, and the harder reforms still remain to be implemented. Politics remains the number one threat to economic reforms but, increasingly, the policymakers and India's corporate world are distancing themselves from political interference. The spin-off effects of sustained economic growth will further hasten this process and we remain hopeful of a revitalized, vibrant nation on the move.

Economic structure

India is blessed with a varied terrain and climate, large mineral reserves, a massive population, a majority of its urban population comfortable with the English language, and an often inventive and entrepreneurial middle class. While it developed a public sector and a reasonably vast industrial sector for a developing nation over the past four decades, it is still a highly agrarian society. Two-thirds of the nation's population is dependent upon agriculture which contributes one third (32 per cent) of the GDP.

Population

Seventy-four per cent of the population live in rural areas and 26 per cent in urban areas (see Figure 16.2). Population expansion is still rapid, although birth rates are declining. Increasing literacy rates should help curb population growth, although it is recognized that this will require considerable effort in time and resources. The need for primary health care, safe drinking water, sanitation and elementary education will put pressure on government expenses.

The rural population still consists of substantial numbers of smallholders and subsistence farmers. Over half of India's farmers have marginal holdings with average holdings of 0.4 hectares. Despite the dependency on monsoons, and the burdens of higher input costs and inflationary pressures, rural incomes have risen in recent years and this sector is increasingly viewed as a 'high potential' market by Indian corporations.

	1970-71	1980-81	1990-91
Total (million)	548.2	685.2	844.3
Rural population (%)	80.1	76.7	74.3
Urban (%)	19.9	23.3	25.7
Male (%)	51.8	51.7	51.9
Female (%)	48.2	48.3	48.1
Density (persons/sq. km.)	166.6	208.3	256.6
Birth rate (per 100)	3.7	3.4	2.6
Death rate (per 100)	1.5	1.3	0.9
Life expectancy at birth (yrs)	41.0	56.0	62.0
Literacy rate (%)	34.4	43.6	52.1

Figure 16.2 India: demographic analysis

Tertiary education standards are high. Although a small proportion of the population achieve these levels, in absolute numbers there are many graduates. This class forms the bulwark of the middle-class population at 150m and is often identified as the single most important reason for foreign investors to review their opinion of India.

Caste and religious distinctions are an important factor in the social fabric of the country. Elections often emphasize and contribute to increasing this divide. Caste and religious violence is now no longer confined to select pockets. However, despite all these impediments, there is hope that the fruits of economic growth will gradually wither away caste and religious divides.

Agriculture

Two-thirds of the nation's population is dependent upon agriculture. A steady increase in irrigated areas has helped improve yields and water supply. However, overall agricultural growth is still dependent on monsoons. India has had four good monsoons in a row and this has, to a great extent, helped contain the possible after-effects of poor overall economic growth in the last couple of years, especially in the industrial sector. However, distortions remain. Self-sufficiency continues to be the overriding objective, distorting productivity. Most inputs used by farmers, including fertilizer, are subsidized. The government is under increasing pressure from multilateral agencies to reduce its subsidy bill but, being a sensitive issue, attempts have been half-hearted. India is now largely self-sufficient in food grains although crop yields are way below international levels and further investment is needed.

Infrastructure

The backbone of the infrastructure—road and railway network, power supply etc.—does exist, but much of it suffers from poor management, political indecision, and overloading. With government finances being stretched, and limited by falling revenues, in the last two years, the reformers have decided to invite private sector investment in infrastructure. However, bureaucratic delays and red tape have frustrated such investment. Bottlenecks in India's infrastructure will be a major impediment to rapid growth. The railway system is extensive (the third largest in the world) but low fares and lack of investment have created pressures on the system. The road system is in urgent need of repair and upgrading. The telephone network is inadequate, of poor quality and fraught with operational inefficiencies. There are only five million lines in operation and, at any one time, the

	1988-89	1989-90	1990-91
Railways			
Route length (km)	61,985	62,211	62,367
Route length electrified (km)	8880	9100	9968
Cost of staff (US$m)	1398.8	1522.6	1645.2
Roads			
Road length surfaced ('000km)	928	960	1001
Road length unsurfaced ('000km)	985	1010	1036
Ports			
Major ports (number)	11	11	11
Merchant shipping tonnage	5906	6027	5939
Airlines			
Revenue tonnes/km (US$m)	26.78	26.30	22.26

Figure 16.3 India: transport & infrastructure

number of customers waiting for telephone connections is estimated to be in excess of two million. India's insistence on self-reliance and its reluctance to import switches and other equipment has created this situation. This policy is now changing and the telephone system in Bombay in particular has markedly improved. The Department of Telecommunication (DOT) has drawn up ambitious plans and the private sector has been invited to tender for major cellular systems and foreign switching technology is also being invited.

There is an urgent need for investment and improvement in power supplies. A major problem here is the low tariffs charged by the State Electricity Boards (SEBs). SEBs are chronically fund-constrained and, therefore, loss making. In turn, their payments to power-generating bodies are overdue and notoriously slow. The World Bank's planned US$2.1bn loan to the National Thermal Power Corporation (NTPC) has made the loan conditional on NTPC reducing its outstandings from SEBs. The government is also inviting the private sector into the power-generating business and a number of joint ventures are planned.

Industry

Industry contributes about 27 per cent of GDP. The bulk of the contribution comes from the manufacturing sector. India has a very diversified industrial base with production activities ranging from cement, auto components, leather goods, automobiles and consumer durables to heavy engineering equipment. However, until recently, quality consciousness has been low—no doubt driven by the vast domestic market and protection from imports. Technological and capital input has been low by international standards. However, recent reforms which have lowered tariff barriers and removed protective restrictions on imports, have induced Indian corporations to look abroad for increased technological support and joint ventures, with the emphasis on quality upgrading. There is also a recognition of the imperative need to source export markets. Recent industrial policy liberalization and the removal of licensing controls will also lead to increased competition in the domestic markets. However, high interest rates are a constraint to improving the cost-competitiveness of Indian industry.

The public sector enterprises constitute a major part of the industrial scene. There are over one thousand public sector enterprises in India, about seven hundred of which are owned by the state. Most of the public sector enterprises are dogged by gross overmanning, huge accumulated losses, low capacity utilization and inefficiency. In most sectors, government enterprises have virtual monopolies or dominant capacities. The nation's entire output of petroleum, lignite, copper and primary lead comes from PSUs. About 98 per cent of zinc, 90 per cent of coal and more than 50 per cent of steel and aluminium is produced by PSUs. Of the 237 central PSEs, only 134 are profitable. They have survived on budgetary support and acted as a major drain on resources. Over the last two years the government has initiated a policy of selective privatization by divesting its stake to Indian shareholders. However, this policy has drawn flak because of divestment to Indian mutual funds (which are again in the public sector) without any change in management control. The crucial issue of retrenchment of excess labour (exit policy) is still not addressed. Recently, the government has given clear directives to the public sector enterprises that budgetary support henceforth will be limited and they will have to approach the capital markets directly to raise resources. In a nutshell, this sector remains a drag and the process of recovery and improved performance will be a long one.

Banks and financial sector

The banking system is dominated by the State Bank of India and the twenty nationalized banks. They function under rigid regulatory mechanisms formulated by the central bank—The Reserve Bank of India. The controls include restrictions on interest rates, banks' investments in government securities, opening of branches and the direction of credit. The nationalized banks are also bound to disburse at least 40 per cent of the total credit to priority sectors including agriculture, small-scale businesses and trade. The controls and inefficiencies of the system including overmanning, a unionized unproductive work-force and dispersal of branches into the rural areas where business prospects are dim, have all led to most of the nationalized banks incurring huge losses. The recent liberalized atmosphere has turned its attention to reforms in the financial sector, too. Guidelines for private sector banks have been announced and capital adequacy norms for banks to reach international standards within a specified time-frame have been proposed. Permission to close unviable branches has also been a recent measure to improve profitability.

Foreign trade

Until 1990, India's foreign trade was dominated by trade with the East European countries. The collapse of rupee trade with this bloc, along with the foreign exchange crisis in 1991, created a rather tenuous situation for the country. A huge domestic market and protected licensing regime had caused a neglect of the export sector. Coupled with India's dependence on oil imports, the balance of payments situation was under continual strain. However, since then, there has been a turn for the better. Exports in 1993 have grown by 21 per cent in dollar terms. Imports, which were subjected to severe compression in 1991 following the foreign exchange crisis, have still remained subdued. The trade deficit, which fell to $3bn in 1992, is now estimated at $4bn (exports $18.8bn, imports $22.9bn). However, capital inflows through IMF borrowings and foreign direct investment have helped stabilize the foreign exchange scenario. Foreign exchange reserves are currently estimated at US$8bn. The optimism needs to be tempered with cau-

MAJOR EXPORTS	*% of total*	*MAJOR IMPORTS*	*% of total*
Garments	21.3	Petroleum	22.9
Engineering goods	11.9	Machinery & transport equipment	7.6
Leather & leather goods	7.9	Chemicals & fertilizers	13.4
Chemicals & pharmaceuticals	7.8	Iron & steel	4.9
Precious stones	4.6	Non-ferrous metals	2.6

LEADING EXPORT MARKETS	*% of total*	*LEADING SUPPLIERS*	*% of total*
CIS	16.1	USA	12.1
USA	14.7	Germany	8.0
Japan	9.3	Japan	7.5
Germany	7.8	UK	6.7

Figure 16.4 India: International trade analysis

tion as the repayment of IMF loans in 1994-95 to 1996-97 will cause strain again on the balance of payments unless foreign direct investment improves dramatically.

Exports as a percentage of GDP are at a mere 7.2 per cent for India, compared to 19 per cent for China, 20 per cent for Indonesia and Korea. There is considerable potential especially for textiles, gems and precious stones, auto components, leather goods and chemicals.

Recent economic performance

After a decade of average GDP growth of 5.4 per cent in the 1980s, there has been a hiccup in recent performance. The budget deficit and balance of payments had been running out of control. The consequent tight fiscal measures and high interest rates forced on the government has led to a sharp slow down in some areas. GDP growth of 5.2 per cent in 1990 fell sharply to 1.2 per cent in 1991, before recovering to 3.0 per cent in 1992. The recovery has been mainly sustained by agricultural performance, thanks to good monsoons.

	1981	1986	1991
Agriculture, forestry, fishing, mining & quarrying	39.6	36.3	33.4
Manufacturing, power & construction	24.4	25.9	27.0
Transport, Communications, Trade etc.	16.7	17.6	18.0
Finance & real estate	8.9	9.5	10.3
Community & personal services	10.4	10.7	11.3

Figure 16.5 India: origin of GDP (%)

Agriculture

Agricultural growth was 3.5 per cent in 1992 compared with a fall of 1.1 per cent in 1991. Food grain production increased by 5.7 per cent to 177m tonnes. For the current year food grain production is slated to cross 182m tonnes.

Industry

Industrial growth of 6.8 per cent in 1990 was maintained at 6.7 per cent in 1991. However, severe import compression and domestic recession saw growth fall drastically to 0.1 per cent in 1992. The recession has continued in cement, steel and infrastructure sectors, being dependent on government expenditure. However, in 1993 cotton textiles, sugar, automobiles and auto component segments did well.

Fiscal deficit

The fiscal deficit has continued to fall from 8.5 per cent of GDP in 1990 to 6.4 per cent in 1991. It is expected to decline to 5.7 per cent by 1993.

Inflation

When the reform process began in 1991, inflation was running high at 16.7 per cent. Thanks to cuts in the fiscal deficit and controls on money supply growth and good harvests, inflation is currently at 7 per cent. The price of administered goods and services are expected to be hiked, with 1993 year-end inflation reckoned to touch 8.0 per cent.

Interest rates

Interest rates, which were running at 18-20 per cent over the last two years, have been brought down in stages to 16 per cent.

External trade and balance of payments

Merchandise exports at US$18.9bn in 1990, US$18.6bn in 1991 and $18.8bn in 1992, have stagnated. In 1993, however, growth was impressive at 21 per cent in dollar terms helped by the devaluation. Exports are expected to reach US$22bn. Imports, which were at US$26bn in 1990, fell to US$21bn in 1991, before going to US$24.7bn in 1992. Severe restrictions have helped curb imports, but suppression of imports can only endure so long and we expect the import bill to rise significantly in 1994.

Foreign exchange reserves

After the crisis of June 1991, foreign exchange reserves have improved from a level of US$1.12bn to US$6.92bn in April 1993. Currently it is estimated at US$8bn and before the 1993 year-end is expected to touch US$9bn. External assistance, increased flow from foreign investment and collections achieved through the India Development bonds, have helped improve the foreign exchange reserves position.

Overall, the economy is slowly emerging from a recession. Current year growth should be 4 per cent increasing strongly in 1994 and 1995 as investments and exports pick up.

The stock market

The Indian stock market has a history tracing back 118 years with the first transaction being dealings in loan securities issued by the East India Company. It is Asia's oldest stock exchange. However, the actual growth can be traced from 1985, as the markets were largely dormant until then. Over-regulation in the economy, coupled with availability of debt, led to low levels of primary market activity until the 1980s. The initial liberalization programmes initiated in 1985 by the Rajiv Gandhi government resulted in a spate of IPOs and rights issues at low prices which in turn resulted in the growth of equity culture. Today, the stock exchanges have emerged as a major source of investment capital, both for existing corporations and for start up ventures. Increasingly, even public sector companies will have to tap this source for resource mobilization. The amount raised in primary issues has increased from about Rs700m during the 1960s, to a total of Rs45bn (US$1.5bn) during 1991-92. It improved to a staggering Rs275bn (US$8.7bn) in the year 1992-93. The number of individual investors has grown from 1m in 1980 to over 20m in 1992. Regulations on the pricing of IPOs and rights issues, which were lifted in 1992, has induced companies to take full advantage and we expect the markets to show a manifold expansion in terms of IPOs.

Another significant transition that the market is undergoing is from a speculative market to a more mature and research based market. The opening up of the markets to foreign institutional investors has broadened the base of market players and created pressures on the exchange authorities to improve the settlement systems.

There are 22 recognized stock exchanges in India in the major cities. Apart from these there is an OTC exchange on the lines of Nasdaq in the USA. The Bombay Stock Exchange accounts for about 70 per cent of transacted volumes. It is considerably more liquid than any other market in India and has about 400 active individual members.

The government has recognized a new stock exchange to be located in Bombay. The exchange, called 'The National Stock Exchange' (NSE) is being co-promoted by the leading Indian financial institutions under the co-ordination of the Industrial Development Bank of India. It is expected to be operational for trading in debt instruments by December 1993.

Regulation of stock exchanges

The day-to-day administration of stock exchanges is the responsibility of individual governing boards for each exchange. The composition of these boards, which used to be heavily weighted towards active stockbrokers, is changing as the Securities and Exchange Board of India (SEBI) has succeeded in getting non-broker directors appointed. These are usually representatives of government, The Reserve Bank of India and the SEBI. The SEBI's responsibilities include:

- regulation and licensing of stockbroker activities;
- regulation of capital issues, including approval of prospectuses;
- regulation of merchant bankers;
- regulation of mutual funds;
- control of insider trading.

Settlement procedures and operating mechanism

The Bombay Stock Exchange has two-hour trading sessions with deals made by open-outcry in a trading ring, during which an average of 90,000 deals are executed per day. There are specialized jobbers offering two-way quotes for scrips. Spreads on highly-liquid scrips are narrow, but in illiquid counters can widen to as much as 15 per cent. Transactions are matched overnight by the BSE's computer system. The BSE plans to introduce screen-based trading for less active scrips in 1994.

Indian stocks are categorized into two groups: specified or 'A' group shares; and unspecified or 'B' group shares. The necessary qualifications for the specified category shares include:

- the company must have been listed for at least 3 years;
- there must be a minimum issued capital of Rs75m;
- there must be at least 10,000 public shareholders;
- payment of dividends must take place;

The normal account period is 14 days. For the 'A' group, positions are permitted to be carried forward, while for 'B' group stocks, transactions have to be settled by delivery and payment at the end of each settlement period.

■ Typical settlement programme

Settlement period:	Day 1-14
Delivery of shares:	Day 22-25
Pay in:	Completion by Day 25-30
Pay out:	Completion by Day 28-33

Settlement for non-specified B group shares is now on a weekly basis. Settlement procedures are a major weakness of the Indian markets. The dated transfer deeds and share certificates which change hands are a major hurdle to the smooth development of markets. Physical delivery of all shares has to be effected together with duly executed transfer forms and the transfer/registration process with companies takes a minimum of 3 months. A bill called 'The Stock Holding Corporation of India Bill' to immobilize securities through a national depository is being considered. It proposes to establish central and regional depositories which, on completion, would alleviate the problem caused by physical transfers.

Stockholding pattern

Broad estimates put the stockbroking pattern amongst the following groups:

- controlling management/family: 25-30 per cent;
- institutions (public sector institution, mutual funds, etc.): 35-45 per cent;
- public (free float): 35-40 per cent.

The recent trend of increasing size and number of IFOs will increase the free float.

Turnover

A rise in the investor base and capital issues has seen turnover on the Bombay Stock Exchange rise from a daily average of Rs0.3bn in 1985, to Rs1.5bn in 1992. Volumes are high only in about 25 per cent of the roughly 1500 actively traded stocks (total listings 6000+).

Market capitalization

From a level of US$7.35bn in 1980, market capitalization has risen to US$70bn in 1993. It is 30 per cent of GDP.

Price/earning multiples

The P/E multiples of stocks have been rising consistently over the past few years and, compared to international trends, have been high. This is primarily because of low float and excess demand for stocks. With an increase in IPOs a more balanced P/E multiple is expected by 1994.

BSE SENSEX	Historic P/E ratio *(based on monthly average)*
1989	18
1990	20
1991	22
1992	37
1993	30

Figure 16.6 India: Historic price/earnings ratios (Bombay Stock Exchange Sensitive Index - SENSEX)

	Mar 90	Mar 91	Mar 92	Mar 93	Oct 93
BSE SENSEX	781.05	1167.97	3487.0	2280.5	2673.7
BSE National	420.62	589.48	1967.71	n/a	1280.7

Figure 16.7 India: Performance of the SENSEX and National indices

Market indices and performance

The most popular index used is the Bombay Stock Exchange Sensitive Index (SENSEX) which is based on 30 major stocks traded on the Bombay Stock Exchange. However, the BSE National Index, which is based on 100 stocks selected on an all-India basis, is more representative.

1992 was a dramatic year for Indian stock markets. The euphoria generated by the reform proposals of the February 1992 budget sparked a major rally. But the discovery of fraudulent transfer of funds from the banking system into the stock market, popularly called the 'scam', pricked the bubble. The shock of the discovery, the arrest of key operators and officials, the combination of poor results and a spurt in primary issues caused an equally dramatic fall. It has since seen a minor recovery fuelled by interest shown by foreign institutional investors. The market is in a transitional phase with merchant bankers and issuers experimenting with new issues under 'free market' conditions and an increasing number of domestic mutual funds and foreign institutional investors taking an active interest.

Capital market developments

Foreign institutional investors

While presenting the budget for 1992-93 in February 1992, the finance minister announced a decision to allow reputable foreign institutional investors to invest in the Indian capital market. Guidelines to give effect to this policy were enumerated in September 1992. The response in terms of the number of institutions registered with the SEBI has been encouraging. To date more than 75 FIIS have registered.

The broad contours of the guidelines are:

- only institutional investors permitted;
- investments permitted in all primary and secondary market instruments;
- initial registration with the nodal regulatory agency—Securities and Exchange Board of India (SEBI) required;
- RBI permission for various exchange control regulations required;
- registration renewable every five years;
- RBI permission will enable FIIs to transact business, operate bank accounts and repatriate capital and profits;
- no lock-in period for investments;
- concessional tax regime—20 per cent on dividend and interest income; 10 per cent on long-term capital gains; 30 per cent on short-term capital gains;
- No FII to hold more than 5 per cent of capital of any company.

The initial response in terms of actual inflows has been poor, partly on account of an overvalued market and apprehension of settlement procedures and relatively high tax rates. Investments to date from September 1992 are estimated at US$400m but, from August 1993, interest has improved. Over 1994, expected inflow is about US$1bn.

Country funds

Until 1993, there were four country funds dedicated to India, all closed-ended. For a significant period they were all traded at heavy to moderate discounts to their net values. With interest picking up in 1993, the discounts narrowed.

- **India Fund:** issued at 1.00 pounds in August 1986. This fund is managed by the Unit Trust Of India and was lead managed by Merrill

Lynch. Incorporated in Guernsey and listed on the London stock exchange the fund's corpus is US$192m. Went open-ended in July 1993.

- **India Growth Fund:** managed by the same partnership as the India Fund, this US$60m fund is traded and listed in New York. It was issued at US$12.00 in August 1988.
- **India Magnum Fund:** managed by Morgan Stanley in association with the State Bank of India. It is the biggest country fund in India with a total initial corpus of US$200m with the 'B' tranche issued in July 1990 at US$26.29 per share.
- **Himalayan Fund:** issued at US$10.50 in June 1990, the US$100m fund is managed by Canara Bank in Bombay in association with Indosuez Investment Services. Its assets are invested 75 per cent in India and 25 per cent in Sri Lanka, Nepal and Bangladesh. It is incorporated in the Netherlands and listed on the London Stock Exchange.

In 1993, more new funds were launched. In keeping with the general trend all these funds are open-ended.

- **India Opportunities Fund**: launched by Martin Currie in August 1993 and jointly managed with Indian Bank in Bombay. Initial offer US$150m.
- **Bombay Fund**: managed by Barclays de Zoete Wedd with an initial offer of US$50m.
- **LG India Fund**: open-ended fund managed by Lloyd George Management in Hong Kong.
- **Indico Fund**: launched and managed by Foreign and Colonial Markets Fund (FC) with an initial offer of US$150m.

Global Depository Receipts (GDRs)

Indian corporations made a start in 1992 with Global Depository Receipts with issues by two of the top ten Indian industrial houses.

- **Reliance Industries**: The global depository receipt for this textile/polyester/petrochemicals group was brought to the market by Morgan Stanley in May 1992, at an issue price of US$16.35. The issue size was US$150m. Reliance has followed up with another euroconvertible issue this year garnering US$1.1bn.
- **Grasim Industries:** The dominant produce of viscose fibre, with cement and sponge iron being other lines of business. Grasim issued US$90m of GDRs in November 1992, at a price of US$12.98.
- **Hindalco Industries:** This aluminium major entered the fray in 1993 with a GDR issue. Essar Group, Jindal Strips, Bombay Dyeing, South-

ern Petrochemicals Industries Corporation (SPIC) and the finance company, SCICI, followed later with euro-currency bond issues at attractive rates of interest and all of them were over-subscribed. The tobacco giant, ITC, sold 4.5m GDRs at a price of US$15.30 per unit and has raised US$91.8m. Many more Indian corporations have ambitious plans for further offerings of GDRs/eurobonds.

Privatization of state-owned enterprises

The government has enunciated a policy of disinvestment of up to 49 per cent of government equity. The initial tranche of disinvestment was made in 1992, but the offers were not directly made to the Indian public but rather to the public sector mutual funds. The second and third tranches, with invitations to individuals also to take up the offer, did not fetch attractive prices. Further offers are slated towards the last quarter of fiscal 1993-94. Major divestments until now have been in the petrochemical, telecommunications and heavy engineering companies. Of the better known and more profitable ones, Bharat Petroleum (30 per cent disinvestment), Hindustan Petroleum (30 per cent), Videsh Sanchar Nigam (20 per cent) have greater investor interest. The government raised US$1bn from the sale of 31 public sector undertakings during 1991-92. In fiscal 1992-93 it raised US$620m.

In addition to the active divestment of its shareholdings, the government is also following other policies, namely:

- a halt on new budgetary support to PSUs;
- the opening-up of most industries to competition.

However, the government has stated its intentions to maintain ultimate majority control of many PSUs, particularly those in the oil sector.

Product	**Units**	**Value (US$m)**
Packaged food		
Soft drinks	20,490m bottles	382.2
Baby milk foods	61,400 tonnes	127.4
Ice cream	50,000 kilolitres	79.6
Chocolates	11,326 tonnes	159.2
Beer	220,000 kilolitres	238.9
Cigarettes	90bn sticks	1271.7
Wine & spirits		442.0
Appliances		
Colour televisions	830,000	n/a
VCRs	150,000	n/a
Refrigerators	1,400,000	n/a
Washing machine	350,000	n/a
Vacuum cleaners	150,000	15.0
Air conditioners	70,000	n/a
Rice cookers	75,000	3.6
Watches	10,000,000	155.0
Personal vehicles		
Cars	165,000	799.2
Motorcycles	430,000	252.7
Scooters	820,000	313.1
Mopeds	415,000	85.3

Figure 16.8 India: national market size for branded products

Company	**Mkt cap. (US$m)**	**Equity (US$m)**	**EPS (Rs)**	**Market price (Rs)****	**Activity**	**Remarks**
Reliance Industries	2469.9	93.08	11.1	265.50	Diversified	World scale, vertically-integrated plants ensuring lower costs.
Hindustan Lever	2117.7	44.58	7.0	474.75	Soaps & detergents	Access to international product range that will ensure steady earnings growth.
ITC Ltd	2081.8	37.18	13.3	560.00	Diversified	Strong export presence / excellent brand image.
Tata Steel	1795.3	104.07	3.9	172.50	Steel	Facing demand recession / not internationally competitive.
Colgate Palmolive	1161.4	16.02	9.6	710.00	Healthcare	Access to international product range that will ensure steady earnings growth.
TELCO	1148.8	41.03	2.3	284.00	Commercial vehicles	Unmatched brand image and easing of demand recession will lead to strong earnings growth.
Grasim Industries	1020.2	21.48	18.5	475.00	VSF/Cement	VSF to do well though cement and sponge iron will have adverse impact.
Bajaj Auto	713.1	11.98	13.8	595.00	Motorcycles	Cost-competitive internationally and excellent brand image. High cash earnings.
Century Textiles*	779.9	13.56	153.8	5750.00	VFY/Cotton/Cement	Strong export presence with high cash earnings though cement will have adverse impact.
Associated Cement*	568.8	24.52	89.4	2280.00	Cement	Industry currently under demand recession, easing of which will lead to strong earnings growth.

**Rs100 paid up (US$3.18)*

***Market rates as at 10 November 1993*

Figure 16.9 India: top ten companies

Chapter 17

Nepal

Population:	19.9m
Gross national product:	$3.0bn
Market capitalization:	$82.8m
Currency/US$:	49.3 rupees

Nepal is a mountainous kingdom on the slopes of the Himalayas, between India and Tibet. Included within its territory is the highest mountain in the world, Mount Everest, at 29,078 feet. Nepal emerged as a separate nation in the middle of the 18th century when it was unified by the warrior Raja of Gorkha who founded the present Nepalese dynasty. For one hundred years, it was ruled by a line of hereditary Rana prime ministers but in 1950 the monarchy was restored. King Mahendra prescribed all political parties in 1960 and introduced a new constitution in 1962. However, recently there has been mass agitation for political reform and this led, in 1990, to the lifting of the ban on political parties and to a new constitution. Nepal's vulnerable strategic position has led to both India and China vying for diplomatic influence in Kathmandu.

One of the major environmental problems facing Nepal is the deforestation which has severely impacted agriculture, and led to widespread flooding. In contrast with Bhutan, its neighbouring Himalayan country, Nepal has been entirely open to tourism which has been the single largest source of revenue. But the rapid increase in population, still growing at over 2 per cent annually, has meant growing pressure on the land resources of the country. Nepal has nevertheless achieved a steady growth in its economy which has raised per capita incomes from $150 to $170 per head, still a very low level, in recent years. Exports have also increased, helped by the steep fall in the Nepalese rupee which halved in value against the US dollar in the past three years.

Against this economic background, it is encouraging to find that the tiny Nepalese stock market has grown steadily, with the number of listed companies doubling since 1988 and the market capitalization approaching US$100m. Daily turnover, however, is still only about $5000 and it is, there-

	1988	1989	1990	1991	1992	1993
Population (m)	17.9	18.4	18.9	19.2	19.5	19.9
GNP (US$bn)	1.4	1.55	1.82	2.1	2.6	3
Real GNP growth (%)	7.2	4.2	6.1	5.5	3.1	2.5
Per capita income (US$)	150	140	180	180	170	170
Exports (US$m)	195.5	156.2	217.9	274.8	390	480
Imports (US$bn)	672.8	571.4	666.6	756.9	907	990
Foreign direct investment (US$m)	n/a	n/a	n/a	n/a	n/a	n/a
Inflation	11	8.1	11.5	9.8	26.1	15
Interest rates (prime)	15	15	14.4	14	13	16
International reserves (US$m)	212.5	206.8	272.9	378.5	438.9	556.7
Market cap (US$m)	54.4	72.2	73.2	67.5	80.3	82.8
No. of listed companies	31	36	41	46	55	59
Index performance in US$ (%)	n/a*					
Price/earnings (P/E) ratios						24.5
Earnings per share (EPS) growth						14
Avg daily turnover (US$)	1936	3368	3736	2932	3456	5712
Dividend yield						3.1
Currency to US$ (rupee)	23.29	27.19	29.37	37.26	42.72	49.3

**No index exists*

Figure 17.1 Nepal: key statistics

fore, extremely difficult for any foreign investor to trade actively in the market.

Exchange address

Nepal Stock Exchange
Dilibazar
Kathmandu
PO Box 1550
Nepal

(Trading hours: Sunday-Thursday: 11.00-13.00, except Mondays: 14.00-15.00. Friday: 11.00-12.00)

Chapter 18

Pakistan

Population:	120.8m
Gross national product:	$52.2bn
Market capitalization:	$8.1bn
Currency/US$:	29.8 rupees

Pakistan was the child of Jinnah's vision of an Islamic state on the north-west frontier of India. Born in 1947, in the tumult of Indian independence, it has achieved a remarkable growth and relative prosperity through its own efforts. A close relationship with the US has also been an important factor. In recent years, the war in Afghanistan, which caused a flood of over three million refugees into Pakistan, has been a heavy cost to the country. With the return of peace on its northern frontier Pakistan's political risk profile has markedly improved and, with it, the investor profile of its stock exchange. Pakistan had a military government from 1977 to 1988. The recent elections in which Mrs Benazir Bhutto regained power were an important development in its steady progression towards a liberal democracy. This has also led to a warming-up of relations with India.

Pakistan's economy has grown steadily in recent years, with an average growth rate of 5 per cent. Inflation has moderated and interest rates are beginning to fall. Against this background, the markets in Karachi and Lahore have had an excellent performance in 1992, rising 172 per cent, stabilizing in 1992 and continuing their upward ascent in 1993. However, the major listed industry of textiles has had a difficult year and this has held back the broader performance of the market. The Pakistani banks and insurance companies have performed well and the market, with over US$8bn of capitalization, is beginning to attract international investors. There are two Pakistan funds listed offshore. Daily turnover now exceeds US$10bn and Pakistan has the potential to rise to the major league of emerging markets.

	1988	1989	1990	1991	1992	1993
Population (m)	103.8	107	110.4	113.8	117.3	120.8
GNP (US$bn)	40	41.5	41.6	46.6	49.2	52.2
Real GNP growth (%)	3.6	4.1	5	3.6	6.5	3.2
Per capita income (US$)	385	388	377	410	419	432
Exports (US$bn)	4.4	4.6	4.9	5.9	6.8	6.6
Imports (US$bn)	6.9	7.2	7.4	8.4	9	9.8
Foreign direct investment (US$m)	162	209	216	246	335	450
Inflation	6.3	10.4	6	12.7	9.6	9.8
Interest rates (lending)	6.3	6.3	7.3	7.6	7.5	12.6
International reserves (US$m)	1359.5	1350.5	1487.7	1510.3	1832.7	1725
Market capitalization (US$bn)	2.2	2.3	2.3	3.1	8.8	8.1
No. of listed companies	265	400	487	511	608	645
IFC Index performance in US$ (%)	13.8	6.4	11.1	172.1	18.4	52.4
Price/earnings (P/E) ratios	40.6	35.3	31.2	27.2	21.7	17.5
Earnings per share (EPS) growth	10	15	13	14.9	24.9	24.3
Average daily turnover (US$m)	1.6	1.2	1.2	3.8	5	9.5
Dividend yield	1.6	1.5	1.3	1.3	1.7	2.4
Currency to US$ (rupees)	17.6	19.2	21.5	22.4	24.9	29.8

Figure 18.1 **Pakistan: key statistics**

Exchange addresses:

Karachi Stock Exchange (Guarantee) Ltd.
Stock Exchange Building
Stock Exchange Road
Karachi

Tel: 9221 233581

Lahore Stock Exchange (Guarantee) Ltd.
17 Bank Square
PO Box 1315
Lahore

Tel: 9242 57265

Company	**Market cap. (US$m)**	*Company*	**Volume (US$ '000s)**
Pauji Fertilizer	670.8	Delwan Salman Fibre	827
Lever Brothers	241.3	Indus Motors	608
ICI Pakistan	188.3	Fauji Fertilizer	292
SUI Northern Gas Ltd	182.3	Bank of Punjab	267
Engro Chemical	178.3	D.G. Khan Cement	174
SUI Southern Gas Ltd	177.9	Pakistan State Oil	141
Pakistan State Oil	177.7	ICI Pakistan	129
Dewan Salman Fibre	171.1	Cherat Cement	140
P.I.A.C.	154.8	Kohinoor Power Company	94
National Refinery	139.8	Pakistan Synthetics	84
National Fibres	131.6	Nishat Mills	66
Packages Limited	108.9	ICP S.E.M.F.	64
Glaxo Laboratories	106.0	Muslim Commecial Bank	62
Bank of Punjab	99.6	Gatron Industries	61
Muslim Commercial Bank	99.3	Ibrahim Energy	59
K.E.S.C.	95.9	Packages Limited	52
D.G. Khan Cement	95.7	Pakland Cement	51
Nishat Mills	92.1	Pioneer Cement	48
Indus Motors	91.1	Bankers Equity Limited	45
Pakistan Oilfields	89.2	Tawakkal Ltd	45

Figure 18.2 **Pakistan: 20 largest companies by market capitalization and average daily volume**

Chapter 19

Sri Lanka

Population:	17.8m
Gross national product:	$9.99bn
Market capitalization:	$1.97bn
Currency/US$:	49 rupees

Sri Lanka, formerly known as Ceylon, is a fertile and attractive island lying in the Indian Ocean off the southern tip of India. Its population is now estimated at nearly 18m enjoying a higher living standard than any of the other countries of the sub-continent. However, the ethnic composition of the people—74 per cent Sinhalese, 18.2 per cent Tamils—has led to continuing conflict in recent years and has undoubtedly held back the foreign investment which Sri Lanka would otherwise attract. The island has many important assets including its fertile soil, favourable climate and well-educated population together with a basically sound infrastructure.

The Colombo stock exchange was originally started by the British and the foundation of the country's prosperity was in tea followed by rubber. In recent years the stock market has been revived as Sri Lanka's thirty-year flirtation with socialism has been discarded. In fact, many of the tea plantations are now being restored to private management under the name 'peoplization'. At the same time, the manufacturing and service sectors have become the engines of economic growth. Textile production has increased. The tourist industry is performing very well and there is considerable interest in investment in the hotel sector. In 1992 foreign direct investment grew nearly 85 per cent to US$115m. Relatively low wages, various government incentives (for example, ten year tax holidays) and Sri Lanka's strategic location were contributing factors to this improvement. Further economic reforms such as liberalization of foreign exchange in 1994 could well boost inflows of foreign direct investment.

Against this background, the stock exchange has performed well although the rupee has continued to depreciate against the international currencies. Sri Lanka has a problem of inflation which reached 22 per cent in 1993. Nevertheless, market capitalization now exceeds US$2bn and there are 200 companies listed. Sri Lanka will undoubtedly benefit from the new-

	1988	1989	1990	1991	1992	1993
Population (m)	16.5	16.8	16.9	17.2	17.4	17.86
GNP (US$bn)	6.2	6.7	7.97	8.73	9.17	9.99
Real GNP growth (%)	3.5	2.3	6.2	4.6	4.3	5.6
Per capita income (US$)	375	391	439	460	494	510
Exports (US$bn)	1.4	1.67	1.9	2	2.39	2.56
Imports (US$bn)	2.08	2.4	2.67	3	3.3	3.45
Foreign direct investment (US$m)	-	-	-	165	116	174
Inflation	15	15.1	19.6	17	13.8	12
Interest rates (lending)	14.8	18	18.5	19.6	20.2	20.4
International reserves (US$bn)	128	446	598	808	1047	1262
Market capitalization (US$bn)	471	427	917	1936	1439	1970
No. of listed companies	176	176	175	178	190	198
Index performance in US$	-26	63	98	66	-36	61.9
Price/earnings ratios (P/E)	8	11	1212	2020	12	15
Earnings per share (EPS) growth	n/a	n/a	n/a	n/a	17	28
Average daily turnover (US$m)	48	28	156	416	456	1850
Dividend yield	n/a	n/a	n/a	1.4	2.3	2.8
Currency to US$ (rupee)	35	38	40	42	46	49

Figure 19.1 Sri Lanka: key statistics

found interest shown by international fund managers in India as a major market in the process of opening up. It is very often the case that Indian country mutual funds will include, say, a 10 per cent weighting in Sri Lanka as a diversification. The key to the island realizing its economic and investment potential will be in the restoration of peace and political stability.

Exchange address

Colombo Securities Exchange (Gte) Ltd.
2/F Mackinnon Building
York Street
Colombo
Sri Lanka

Tel: 941 25686

Company	**Market cap. (US$m)**	*Company*	**Volume (US$ '000s)**
DFCC	96.4	John Keells Holdings	409
John Keells Holdings	71.4	Pure Beverages	302
Ceylon Grain	69.3	Aitken Spence	257
National Development Bank	62.1	Lanka Milk	232
Hayleys	61.8	NDB	
Commercial Bank	59.5	Beruwala Walk	162
Asian Hotels Corporation	59.2	Asian Hotels	161
Hatton National Bank	54.9	Fort Land	145
Colombo Drydocks	49.0	Pelwatta	137
Aitken Spence	46.7	Riverina Hotels	90
Distilleries	39.3	Blue Diamonds	87
Trans Asia Hotels	35.7	Merchant Bank	84
Sampath Bank Ltd.	29.3	ACL	
Lanka Orix Leasing	28.3	Sampath Bank	70
Colombo Pharmacy	27.9	CT Land	68
PDL	27.5	Lanka Tiles	52
Nestle	27.4	Kapila Heavy	45
Lanka Ceramic	25.7	Hotel Services	21
Galadari Hotels	25.0	Distilleries	13
Seylan Bank	21.4	Bogala Graphite	12

Figure 19.2 Sri Lanka: 20 largest companies by market capitalization and average daily volume

PART IV

Latin America

THE EMERGING MARKETS OF LATIN AMERICA

Chapter 20

Latin America - Introduction

The transformation of Latin America as a destination for investors in the past ten years is nothing short of remarkable. Beginning in the late 1970s under the inauspicious rule of the dictator, Pinochet, Chile pioneered the way back from state interventionism towards free market reforms. The success of Chile's economic revival was widely noted by its neighbours. Argentina, which had perhaps the worst problems of hyperinflation, political corruption and decline, successfully followed the Chilean example in the late 1980s with the return to power of the unlikely figure of the Peronist Menem. With the help of his able finance minister, Domingo Cavallo, the new Argentine government was able to bring the inflation rate down from over 1000 per cent to less than 10 per cent, to stabilize the peso against the dollar (effectively at a 1:1 rate) and restore confidence in Argentina with the result that an estimated US$10bn has flowed back into the country in the last four years.

More recently, and again under an authoritarian government, Peru has, within twelve months, restored its fortunes in the eyes of international investors by cutting its budget deficit, reducing inflation and largely emulating the market reforms which had been so successful among its southern neighbours. Even the most isolated and recalcitrant dictatorship such as Paraguay has finally felt the mood of change move towards democracy and opened its economy to foreign investment. A large question mark still hangs over the giant of the Latin American continent—Brazil—which is still struggling in the aftermath of the corruption scandal which brought down President Collor who had promised so much when he was elected in 1990. Instead, the government in Brasilia stumbled on from crisis to crisis, from finance minister to finance minister. The inflation rate continues at 30-40 per cent monthly. The cruzeiro falls at a steady and accelerating rate against the dollar and urban crime in Rio and São Paolo has become more and more rampant as the cases of violence between police and impoverished street children attest. There is a complete lack of international confidence in Brazil's ability to tackle these problems. Nevertheless, the Brazilian stock market has repeatedly anticipated an improvement, and many international fund managers and pundits, such as Barton Biggs of Morgan Stanley, have increased their exposure to Brazil on the basis that it can and it must tackle

	Argentina	Brazil	Chile	Colombia	Mexico	Peru	Uruguay	Venezuela
Population (m)	33.4	153	13.5	34	84	23	3.17	20.5
GNP (US$bn)	237.3	431	41.2	51.4	338	24	12	63.7
Real GNP growth (%)								
1992	8.7	1.3	10.4	3.6	2.6	1.9	7.4	7.3
1993	5	4	6	4.5	1.9	4	3.1	3.5
1994[F]	5	5	5.5	5.5	3.5	5	3.6	4.2
Per capita income (US$)	7105	2817	3052	1512	4024	1087	3785	3107
Exports (US$bn)	13	39	9.8	7.6	29.9	3.55	n/a	14
Imports (US$bn)	15	25	10.7	7.64	51.1	4.05	n/a	11.4
Foreign direct investment (US$m)	n/a	n/a	n/a	n/a	6200	n/a	n/a	n/a
Inflation	9	2550	12	22	8.5	45	50	37
Interest rates	9	31.9	7.5	26.2	13.9	5.8	n/a	38.9
Market capitalization (US$bn)	26	74.4	35.2	10.2	142	3.8	0.45	6
No. of listed companies	179	692	258	80	188	250	n/a	66
Index performance in 1993 (%)	67.3	91.3	29.5	31.7	46.2	34.9	n/a	(10.5)
Price/earnings (P/E) ratios								
1993[e]	15	17.1	16.9	13.8	11.7	20.8	n/a	22.4
1994[f]	11.2	10.8	14.7	12.1	9.3	16	n/a	12.2
Earnings per share (EPS) growth								
1993[e]	21	42.9	5.3	12	7	0	n/a	21.9
1994[f]	11.2	39.1	14	14	16	26	n/a	n/a
Avg daily turnover (US$m)	70.1	180	9.1	2.8	250	5.5	n/a	10.5
Dividend yield	4.2	0.6	4.1	n/a	1.7	n/a	n/a	0.8
Stock market performance , '88-'93 (%)	793	106	391	542	644	n/a	n/a	230
Currency to US$ perf., '88-'93 (%)	(60,636)	(43,261k)	(66.6)	(103.1)	(33.8)	(146,531)	(892)	(181)

Figure 20.1 Latin America: country statistics (31 December 1993)

its problems and that the result will be a tremendous re-rating of the Brazilian market in line with the enormous size of the industrial base in and around São Paolo.

Nowhere else in the world is the unlocking of capital flows so obviously beneficial as between the US and South America. The 1982 debt crisis, which affected not only Mexico but all of Latin America, effectively froze the flow of lending and investment to the Latin American countries for almost a decade. It was called 'the lost decade' of Latin America. The Falklands War of March to June 1982, between Argentina and Britain, also was a cathartic turning point which led to the fall of the military junta in Buenos Aires and consequently weakened dictatorships everywhere in the continent.

The investor approaching Latin America is initially confronted with a bewildering variety of different countries and markets: the vice-royalties of new Spain, centred on Peru and Argentina (Brazil is, of course, the exception in the whole continent in being Portuguese-speaking rather than Spanish). These two large former colonies broke up in the 1820s into innumerable small countries and there have been few subsequent changes, although Latin America has known its civil wars like the Chile Peru war of the 1860s and the Paraguay Argentina war of the 1870s.

Broadly speaking, there has been peaceful evolution in Central America but the attempts to unify the small republics of Guatemala, Nicaragua, El Salvador, Costa Rica and Paraguay have all failed and, consequently, we are faced with a lot of small economies struggling to compete in world markets frequently with one export commodity. In addition, social and political instability has plagued these countries so that, with the exception of Costa Rica, they have not had a continuing record of democracy and economic growth.

No-one can doubt, however, the enormous economic potential of the Latin American hemisphere. With the signing of the North American Free Trade Agreement in late 1993, the opening up of new markets to US capital and goods and the reduction of import tariffs is having a very positive effect on the countries of the region especially Argentina, Chile and Brazil which have formed themselves a free trade agreement under the 'Southern cone'. British investors in particular have, in the past, put a great deal of capital into Latin America, not always with happy results. Not only the endemic inflation of the past forty years and the tradition of Caudillos or corrupt dictators, but also the history of debt repudiation must cause some reflection on the risk involved in lending and investing in this region of the world. The famous instance of 1893 when Baring Brothers almost went bankrupt as a result of their Argentina exposure has been repeated at regular intervals of about a generation: in the 1930s, widespread debt repudiation and again in the 1982 Mexico debt crisis. It may be, however, that in the 1990s with the shift from bank lending to direct investment and equity financing, both domestic and foreign investors in South American shares may have a better hedge against inflation and a better chance of reaping the rewards of economic growth than the international banks did in the 1970s and 1980s. The movement towards free trade implies a trend towards free capital movements in and out of these new exchanges.

Latin America stock markets are essentially European in culture and their stock exchanges in Buenos Aires, São Paolo and Santiago are very similar to those in Paris, Madrid and Milan. Some of the same liquidity constraints are apparent. Sometimes the influence of the banks is greater than in the Anglo-Saxon exchanges such as New York or London. Nevertheless, the trend towards privatization, which has been especially marked in Mexico, where it is estimated US investors have put over US$5bn in the last two years, is also striking in considering Argentina and Chile where the telephone companies, the airlines and electricity power utilities have all been successfully floated on the stock exchanges. In Brazil this trend is yet to start in a major way.

Chapter 21

Argentina

Population:	33.4m
Gross national product:	$237.3bn
Market capitalization:	$26bn
Currency/US$:	.9995 pesos

More than any other Latin nation, Argentina's history and development has been shaped by the diversity of the immigrants who have flocked to the port of Buenos Aires throughout the last two hundred years. The effects of this human capital contributed to Argentina's status as one of the ten wealthiest nations in the world at the turn of the century.

The Spanish actually began arriving in Argentina as early as 1516. Colonization was slow, however, as almost all early developments were concentrated in Peru and Bolivia—the region richest in gold and silver ore deposits. It was not until 1776 that the viceroyalty of the River Plata, with Buenos Aires as the capital, was established. It was during those 250 years, however, that the transfer of Spanish customs, politics, and ideals to the region was almost complete.

As the Spanish empire and influence declined in the early 1800s, the Argentines declared their independence in 1816. Yet, unification of this vast area, which still operated under the traditional Spanish feudal system, proved extremely difficult. The years that followed were marked by social unrest and it was not until 1880 that the nation was united with Buenos Aires as the capital. Horses and cattle dominated the economy, with the livestock *estancia* the symbol of power.

Argentina prospered under this system, making breakthroughs on the world trade markets—particularly in grains and beef. This recognition caused not only inflows of needed foreign capital into their system but encouraged large scale immigration—from Spain and Italy in particular—which doubled in the 1880s. This new wealth and influx of culture (even the French left their influence in art, architecture, literature, and politics) greatly changed the social fabric of the country.

The first truly democratic political group to establish themselves in Argentina was the Radical Party. Positioning themselves as anti-establishment

	1988	1989	1990	1991	1992	1993
Population (m)	31.5	31.9	32.2	32.6	33	33.4
GNP (US$bn)	98.7	58.3	134.7	189.4	228.6	256.8
Real GNP growth (%)	-1.9	-6.2	0.1	8.9	8.7	50.0
Per capita income (US$)	3110	1815	4172	5801	6923	7693
Exports (US$bn)	9.1	9.6	12.4	11.9	12.2	13
Imports (US$bn)	5.3	4.2	4.1	8.3	14.8	15
Foreign direct investment (US$m)	1147	1028	1836	2439	4179	6120
Inflation	342.7	4923.7	1343.9	84	17.5	9.3
Interest rates (term deposits)	n/a	663.6	80.4	15.6	13.2	10.6
International reserves (US$bn)	2.5	0.8	3.6	7.5	11.5	13.3
Market capitalization (US$bn)	5.2	17.9	4	21.7	18.6	26
No. of listed companies	194	184	179	171	175	179
Index performance in US$ (%)	38.8	175.9	-36.5	369.9	-26.5	67.3
Price/earnings (P/E) ratios	11.3	22.1	3.1	38.9	16.9	15.1
Earnings per share (EPS) growth	-	-	-	-	50	36.4
Average daily turnover (US$m)	n/a	4.9	3.2	18.4	41.6	50.1
Dividend yield	3.6	4.7	0.9	0.3	1.9	4.2
Currency to US$ pesos	0.00163	0.136	0.567	0.999	0.998	0.995

Figure 21.1 Argentina: key statistics

and composed primarily of the middle class and recent immigrants, they held the reins of power from 1916 to 1930. The conservatives, unhappy during these years, helped to bring about a military coup in 1930.

World War II ushered in economic hardship, causing the military to lead another coup in 1943. Of the military officers that took power, Colonel Juan D. Peron came to the forefront with his populist policies aimed at the working class—hence the creation of Peronism and the Peronist Party (PJ).

Officially elected in 1946, the goal of his leadership was to create social justice through the redistribution of income and state intervention. The unions were given political party status and widespread nationalizations in such areas as oil, telecommunications, and energy took place. These ideas were well received by the populace as they were considered to be foundations of nationalism. The expenses of the new programmes, however, soon began to bankrupt the economy. With his support dwindling, Peron's confrontation with the Catholic Church in 1955 was reason enough to have him overthrown by the military and sent into exile.

What followed were unstable years of mainly military rule, as they were the only group with the power to hold the fragmented society together. Economically, the military was unsuccessful, which eventually led to

Peron's return in 1973. By this time the country had deteriorated to such a point that neither Peron (who only lived one more year) nor his wife Isabel, who succeeded him, could hold the pieces together. Politics had digressed to the point that factions were created with guerrilla groups on the left and radical death squads on the right. When tensions reached a dangerous level the military stepped in with two aims in mind: elimination of the guerrilla groups and re-organization of the economy.

The military was effective in eliminating the guerrilla groups, but their methods were questionable. Called 'the dirty war' for the number of human rights violations involved, today there are still people who march on the Plaza de Mayo in honour of those who 'disappeared'. Unfortunately, their economic policies were less effective, bringing in 100 per cent inflation and negative economic growth. This, combined with their poor performance in the South Atlantic (Falkland Islands) War in 1982, made it necessary for them (under intense public pressure) to open dialogues with a multi-party commission. These talks eventually lead to the democratic elections held in 1983.

The elections brought in Dr. Alfonsin of the Radical Party. Although he was able to maintain social stability, the economy was once again marked by bouts of hyperinflation. In 1989, the electorate voted in Dr. Carlos Menem of the Peronist party. Ironically, he proved successful by introducing policies that were counter to the Peronist tradition—primarily, reduction of state intervention in order to improve productivity and efficiency. Large scale privatizations of telecommunications, oil, and energy were initiated as well as the famous Convertibility Plan placing the peso on a 1 to 1 parity with the US dollar. These policies have proved successful.

Under the leadership of Menem and Domingo Cavallo (Menem's finance minister credited with authorship of the Convertibility Plan) Argentina has achieved consistent and substantial GDP growth, low inflation, improving trade balances, and a fast-developing capital market that is drawing capital flows to the country from all over the world.

Economy

Argentina is a country of tremendous natural resources. With the Andes, the Arctic circle, the farming regions of the Pampas and the oil and natural gas reserves of Patagonia, Argentina is resource-rich. A country of 33m people, 13m of which live in metropolitan Buenos Aires, there are great tracts of open land famous for the production of wheat, sunflower seeds, sugar cane, grain, tobacco, sorghum, and rice. The hilly north-west is home to wine, olive, vegetable and fruit production.

At present, 60 per cent of export earnings still come from agricultural products. Despite the projected growth of the manufacturing and industrial

Company	**Market cap. (US$m)**	*Company*	**Volume (US$m)**
YPF	9355	Perez Companc	6.1
Telefonica	4515	Acindar	4.4
Telecom	4302	Cidea	3.3
Perez Companc	2749	Astra	3.2
BCO Galicia	959	Molinos	2.3
BCO Frances	916	Commercial del Plata	2.0
Baesa	856	Telefonica	1.7
Ciadea	767	BCO Frances	1.5
Astra	713	YPF	1.4
Sevel	667	Telecom	1.4
Commercial del Plata	621	Siderca	1.3
Siderca	469	BCO Galicia	1.3
Massalin P.	439	Alpargatas	1.1
Molinos Rio	395	Ledesma	0.8
Bagley	328	Bagley	0.8
Acindar	289	Nobelza Piccardo	0.7
Ledesma	260	Sevel	0.3
Corcemar	238	Celulosa	0.2
IRSA	193	Baesa	0.2
Alpargatas	189	IRSA	0.1

Figure 21.2 Argentina: 20 largest stocks by market capitalization and average daily volume

sectors, this percentage will probably be maintained as there is tremendous under-utilized agrarian potential. The use of fertilizers and technology thus far has been modest while there are still large tracts of uncultivated farm land.

As the standard of living rises the Argentine people will continue to demand more from the manufacturing sector which unfortunately suffers from outdated machinery and intense international competition. As investment flows increase—particularly from foreigners—this area should improve. The transport and communications sectors have taken the lead already.

The stock market

There are five stock exchanges in Argentina that are able to function independently: Mendoza, Cordoba, La Plata, Rosario, and Buenos Aires. The largest is the Bolsa de Commercio de Buenos Aires, founded in 1954, where only the 250 members are allowed to trade. The market deals with forward basis transactions, options, futures, and 30-day interest rate contracts. There are two equity market indices: the General Index and the Merval. The General includes all 176 companies and is weighted on a market capitalization basis. The Merval index uses the most active stocks based on 2 criteria: the ratio of a stock's traded value to the whole market and the ratio of the number of transactions to the whole market's transactions.

At a market capitalization of only 10 per cent of GDP, the market has considerable scope for growth with daily trading volumes quadrupling since 1991 to more than US$60m per day. It tends to have a low price to book value in relation to the other Latin American markets, with the only concern being the average Argentine's lack of faith in their market. (At the first sign of trouble they sell everything, giving the Bolsa an unflattering volatility.)

Technical notes

- Floor trading is from 11.00 to 15.00 every business day. Continuous trading system transactions take place from 11.00 to 17.00.
- Settlement of a share occurs in 72 hours with the costs—including duties, fees and taxes—are 0.06 per cent for a purchase and 0.17 per cent for a sale.
- Settlement of a transaction in government securities is in cash and the costs are 0.06 per cent for a purchase and 0.06 per cent for a sale.
- Securities are held at the Caja de Valores, principal custodians of the stock exchange.
- Commissions are negotiable and there are no income or capital gains taxes for foreign investors.

Chapter 22

Brazil

Population:	153m
Gross national product:	$431bn
Market capitalization:	$74.4bn
Currency/US$:	326 real cruzeiro

Brazil epitomizes the promise and opportunity as well as the risks and volatility of emerging market investment. Known, since its discovery in 1500 by Pedro Alvarez Cabral, as the land of the future, it is today a vast, rich, developing nation with over 150m people, a well-established industrial base around São Paolo, a strong and growing export sector and a sad history of political ineptitude and endemic inflation. The stock exchanges in Rio de Janeiro and São Paolo are among the most modern and efficient of any, yet the failure of the government to implement fully the privatization programme has held back the potential of the capital market which is still only 17 per cent of GNP.

Brazil's first boom really started in the 18th century when gold and diamonds were discovered in Minas Gerais. Following independence in 1822, Brazil became an empire and was ruled by the benevolent Pedro II from 1831 until his abdication in 1889 following the abolition of slavery. During his reign, Brazil expanded geographically to its present boundaries with vast areas of the Amazon and Mato Grosso becoming open for colonization. The new wealth of the country at the time of the establishment of the republic in 1889 stemmed mainly from coffee. Both British and international investment into this developing young country was growing fast in 1890. A rubber boom in the Amazon region in the 1890s also helped to develop the infrastructure and establish many new towns in the interior, including Manaus with its famous opera house two thousand miles up the river.

The industrialization of São Paolo began early in the century and attracted major European and US multinationals to establish subsidiaries there. Today it has, for example, a large car industry producing over 700,000 vehicles per annum, a large steel industry, textiles, machinery and other sectors based on its agricultural wealth.

	1988	1989	1990	1991	1992	1993
Population (m)	139	141	144	146	149	153
GNP (US$bn)	329	400	399	419	420	431
Real GNP growth (%)	0.1	3.3	4.4	0.9	1.3	4
Per capita income (US$)	2367	2837	2771	2870	2819	2817
Exports (US$bn)	33.8	34.4	31.4	31.6	36.2	39
Imports (US$bn)	14.6	18.3	20.4	21	20.5	25
Foreign direct investment (US$m)	n/a	184	517	695	1325	1500
Inflation	892	1636	1639	459	1170	2550
Interest rates (term deposits)	1050	2299	1281	635	1185	31.9
International reserves (US$bn)	8	8.5	8.7	8.6	16.7	22
Market capitalization (US$bn)	19.6	44.1	15.4	43.6	45.3	74.4
No. of listed companies	630	629	612	598	593	692
Index performance in US$ (%)	125.6	39.9	65.7	170.4	0.3	91.3
Price/earnings (P/E) ratios	n/a	6.8	7	147.8	26.7	17.1
Earnings per share (EPS) growth					1051.5	42.9
Average daily turnover (US$m)	71.9	67	65.4	131	82.1	180
Dividend yield	1.5	1.1	6.3	0.7	1	0.6
Currency to US$ (cruzeiros*)	0.731	11.3	161	1090	12,243	326

Figure 22.1 Brazil: key statistics
**1987-89: new cruzeiro/US$; 1990-92: cruzeiro/US$; 1993: real cruzeiro/US$*

Immigration was a key to the rapid development of Brazil in the early 20th century. Over one million Japanese live around São Paolo today and there are strong links with Japan. The Italian community is especially strong around São Paolo. In the three southern cities of Parana, Santa Katarina and Rio Grande de Sul, the German element is strong and the population predominantly European. About 56 per cent of the population is European in origin, 38 per cent of mixed race and 5 per cent African. Brazil's population is young, with 35 per cent under 14.

Between 1930 and 1945, Brazil was ruled by Getulio Vargas who was much influenced by the Fascist movement in Italy. His economic policy was based on nationalizing most of the major utilities and industries and, like Peron in Argentina, encouraging the growth of unions. He was succeeded by Juscelino Kubitschek who moved the capital from Rio de Janeiro to Brasilia in 1960, which produced a rapid economic development of the central part of the country. There was rapid economic growth averaging 9 per cent per annum under a pro-business government by technocrats. Brazil was hit hard by the oil crisis in 1979-80 and the 1980s was a period of slower growth and higher inflation. The new civilian government was unable to implement the hard measures needed to reduce inflation and cut back gov-

Company	**Market cap. (US$m)**	*Company*	**Volume (US$ '000s)**
Telebras PN	9321	Telebras PN	81136
Telebras ON	8011	Telebras ON	12821
Electrobras PNB	7581	Petrobras PNB	10185
Electrobras ON	7581	Petrobras PN	7110
Petrobras PN	6092	Cemig	6561
Telesp PN	4880	Vale do Rio Doce PN	5190
Cesp PN	4759	Brasil PN	2990
Telesp ON	4195	CSN ON	2989
Bradescon PN	4105	Telesp PN	2411
Petrobras ON	3960	Paranapanema PN	2242
Bradesco ON	3757	Bradesco PN	2149
Vale Rio Doce ON	3675	Usiminas PN	2136
Vale Rio Doce PN	3568	Light ON	1627
Itaubanco PN	2739	Telebras ON	1387
Light ON	2611	Brahma PN	1128
Itaubanco ON	2590	Sid. Tubarao	987
Souza Cruz ON	2181	Itaubanco PN	803
Cemig PN	1988	Paul Forca e Luz ON	795
Cemig	1755	Mosbla PN	687
Brahma ON	1523	Banespa PN	633

Figure 22.2 Brazil: 20 largest stocks by market capitalization and average daily volume
Note: PN = Partcipating Preferred Registered; ON = Common Registered Voting

ernment spending. Inflation averaged 356 per cent per annum during the 1980s, which were frequently described as the 'lost decade' for Latin America and especially for Brazil. GDP growth was only 2 per cent per annum. Nevertheless, Brazil managed to generate a growing trade surplus with its fast growing exports trade. From 1983 onwards it was US$12bn per annum.

The economic history of Brazil in the past thirty years reflects first the period of military rule between 1964 and 1985.

The election of Fernando Collor in November 1989 led to a new economic policy to open up the country to the rest of the world, improve productivity and provoke greater competition. Measures were taken to eliminate non-tariff barriers and reduce tariffs from an average of 40 per cent in 1990 to an average of 14 per cent in 1994. Imports grew as a result of these measures and Brazilian companies have considerably improved their productivity. The government also took measures to attract foreign capital, reducing dividend taxation and allowing investment by foreign institutions into the stock market from May 1991. This last measure has been quite effective with over US$2bn invested in the first two years. In addition, Brazil's foreign debt was completely re-scheduled with the international banks, and the first privatizations were undertaken in 1991 with Usiminas beginning with a large market value of US$1.4bn. During the next two years a further twenty five companies were privatized raising over US$5bn. Nevertheless, compared with the successful economic reforms in Chile and Argentina (where inflation had been brought from 1000 per cent to less than 10 per cent in three years) Brazil's economic and financial outlook remains clouded in the eyes of many international investors. No-one can doubt the potential of the country yet few have faith that the politicians will enable that potential to be realized.

Per capita income is an impressive US$2650, ahead of Mexico, Argentina and Chile and compares favourably with Asian countries such as Malaysia and Indonesia.

The key decision for an international investor looking at Brazil is one of timing in regard to the currency and inflation. Such is the rate of inflation that it is estimated, for example, that the São Paolo stock market must go up 4 per cent on Mondays to make up for the inflation over the weekend. The IFC Dollar Index has shown a characteristic volatility of between 40 and 180 during a period of less than twelve months. Even the New York -listed ADRs of Telebras and other Brazilian stocks reflect this intensely volatile pattern of trading, which makes it much harder for a long-term investor to make an intelligent decision. Nevertheless, the probability must be that the Brazilian government will see the advantages of bringing in more foreign capital which will allow privatization to proceed and the stock market, now about US$75bn, to reflect the growing GNP of over US$400bn and the export surplus of US$16bn annually, coming from the tremendous wealth in coffee, vehicles, soya beans, oranges, sugar, auto parts, steel and household appliances.

Chapter 23

Chile

Population:	13.5m
Gross national product:	$41.2bn
Market capitalization:	$35.2bn
Currency/US$:	428.5 pesos

The first outside influence on the Indians of Chile occurred during the 1500s when the Europeans—primarily Spanish—began arriving in their search for silver and gold. These explorers were followed by Jesuit priests, craftsmen, architects, engineers, pharmacists, weavers, painters and sculptors of whose influence can still be seen in the cities and towns of Chile.

When the Spanish rule declined in the western world following both the French and American Revolutions, the Chileans proposed their own constitution and independence in 1810. Spain promptly sent an army attempting to retain their empire but were defeated in 1818 by Chilean forces, under the leadership of army commander Bernardo O'Higgins. The early years of independence were unstable with a civil war in 1828-30, but they did produce the 1833 Portalian Constitution which allowed for a strong central government while strengthening the three common branches of government. This was consequently followed by 50 years of peaceful and democratic civilian rule.

The War of the Pacific (1879-83), against both Peru and Bolivia over the nitrate-rich lands in the north, was a Chilean success and effectively took away Bolivia's access to the sea—a point of contention to this day. Unfortunately, the profit from these lands was short-lived as the development of synthetic substitutes in the early 1900s destroyed the demand for nitrates.

The 1920s and 30s saw an increase in tensions between the two traditional political factions composed of the *laissez-faire* liberals and radicals against the conservative land owners and Catholic Church. Ironically and perhaps prophetically it was the military that was called in during these times to keep the peace.

Chile returned to democratic rule in 1932 but political stability remained elusive as new parties formed in the 50s and 60s. On the left were the socialists and communists following Marxist-Leninist ideology, while the

	1988	1989	1990	1991	1992	1993
Population (m)	12.5	12.7	12.9	13.1	13.3	13.5
GNP (US$bn)	27.3	30	30.7	32.6	36	41.2
Real GNP growth (%)	7.4	10	2.1	6	10.4	6
Per capita income (US$)	2184	2362	2380	2489	2707	3052
Exports (US$bn)	7	8.1	8.3	8.9	9.9	9.8
Imports (US$bn)	4.8	6.5	7	7.3	9.2	10.7
Inflation	12.7	21.4	27.3	18.7	12.7	12
Interest rates(lending)	7.7	11.7	9.2	7.7	8.8	9.1
International reserves (US$bn)	2.5	2.9	5.3	6.6	9	9.6
Market capitalization (US$bn)	7	9.5	13.6	28	29.7	35.2
No. of listed companies	203	213	215	223	244	258
Index performance in US$ (IFC) (%)	37.1	51.2	40.4	98.1	16.2	29.5
Price/earnings (P/E) ratios	4.4	6.4	11.1	14.7	19.4	20.1
Earnings per share (EPS) growth						
Average daily turnover (US$m)	2.4	3.5	3.1	7.6	8.2	9.1
Dividend yield	9.4	9.5	5	3.5	3.8	4.1
Currency to US$ (peso)	245	267	304.9	349.2	362.6	428.5

Figure 23.1 Chile: key statistics

centre was taken over by the Christian Democrats with strong links to the Catholic Church and middle classes.

The year of 1970 brought in Salvador Allende, an avowed Marxist, by a slim controversial vote. As he lacked a parliamentary majority, he proceeded to instate policies by bypassing the law completely. His most extreme measures included wide-spread nationalizations and his support for *tomas*—illegal land seizures. To ensure his party, the Unidad Popular, won the 1973 elections he called for state-wide wage increase and insisted companies under state control take on new workers. The party's influence increased from 37 per cent to 43 per cent but Allende's policies caused hyperinflation and queues for basic food items. This allowed the opposition to increase their campaigns and finally, in September 1973, the military stepped in. President Allende died in the battle which ensued at the presidential palace leaving General Pinochet unquestionably in charge.

Under General Pinochet's rule political parties were banned, strict censorship laws were imposed, and all remnants of Marxist influences were purged. Free market principles were introduced with government influence minimized following the principles of Nobel Prize winner Milton Friedman. Many of the new economic leadership had been educated in Chicago under Friedman and though the new export-led economy was not without its problems, the systems remained in place with Pinochet remaining in power until 1988, when a plebiscite was held allowing the return to democracy.

In 1989, Patricio Aylwin, a Christian Democrat at the head of a 13-party coalition, *Concertacion*, was elected president in the first election in two decades. With his finance minister Alejandro Foxley, Aylwin interestingly maintained Pinochet's free market policies with little changes besides occasional tightening of monetary policy in efforts to curb inflation. They have invested considerable political capital ensuring Chile's access to new markets for export growth and is the next country in line to join Nafta.

Economy

A country of 13m people, 6m of which are based in the Santiago metropolitan area, Chile is rich in export products: copper (40 per cent of export earnings), fish and fish products, wood, wines, fruits, juices, vegetables. Unfortunately, the weak commodity prices world-wide hurt the export market in 1993 causing a trade deficit—the first in over a decade. The lingering high inflation rate can be attributed to the indexation of wages, rents, etc. that occurs on a yearly basis, yet, with a GNP growth rate at 6 per cent, international reserves of $9.6bn, a low unemployment rate, and a diversifying corporate base moving into manufactured products, the Chilean economy is fundamentally very strong.

The stock market

Founded in 1893, the Santiago Stock Exchange now has 258 companies with a market capitalization of US$35.2bn. Forty brokerage houses sit on the exchange which is technically a private company composed of 46 shareholders. The Valparaiso Stock Exchange was founded in 1892 but accounts for only 4.7 per cent of the equity market, while the Electronic Stock Exchange was founded in 1989 and now handles 26.7 per cent. During the Pinochet years, stringent rules were placed on the market in order to keep away speculators. Fortunately, these are slowly being changed which will greatly enhance the market attractiveness.

The Chilean stock market's liquidity is enhanced by the AFPs—Chile's mandatory pension fund system, whereby every working citizen makes payments (10 per cent of earnings) to whichever fund they choose (there are 20 approved). The amount added to the system is at least US$300m monthly and, as the AFPs are required to invest the majority of this in the equity and fixed-income markets, the Chilean stock market capitalization is now 98 per cent of GNP.

Company	**Market cap. (US$m)**	*Company*	**Volume (US$m)**
Endesa	3139	Endesa	350
Copec	3131	Telefonosa	298
Telefonosa	2849	Enersis	166
Cartones	2099	Chilgener	119
Enersis	1834	Chilectra	63
Vapores	844	Entel	57
Cervezas	820	Copec	50
Chilectra	705	San Pedro	49
Minera	691	Cartones	48
CCT	657	Masisa	42
Chilgener	610	Vapores	37
Melon	608	Cap	35
Electricid	574	Soquimich	31
Entel	542	Mantos	30
Colbun	483	Labchile	30
Emos	476	Iansa	27
Pehuenche	440	Santa Rita	27
Madeco	410	Itata	26
Pasur	397	Luz-A	24
Cap	372	Provida	23

Figure 23.2 Chile: 20 largest stocks by market capitalization and average daily volume

The market unfortunately has little depth. The top ten stocks account for almost 54 per cent of total market capitalization and 58 per cent of trading. As institutional investment was traditionally limited to particular issues, it was not uncommon to find 20 per cent of their holdings in the electrical utilities alone. Recent changes, however, will now allow the AFPs to expand their investments into new issues, smaller issues, and even venture capital funds.

Capital repatriation is restricted to one year for direct investments and five years for fund investments. Profits are subject to relatively high tax rates (32 per cent on direct investments and 10 per cent on foreign investment funds). As a result, the two best vehicles for investment are either the foreign investment funds or shares of Chilean companies listed abroad—ADRs.

There are two types of indices in the Santiago Stock Exchange: The General Index of Stock Prices (IGPA) and the Selective Index of Stock Prices (IPSA). The IGPA includes almost all the stocks on the exchange (255 included in June 93) based on market capitalization. It is a very good indicator of the strength of the economy. The IPSA includes the 40 stocks with the highest trading volume and liquidity. It is adjusted every quarter.

Technical notes:

- Trading hours: 10.30 to 11.20, 12.30 to 13.20, 16.00 to 16.30
- Transactions are settled two exchange business days following the operation.
- Brokers commissions are negotiable and range from 1 per cent to 0.35 per cent.
- Transaction costs are 0.5 per cent maximum and decrease according to the volumes traded.
- Value-added tax of 18 per cent is added to both brokerage and stock exchange commissions.

Exchange address

Physical address:

Santiago Stock Exchange
La Bolsa 64
Santiago—Chile

Tel: 56-2 698 2001 & 56-2 695 8077 / Fax: 56-2 672 8046

Mailing address:

PO Box 123-D
Santiago—Chile

Chapter 24

Colombia

Population:	34m
Gross national product:	$51.4bn
Market capitalization:	$10.2bn
Currency/US$:	802 pesos

Gran Colombia, with a coastline stretching from the Orinoco at the Atlantic to Northern Peru in the Pacific, was a successor state to the old Spanish viceroyalty of New Granada. In 1819, Simon Bolivar (1783-1821) established the republic of Gran Colombia which consisted of the territory known as Colombia, Panama, Venezuela and Ecuador. Venezuela and Ecuador withdrew in 1829 and, in 1861, the name Colombia was adopted. Panama seceded in 1903 with US support. The largest share of Gran Colombia's population lay in Colombia itself and today exceeds 33m, with a GNP capitalization of US$1200. The capital, Bogotá, accounts for a large share of the population with over 5m. It is situated at nearly 9000 feet above sea level, other major cities being Medellin with 2.4m and Cali with 1.8 m.

Political instability over the last 150 years has held back economic growth although Colombia is rich in resources, especially minerals. In addition, hyperinflation has deterred foreign investment. A new constitution was approved in 1991, expanding individual rights and establishing the election of a president for four years with legislative power being held by a congress of 160 members. President Cesar Gaviria was elected in 1990.

Despite the continuing problems of the drug-trading cartel based in Medellin, which has violently challenged the government's right to rule the country, Colombia's economy has, nonetheless, expanded at a steady rate. In the last two years significant oil discoveries have been made by BP, amongst other international oil companies, which will do much to boost exports in the future. A free trade agreement came into effect with Venezuela, Ecuador and Bolivia in 1992.

	1988	1989	1990	1991	1992	1993
Population (m)	31.2	32.4	33	33.6	33.8	34
GNP (US$bn)	39.2	40.8	42.6	44	47.7	51.4
Real GNP growth (%)		3.2	4.2	2.2	3.6	4.5
Per capita income (US$)	1256	1259	1290	1336	1411	1512
Exports (US$bn)	5	6	7.1	7.2	7.1	7.6
Imports (US$bn)	4.5	4.5	5.1	4.8	6.7	7.64
Foreign direct investment (US$m)	159	547	484	133	938	1116
Inflation	28.1	25.8	32.4	26.8	25.1	22
Interest rates (term deposits)	42.7	43	47	40	22	26.2
International reserves (US$bn)	3.7	3.9	4.6	6.4	7.8	8.1
Market capitalization (US$bn)	1.1	1.1	1.4	4	5.7	10.2
No. of listed companies	142	130	166	172	180	182
Index performance in US$ (%)	-12.3	12.2	37.5	191.3	39.1	31.7
Price/earnings (P/E) ratios					16.1	13.8
Earnings per share (EPS) growth					26	12
Average daily turnover (US$m)	0.25	0.3	0.3	0.8	2.3	4.1
Dividend yield						1.2
Currency to US$ (pesos)	336	423	523	632	738	802

Figure 24.1 Colombia: key statistics

The stock market

The Colombian stock market consists of three exchanges, Bogotá, Medellin and Cali. By the end of 1993, market capitalization was over US$10.2bn—equivalent to 20 per cent of GNP. The government has recently done much to encourage companies to use equity as a resource of finance, eliminating capital gains tax and wealth tax. Foreign investment regulations have also been liberalized in 1991. There are now over 182 companies listed on the three exchanges and average daily volume has expanded to over US$4m a day.

Exchange addresses

Bolsa de Bogotá
Carrera 8
#133-82, 7/F
Apdo Aereo 3584
Santafe de Bogotá

Tel: 57 1 243 6501 / Fax: 57 1 281 3170

Bolsa de Medellin
Carrera 50
#50-48, 2/F
Apdo Aereo 3535
Medellin

Tel: 57 4 260 3000 / Fax: 57 4 251 1981

Bolsa de Occidente
Calle 8
#3-14, 17/F
Cali

Tel: 57 2 381 7022 / Fax: 57 2 381 6720

	Market value (US$ million)
Bavaria	954
Cementos Argos	675
Suramericana	537
Banco Bogotá	466
Cementos del Caribe	378
Coltabaco	372
Cementos del Valle	369
Bic	335
Cadenalco	319
Banco Ganadero	236
Coltejer	209
Cementos Rio Claro	161
Bancoquia	133
Fabricato	128
Colseguros	58
Avianca	38
Tejicondor	32
Paz del Rio	24
Productos Familia	18
Alumina	19

Figure 24.2 Colombia: 20 largest stocks by market capitalization
Source: Baring Securities Ltd.

Chapter 25

Mexico

Population:	84m
Gross national product:	$338bn
Market capitalization:	$142bn
Currency/US$:	3.1 pesos

History shows that, of all the Latin American countries, Mexico has had the most advanced Indian civilizations, from the Olmecs (1000 to 500BC) to the Mayas (1500BC to 1000AD) to the Aztecs (1276 to 1500AD). Today's Mexican countryside is still a testament to the extraordinary cultures that existed before the Spanish colonization in 1521.

Hernan Cortes was the first conquistador to land and be invited into the Aztec city of Tenochtitlan—now Mexico City—as a god. With the other conquistadors, he was able to conquer the Aztecs and begin the transformation of this new colony into 'New Spain'. The first Franciscan monks began arriving in 1523, with the Dominicans and Augustines to follow soon after.

Silver mining became the major source of wealth in New Spain with agriculture a close second. By 1804, silver production was greater than that of the rest of the world combined, and New Spain was growing rapidly in land and wealth. Its army conquered what is now California and Texas, making New Spain second only to Brazil in size. Mexico City grew to 100,000 inhabitants, becoming one of the largest and most cosmopolitan cities in the world.

Encouraged by their new wealth, the Mexicans followed the examples of the American and French Revolutions and declared their independence in 1810. It brought chaos and over 50 governments in the years to 1857. The young country lost much in this time—including 890,000 square miles to the US, comprising what is now Texas, New Mexico, and California.

A Liberal party emerged but, by 1864, the Conservatives had invited in the French, with Maximilian of Hapsburg as Emperor, to help consolidate their power. Ironically, Maximilian arrived in Mexico and began implementing liberal policies. He decreed religious tolerance, issued laws on wages and work conditions, and established a decimal system. When the French troops were recalled from Mexico to help France against the threat

	1988	1989	1990	1991	1992	1993
Population (m)	78.8	79.5	81	82.5	83.2	84
GNP (US$bn)	165.6	173.2	235.3	275.3	321.5	338
Real GNP growth (%)	1.4	2.9	3.2	3.6	2.6	1.9
Per capita income (US$)	2232	2529	2790	3150	3864	4024
Exports (US$bn)	20.6	22.8	25.8	27.1	27.7	29.9
Imports (US$bn)	18.9	23.4	28.5	38.1	47.8	51.1
Inflation	51.7	19.7	29.9	22.7	11.9	8.7
Interest rates (av. cost of funds)	67.6	44.6	37.1	22.5	18.8	18.7
International reserves	6.6	6.9	10	12.1	18.9	22
Foreign direct investment (US$m)	3157	2500	3400	4742	5366	6200
Market capitalization (US$bn)	15.3	28.9	42.7	101.8	138.1	143
No. of listed companies	203	203	199	209	195	197
Index performance in US$ (IFC) (%)	108.3	73.3	29.7	106.8	21.2	
Price/earnings (P/E) ratios	5	6.2	13.2	14.5	13.5	13.8
Earnings per share (EPS) growth					15	8
Average daily turnover (US$m)	22.9	24	49.3	126.9	178.3	250
Dividend yield	3	2	3.4	1.3	1.3	1.7
Currency to US$ (peso)	2.27	2.47	2.83	3.07	3.12	3.17

Figure 25.1 Mexico: key statistics

of Prussia, the Liberal armies overthrew Maximilian, executing him in 1867. General unrest followed this period, as the economy tried to absorb over 100,000 soldiers unused to civilian life and unwilling to return to badly paid agrarian or city work. General Porfirio Diaz took over the presidency in 1877 and, with a strong hand, was able to quell the unrest.

Famous for his slogan and policies of 'little politics and much administration', Diaz can be credited with the development of railways, postal, telegraph, and telecommunication services, ports, a banking system and the expansion of Mexico's industries. Despite these achievements, there was an increasing gap between rich and poor. Political unrest increased as an unhappy middle class decried their lack of political representation. Diaz, himself, became increasingly oppressive against his advocates.

Unsurprisingly, the people rebelled in 1910 led by middle-class hero Francisco Madero. A true idealist and believer in democracy, Madero failed to consolidate his power and was assassinated in 1913. The post revolutionary chaos that ensued saw the rise and fall of over five leaders who unsuccessfully attempted their hands at the presidency.

The year of 1920 marked the beginning of a peaceful era. Despite his military background, Alvaro Obregon well represented the middle class and began his term with much-needed agrarian and labor reforms. Most notable during this period was the consolidation of the PNR (the forerunner of the PRI—Partido Revolucionario Institucional) which became the 'official' party, designed to incorporate the different interest groups of society in a peaceful manner. This party machine would prove more stable than Mexico itself and would serve to put one of its members in the presidential seat every six years—the present Carlos Salinas included.

The PRI candidate of 1934, Lazaro Cardenas, consolidated the working-class party representation into three sectors—workers, farmers, and bureaucrats—nationalized the railways, and expropriated the oil companies from foreign ownership. This period, from 1920 to 1940, is now referred to as the 'reformist years' since it set the stage for the growth that would occur in the next three decades.

The presidents of the 1940s began a period of economic reform through development of previously uncultivated land, oil production increases, technological advancements in the manufacturing sectors, and acceptance of foreign investment. These factors combined to produce a GNP growth of over 6 per cent per annum.

The 1970s showed the first crack in the 'Mexican Miracle'. As world-wide inflation increased in 1973, exports and tourism receipts decreased faster than imports, causing a jump in the deficit from \$890m in 1971, to \$3.7bn in 1975. The subsequent loss of international confidence caused an outflow of foreign exchange and a decrease in public investments that required the government to borrow at the international level to meet their budgetary needs. The external debt moved from \$4.2bn in 1971, to 11.6 in 1975.

Large and important discoveries of new oil and gas reserves were made in the Gulf of Mexico in 1977, taking the nation's oil reserves from 5.4bn barrels in 1973 to 60bn in 1980. This treasure chest seemed the answer to Mexico's problems and the Portillo administration embarked on a spending and borrowing program in order to finance their variety of social projects. Unfortunately, the high oil prices of the late 70s could not last. When oil prices fell in 1982 and the peso devalued 600 per cent, Mexico was required to declare a *de facto* moratorium on its foreign debt triggering the international debt crisis. Mexican government debt had risen from \$19.6bn in 1976 to \$33.8bn in 1980. Portillo's response was to introduce total exchange controls and nationalize the banking system.

President Miguel de la Madrid inherited this situation upon his inauguration in 1982. Facing over 100 per cent inflation, negative GDP, and protectionist policies he took the offensive through debt renegotiations, liberalization of imports, removal of import tariffs, tariff reductions, privatizations, encouragement of foreign direct investment, and the introduction of the Economic Solidarity Pact. These policies proved effective, but were unfortunately limited by the 1985 earthquake and 1986 oil plunge.

When President Carlos Salinas de Gotari began his term in 1988, he inherited 160 per cent inflation on the back of the Crash of 1987 and a constant devaluation-deficit-inflation cycle. However, with his finance minister, Pedro Aspe, he was able to encourage growth while decreasing inflation through the acceleration of privatizations and tight control over government finance. They have also reduced both corporate and personal taxes to international levels, lowered tariffs and import permits, renegotiated external debt under the Brady plan, and created more simple and expansive rules and regulations for foreign investors. His other notable achievements have been the launching of his successful anti-corruption campaign and the encouragement of political diversity—despite the risk to his own party, the PRI. This has led to the growth and strengthening of both the National Action Party (PAN), a right-wing party with Catholic overtones, and the Party of Democratic Revolution (PRD), a more liberal left wing party.

Negotiations concerning the North American Free Trade Agreement (Nafta) began in 1990. It has been the focus of stock market movements since 1992, leaving the market a prisoner to the many bumps in the long negotiation processes. Yet with or without Nafta, Mexican companies have risen to a new level of international competitiveness under the Salinas-Aspe administration that will promise continued economic successes.

Recent developments

The last months of President Salinas' successful six-year term have been marred by a number of events which have also severely impacted confidence in the Mexican stock market. In February 1994, there was a peasant uprising in the southern province of Chiapas, which was contained and subsequently quashed by units of the Mexican army. Nevertheless, it raised questions as to how far the economic reforms of the present administration had benefited the poorest people in the country, especially the peasants.

Secondly, there was the assassination of the presidential candidate, Luis Donoldo Colosio, in April 1994, which threw the succession of the PRI into confusion and caused a severe loss of confidence, especially as it emerged that there was an apparent conspiracy involved in the assassination. A leading Mexican businessman was kidnapped shortly thereafter and, together with the rise in US interest rates, these events caused the Mexican market to fall nearly 20 per cent in the first four months of the year. The downward spiral was further accentuated by the weakening of the Mexican peso against the US dollar. The government was forced to move up the interest rate on 30-day deposits, from 11 per cent in January 1994 to 16 per cent in May 1994, to prevent a further outflow of capital.

The election of Ernesto Zedillo as the new president has been well received by public and investors alike.

Economy

With a population of 84m, nine million of whom live in Mexico City, Mexico has traditionally been dependent upon its oil exports. In 1981, oil accounted for 75 per cent of export earnings alone. However, with the growth and diversification of the Mexican economy, oil now accounts for only 16 per cent with manufactured goods at 75 per cent—a remarkable transformation (similar to those of Indonesia and Thailand in the 1980s). Mexico's close proximity to the United States, its inexpensive labour and relaxed trade conditions have encouraged many US corporations to set up subsidiaries and joint ventures which have contributed greatly to the growth of the manufacturing sector.

Mexico is rich in minerals and a world leader in the production of silver, lead, iron ore, and copper. Many of their agricultural products—particularly fruits and vegetables—are presently exported, and automobile production has become a tremendous growth industry.

Recent governmental efforts have succeeded in reducing inflation (now below 10 per cent for the first time in 21 years), stabilizing the currency, decreasing interest rates and improving the trade balance. Unfortunately, these measures have occurred at the expense of GDP growth, which slowed to a paltry 1.8 per cent in 1993. The administration saw this cost as necessary, but temporary, and we can now look forward to stronger economic growth in 1995.

The stock market

The Mexico Stock Exchange, located in Mexico City, was established in 1894 and is presently owned by 26 stockbroking companies. All shares of Mexican companies must be registered. A Mexican company will typically issue three different types of shares: A shares—which may be held by Mexicans only; B shares—which may be held by foreign investors; and C shares—which may be held by anyone giving all corporate rights but no voting. In some instances Mexican financial institutions may issue 'N' or 'Neutral Shares' corresponding to A shares they have in trust. These shares carry only economic rights but not voting rights. Lastly are the 'L' shares which carry economic rights but limited corporate rights. They are 32 companies that trade as ADRs.

The MSE (Mexican Stock Exchange Index) is revised every two months and is composed of stocks selected for liquidity and weighted by market capitalization. It consists of approximately 35 companies.

Company	Market cap. (US$m)	Company	Volume (US$m)
Telmex	28448	Telmex	45.24
Banacci	9455	GCarso	7.51
Cifra	7535	Cemex B	7.4
Televisa	7197	Cifra C	6.27
Grupo Carso	5841	Femsa	5.98
Cemex	5760	Cemex A	5.33
GFB	5603	GFB C	5.09
Ttolmex	4066	Ttolmex B	4.73
Kimberly Clark	2652	Banacci	4.58
Femsa	2630	Cifra B	4.42
Bimbo	2066	Vitro	4.23
ICA	1922	Televisa L	4.06
Vitro	1916	Cemex C	3.77
Liverpool	1873	Indetel B	3.54
Apasco	1711	GFB B	3.33
Desc	1121	Banacci C	3.16
Alfa	1117	Apasco A	2.97
Penoles	1001	Gfserfin B	2.87
GMexico	908	Alfa A	2.06
Maseca	895	GGemex BCP	2.02

Figure 25.2 Mexico: 20 largest companies by market capitalization and average daily volume

Technical notes

- Trading hours are from 08.30 to 16.30 Mondays through Fridays and the Bolsa will suspend trading for one hour when change in the given price of a share exceeds 5 per cent of the last price.
- Settlement is in cash within 48 hours. The Indeval, or Institute for the Deposit of Securities, functions as the clearing house and depository for securities traded in Mexico.
- Commissions for foreign investors range between 0.5 per cent and 0.85 per cent.
- Foreign investors are not subject to taxes on capital gains or dividends.

Exchange address:

Bolsa Mexicana de Valores
Paseo de la Reforma No 255
Col Cuauhtemoc
06500, Mexico D.F.

Tel: 52 57 26 67 35 / Fax: 52 57 05 47 98

Chapter 26

Peru

Population:	23m
Gross national product:	$24bn
Market capitalization:	$3.8bn
Currency/US$:	2.16 nuevos soles

Peru was the creation of Francisco Pizarro (1478-1541) who, with only twenty followers, and in one of the most remarkable feats of modern history, subjugated the Inca Empire which had ruled the country for 500 years previously. For three centuries thereafter Peru, with Lima as its capital, was the centre of the Spanish empire in Latin America. After the revolutionary war of 1821, independence was declared and Peru became one of the first independent countries in the continent, with an initial population of 1.2m, half of whom were Indians.

Deeply conscious of its former imperial glory, Peru was anxious to expand its territory into the neighbouring areas of Bolivia and Ecuador with whom it fought intermittent wars in the 19th century. In fact, during the War of the Pacific, 1879-1882, Peru lost territory to both Chile and Bolivia. At the end of the 19th century foreign investment began to come to Peru for the first time after the country had negotiated the transfer of its external debts to a newly-formed London company, known as the Peruvian Corporation. In return, the corporation took over all Peru's railways and some shipping lines of Lake Titicaca, in addition to some guano revenues. In the early 20th century, US investment started to come into the mining and railway sectors.

The major problem affecting Peru's economy in recent decades has been rampant inflation, although this has recently been brought under greater control and is now running at around 20 per cent. In addition, there has been the threat of terrorism with the Maoist Shining Path Movement having claimed many lives. The election of President Fujimori began to reverse this trend and in April 1992, the president—with the help of the army—suspended the constitution. The leader of the Shining Path Movement, Guzman, was arrested and the country's fortunes began to improve.

	1988	1989	1990	1991	1992	1993
Population (m)	20.7	21.1	21.5	22	22.3	23
GNP (US$bn)	26.3	24.3	21.3	21.8	21.2	24
Real GNP growth (%)	-8	-12	-4.9	2.5	-1.9	4
Per capita income (US$)	1270	1150	990	990	950	1080
Exports (US$bn)	2.7	3.5	3.2	3.3	3.5	3.5
Imports (US$bn)	2.8	2.3	2.9	3.5	4	4.1
Foreign direct investment (US$m)	26	59	41	-7	127	1750
Inflation	862	1388	7649	139	57	45
Interest rates (lending)	174.3	1516	4775	752	174	73
International reserves (US$bn)	-0.25	0.5	0.75	2	2.5	3.8
Market capitalization (US$bn)	n/a	0.9	0.8	1.1	2.6	3.8
No. of listed companies	236	256	294	298	287	291
Index performance in US$ (%)						37.2
Price/earnings (P/E) ratios	n/a	n/a	n/a	n/a	34.7	28.1
Earnings per share (EPS) growth	n/a	n/a	n/a	n/a	791	0
Average daily turnover (US$m)	0.2	1.2	2.7	2.5	4.6	9.3
Dividend yield	n/a	n/a	n/a	n/a	3.7	3.1
Currency to US$ (nuevos soles)	0.00013	0.0032	0.254	0.8042	1.3033	2.16

Figure 26.1 Peru: key statistics

	Market capitalization (US$)
Telefonos B	513,609,617
Backus	473,450,575
Backus Labour	243,410,133
Banco de Creditor	205,129,655
Telefonos A	148,619,730
Southern Labour	130,349,192
CNC	n/a
Banco Wiese	89,026,911
San Juan	57,413,297
CNC Labour	49,857,563
Milpo	n/a
Cementos Lima Labour	37,533,851
Cerv del Norte	23,899,976
Buenaventura	21,133,306
Cerv Trujillo Labour	13,737,372
Milpo Labour	13,127,517
Ferreyros	12,400,968
Norte Pacasmayo Labour	12,356,659
Textile Piura	11,761,692
San Juan Labour	10,984,029

Figure 26.2 Peru: 20 largest companies by market capitalization

Source: Baring Securities Ltd.

Chapter 27

Uruguay

Population:	3.17m
Gross national product:	$12bn
Market capitalization:	$450m
Currency/US$:	3.95 pesos

Uruguay used to be known as Banda Oriental, the Eastern bank of the River Plate. Originally under Paraguayan rule, it was captured by the Spanish in 1726 and formed part of the viceroyalty of the River Plate. Captured by Argentina in 1814 and afterwards by the new Brazilian empire, it was the cause of the Argentine-Brazilian war in 1828. With British support Uruguay was declared an independent state in 1828 and subsequently became a kind of South American Switzerland, with the characteristics of a buffer state. With a population of only three million it, nevertheless, has high living standards with per capita income of US$2600. About one quarter of the inhabitants live in the capital city of Montevideo.

Like Argentina, Uruguay suffered from a urban guerrilla movement, known as the *Tupamaros*. This led to military government during the 1970s and early 1980s. Democracy was finally restored in 1989 and the traditional two-party system of the Blancos and the Colorados was superseded by the establishment of a new third party. There are no foreign exchange controls, no capital controls, no restrictions on foreign investment and no income taxes in Uruguay. All of this makes Uruguay quite an attractive place in which to invest. However, its small economy is highly dependent on exports, with Argentina and Brazil being the principal destinations. Uruguay signed the Mercosur Agreement in 1991, which led to the establishment of a common market with Brazil, Argentina and Paraguay, aimed at complete free trade among the members by 1996. Uruguay has also headed the process of reform and liberalization among the Latin American countries.

The privatization programme has included the port services, the airline, Pluna, and the gas company, although the telephone company has yet to be listed. High inflation has also led to rapid depreciation of the new peso, from 359 in 1988 to 3500 in 1992. Inflation is still running at a high rate of over 50 per cent. The number of companies listed on the Montevideo stock

	1988	1989	1990	1991	1992	1993
Population (m)	3.06	3.08	3.1	3.11	3.13	3.17
GNP (US$bn)	7.9	7.5	7.9	9.2	11.1	12
Real GNP growth (%)	n/a	n/a	0.9	2.9	7.4	3.1
Per capita income (US$)	2580	2435	2548	2958	3546	3785
Exports (US$bn)	1.4	1.6	1.7	1.6	1.7	n/a
Imports (US$bn)	1.1	1.1	1.3	1.5	1.9	n/a
Foreign direct investment (US$m)	44.5	n/a	n/a	n/a	n/a	n/a
Inflation	n/a	n/a	129	81.5	58.9	50
Interest rates (lending rates)	102	127.6	174.5	152.9	117.8	n/a
International reserves (US$bn)	2.5	2.3	3.7	3.65	3.88	4.2
Market capitalization (US$m)	24	27	38	44	369	450
No. of listed companies	40	39	36	28	26	n/s
Avg daily turnover (US$ '000s)	8	4	4	8	36	n/a
Currency to US$ (pesos)	0.45	0.81	1.59	2.49	3.48	3.95

Figure 27.1 Uruguay: key statistics

exchange has actually fallen during the past five years and is now only 26, although it is expected to grow again in the next few years.

Exchange address

Bolsa de Valores de Montevideo
Misiones 1400
Montevideo

Tel: 598 95 1906 / Fax: 598 96 1900 / Tlx: Bolsa UY 26996

Chapter 28

Venezuela

Population:	20.5m
Gross national product:	\$63.7bn
Market capitalization:	\$6bn
Currency/US\$:	106.2 bolivars

Venezuela was liberated by Simon Bolivar and became independent from Spain in 1830. It has a much higher living standard than most of the South American countries, with a per capita income of \$2500, owing to its large petroleum industry which contributes about 83 per cent of foreign exchange income. However, the oilfields were nationalized in 1976 and this has led to a steady decline in oil production, which is now about 2m barrels per day compared to 3.3m in 1970. Venezuela is also rich in minerals including aluminium, iron ore and diamonds. The population is nearly 20m and the educational level is quite high.

The stock market

The first stock exchange in Caracas may have been established in the early 19th century, but it was not until 1947 that trading activity started in an initial listing of 18 stocks and six government bonds. A second exchange was established in 1958, although this was later merged in 1974 with the main stock exchange. The volatile characteristic of Latin American emerging markets was reflected in the halving of prices after the overthrow of President Jimenez in 1958 and sluggish trading for the next ten years. In 1973, a new capital market law was enacted establishing a Securities Commission and introducing mutual funds. After 1986, however, it was apparent that the government's attitude towards the stock market changed, to being more positive.

The Securities Commission minimized the new listing procedures and a new stock exchange was established in Maracaibo, although the volume on that exchange was less than 1 per cent of the Caracas Stock Exchange. In 1988-9, the stock market reflected problems in the country's economy, with very low volume and weak prices. However, once a new economic pro-

	1988	1989	1990	1991	1992	1993
Population (m)	18.4	18.8	19	19.3	19.9	20.5
GNP (US$bn)	26.3	38.5	48.9	54.2	61.9	63.7
Real GNP growth (%)	3.6	8.6	6.5	10.4	7.3	3.5
Per capita income (US$)	1429	2048	2574	2808	2965	3107
Exports (US$bn)	10.7	12.9	17.4	14.9	13.9	14
Imports (US$bn)	13.7	7.3	6.8	10.1	12.3	11.4
Foreign direct investment						
Inflation	[illegible]	[illegible]	[illegible]	[illegible]	[illegible]	[illegible]
Interest rates (term deposits)	9.5	23.5	36.5	31	33.1	38.9
International reserves (US$bn)	6.4	6.9	9.1	14.1	12.7	11
Market capitalization (US$bn)	1.8	1.5	8.4	11.2	7.6	6
No. of listed companies	110	60	60	66	66	6.6
Index performance in US$ (%)	24.2	33.1	601.6	44.6	42.3	(10.5)
Price/earnings (P/E) ratios	11.4	6.4	29.3	30.5	20	22.4
Earnings per share (EPS) growth	n/a	n/a	n/a	n/a	46.5	21.9
Average daily turnover (US$m)	0.8	0.4	8.6	12.4	2.6	10.5
Dividend yield	1.1	2.2	0.7	0.57	1	0.8
Currency to US$ (bolivars)	37.2	43.5	49.7	61.6	79.8	106.2

Figure 28.1 Venezuela: key statistics

gramme was adopted, following elections which brought President Perez back to power, the market had a spectacular rise in 1990, followed by consolidation in 1991. There are now over 139 listed companies with a market capitalization of about 11bn, representing 17.6 per cent of GNP. Average monthly trading volume is US$226m. The banks and utilities make up a large part of the turnover and market capitalization. Mutual funds have become important investors since 1989 when restrictions on foreign investments were largely lifted. Major banks include the Banco de Venezuela, Banco Latino and the Banco Provincial.

Exchange address

Venezuela Stock Exchange:
Bolsa de Valores de Caracas
Edificio Atrium
Calle Sorocaima, Urbanizacion
El Rosal, Piso 1
Caracas

Tel: 582 905 5511. Fax: 582 905 5829/5707

Company	**Market cap. (US$m)**	*Company*	**Volume (US$ '000s)**
Electricidad de Caracas	1404	Electricidad de Caracas	4420
Banco Provincial	386	Mavesa	386
Vencemos	355	Vencemos	372
Corimon	261	Mantex	369
Mavesa	250	Ceramica Carabobo	282
Venprecar	232	Corimon	255
Sivensa	206	Sudamtex	56
Banco Mercantil	194	Venepal	23
Ceramica Carabobo	129	Madosa	22
Venepal	95		
Cervicera Nacional	84		
Sudamtex	77		
Madosa	57		
Ron Sta Teresa	42		
Mantex	39		
H.L. Boulton	37		
Dominguez & Cia	34		
Vanaseta	30		
Invers. Aledo	29		
Envases Venezolanos	24		

Figure 28.2 Venezuela: 20 largest stocks by market capitalization and nine largest by market turnover

PART V

The Mediterranean and North Africa

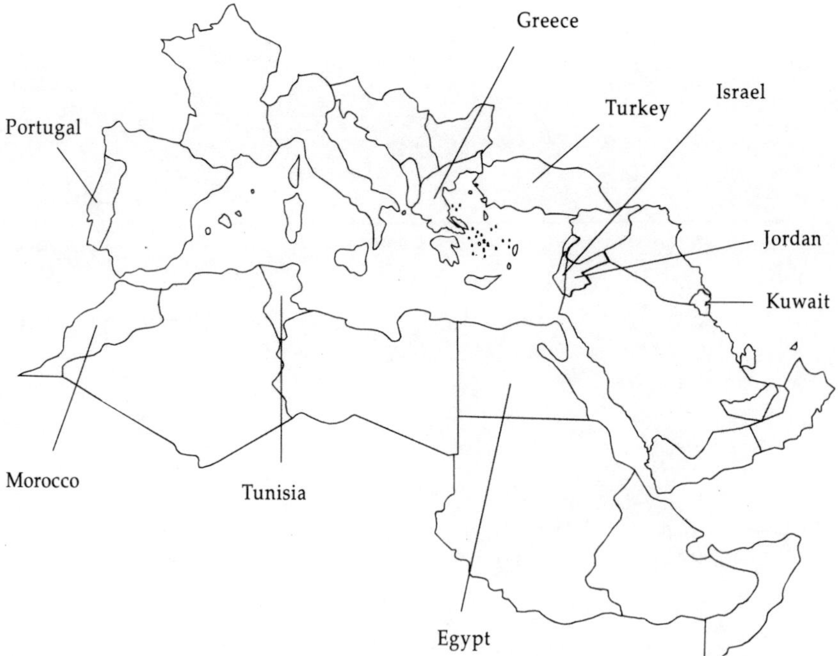

THE EMERGING MARKETS OF THE MEDITERRANEAN & N. AFRICA

Chapter 29

The Mediterranean and North Africa - Introduction

In the Islamic world it has been rather rare to see stock exchanges develop—for the same reasons that the banking system has been slow to develop. The Koran specifically forbids the payment of interest. The Islamic fundamentalists would like to impose *Sharia* on the economies of the Muslim world. They would impose severe restrictions on lifestyles, the role of women and other secular aspects of life. In many respects, it is comparable to early modern Europe when the first stirrings of the modern capitalist system emerged in Milan, in Augsburg, with the Fuggers, in Paris and London. The development of stock exchanges, nevertheless, has begun in as diverse places such as Morocco, Tunisia, Egypt, Jordan, Iran and Kuwait. Kuwait's example of the classic rise and fall of the bubble market in the *souk* in the early 1980s illustrated the potential of oil wealth and savings being channelled into listed securities. In Saudi Arabia, however, this trend has been slower. But a stock exchange may begin to develop because the Saudi government is now feeling the need to raise funds as its oil revenues decline. A working capital market, open to foreign investors, may be the best solution.

The remarkable breakthrough of peace between Israel and Palestine, in September 1993, has great economic implications and the stock market of Tel Aviv may be one of the clear beneficiaries. In a wider sense, however, capital will begin to flow towards these new areas of the Arab world, not only in Palestine but also in Egypt and North Africa, which have been held back by the frozen political relations between Israel and the Arab world. Trade and investment has now begun to flow. Tourism will also be a major beneficiary.

At the western end of the Mediterranean, nations such as Morocco and Portugal which are both much more closely linked to the European Community, have benefited from growth in trade in investment with the EC, but have also recently felt the effects of the deep recession in Germany and France. Portugal, in particular, has undergone the experience of a rapid withdrawal from its empire, ten years of socialist government, and then a return to free market policies and a restoration of the stock exchange. While

	Greece	Turkey	Portugal	Jordan	Morocco	Tunisia	Kuwait	Israel	Egypt
Population (m)	10.06	58.5	10.6	4.3	27	8.55	2.11	5.3	55.16
GNP (US$bn)	74.5	120.7	64.8	4.64	28	12.9	24.6	68.7	42.3
Real GNP growth (%)									
1992	1.3	5.3	1.5	-	-2.9	8.4	-	4.7	-
1993	1.2	6.8	0.5	-	3	-	-	4.7	-
Per capita income (US$)	7276	2063	6113	1005	1008	1509	11,659	12,962	767
Exports (US$bn)	9.1	15.5	16.8	1.1	4	3.8	6.6	22.2	3.3
Imports (US$bn)	19.8	29.5	25.1	2.5	7.4	6	6.3	28.8	7.1
Foreign direct investment (US$m)	-	-	4	-25.6	504	-	-	-	-
Inflation	18.9	70.1	8.9	8.2	4.9	5.4	-	10.5	13.6
Interest rates	29.5	64	14.5	8.5	-	11.7	-	13	16
Market capitalization (US$bn)	9.9	37.6	10.6	5.3	2.8	1.1	-	46.9	2.2
No. listed companies	175	142	175	125	66	18**	-	550	627
Index performance in '93 (%)*	16.1	213.7	30.9	20.8	18	13.1	-	11.9	-
Price/earnings (P/E) ratios									
1993^{e}	9.4	13.1	15.3	18	14.8	13.5	-	21	7.5
Earnings per share (EPS) growth									
1993^{e}	3.4	24.9	1.3	20	5	3.43	-	18	8
Turnover per annum (US$bn)	2.2	22	57.1	1.4	0.15	-	-	0.235	0.22
Dividend yield	4.8	5.2	3.6	2.7	2.7	4	-	0.2	0.2
Stock market performance ('88-'93)	97.3	286.4	(4.5)	46.2	56.3	53.5	-	-	-
Currency to US$ perf. ('88-'93)	(68.8)	(707.2)	(20.4)	(44.6)	(16.8)	(16.5)	(6.2)	(82.8)	(43.1)

*Notes: *) IFC indices used where available; **) 528 on second board*

Figure 29.1 Mediterranean & North Africa: country statistics (31 December 1993)

in some respects the recovery has been swift, in others it appears that it will take some years for the health of the Portuguese corporate sector to be fully restored.

Greece has also continued to disappoint international investors, as the Athens government lurches from Left to Right and back to Left again. Its strategic position, however, should have greatly improved with the collapse of communism in its neighbours such as Bulgaria, Yugoslavia and Albania. Greece has also had to grapple with environmental problems which may impact its undoubtedly successful tourist sector. The level of foreign direct investment coming from the rest of the EC has, so far, been disappointing. The Athens stock market, therefore, has not been a magnet for foreign money.

The potential investment giant of this whole region has to be Turkey. Like Brazil in the Latin American region, it has been late to reform, but continues to run a high rate of inflation with consequent rapid currency depreciation; yet the Istanbul stock market had a remarkable performance in 1993 and promises to be a winner in the years to come. Of all the Muslim countries, Turkey is by far the most modernized and closest to Europe. Its complex cultural origins, of course, include not only the Greek coastal communities, but also the Byzantine and Christian centuries. The tradition of Ataturk, who modernized Turkey and made it a secular state in the 1920s, is still a vital element of Turkish political life. Thus we could see Turkey playing an important economic role in the recovery of many of the Turkish-speaking regions of southern part of the former Soviet Union, such as Uzbekistan.

The recent launch of the first Near Eastern Equity Investment Fund is perhaps a positive sign of things to come in that international investors who, for many years, have been restrained from committing capital to the area by the political turmoil of the Middle East, will now, in the wake of the breakthrough between Israel and its neighbours, start to consider the Middle East as it should be—an area of great promise, of ancient cultures and of able and enterprising people. There is plenty of capital available in the oil rich states of the Gulf which has hesitated to invest in its closest neighbours because of political uncertainty. Certainly, among the political risks still overhanging the region are those which emanate from Iraq and Iran. On the one hand, since the Gulf War of 1990-91, Iraq appears to have been militarily neutralized, but it is still ruled by the unsavoury dictator, Saddam Hussein. On the other hand, the fanatical followers of Khomeini are ruling in Tehran although, after nearly fifteen years, the economic consequences of their rule are clear for all Iranians to see. There are rumours that the Teheran Stock Exchange may be revived as the need for international capital becomes more pressing. Above all, economic progress and, therefore, investor confidence, will depend on peace in the region.

Chapter 30

Egypt

Population:	55.2m
Gross national product:	$42.3bn
Market capitalization:	$2.2bn
Currency/US$:	3.33 pounds

Egypt's long and splendid cultural history has not always been accompanied by economic growth and dynamism. In recent years, the rapid growth of the Egyptian population, which is now at 53m and estimated to reach 75m by 2010, has severely restricted the per capita income growth of the country.

It has often been said that Egypt is the gift of the Nile and the vast majority of its population live on and around the river, the rest of the land being mainly desert. The Nile has a total length of 4145 miles, of which 960 miles run through Egypt. Since the completion of the Aswan High Dam, in 1965, there has been no flooding downstream of the Nile and the water level remains almost constant throughout the year. The area of fertile land, which is a 5-15 mile wide strip in the Nile valley and some of the Nile Delta, has been increased by the opening of the dam which has allowed the reclamation of about 1.3m acres. However much of Egypt's economy is centred on Cairo, the population of which is now estimated at nearly 15m, and Alexandria, at about 5m.

Egypt has fought three wars with Israel, in 1956, 1967 and 1973 and there have been clear economic benefits for Egypt since the 1989 Camp David Treaty between President Sadat and Prime Minister Begin. Following the assassination of President Sadat in 1981 President Hosni Mubarak came to power and has remained president ever since. This has meant a new period of stability and economic growth for Egypt. Reforms under the Mubarak government, agreed with the IMF, include the commitment of the free market, convertibility of the Egyptian pound (resulting in a drastic devaluation), removal of interest rate controls and price liberalization. However, there has been little progress on privatization of the public sector, which accounted for 54 per cent of GDP as recently as 1991.

	1988	1989	1990	1991	1992	1993
Population (m)	50.27	51.48	52.69	53.92	55.16	56.4
GNP (US$bn)	77.9	77	50.9	35.8	42.3	n/a
Real GNP growth (%)	5.4	4.9	5.7	1.1	4.4	n/a
Per capita income (US$)	1550	1496	966	664	767	n/a
Exports (US$bn)	5706	5213	3477	3533	3272	n/a
Imports (US$bn)	20,970	13,602	11,172	6710	7053	n/a
Foreign direct investment (US$m)						
Inflation	17.7	21.3	16.8	19.8	13.6	n/a
Interest rates (lending)	17	18.3	19	n/a	n/a	n/a
Market capitalization (US$m)	1760	1713	1835	2527	2594	n/a
No. of listed companies	483	510	573	627	656	n/a
Turnover per annum (US$m)	115	81	126	262	293	n/a
Dividend yield						
Currency to US$ (pound)	2.3555	2.56	2.8736	3.3371	3.328	3.33

Figure 30.1 Egypt: key statistics

The stock market

The Cairo Stock Exchange has grown rapidly in recent years. In the ten years to 1991, the number of listed companies grew from 64 to 627 with a market capitalization of nearly US$1bn. However, trading volume is very small and foreign investors have hardly been active.

Exchange addresses

Cairo Stock Exchange
4a Sherifen Street
Cairo

Tel: 20 2 392 1447 & 8968 / Fax:20 2 392 8526

Alexandria Stock Exchange
11 Talat Harb Street
Menshia, Alexandria

Tel: 20 3 483 5432

	Market capitalization (US$ million)
Suez Cement Company	200.60
Abu Feir Fertilizers & Chemicals	113.43
Misr Indust. & Hoteliere	22.39
Kabo	22.15
Uniarab Spinning & Weaving	19.50
Kima	13.97
Misr for Soft Drinks - Food Presser	11.08
El Shams Housing & Development	6.52
Ceramic & Porcelaine	5.73
United Housing & Development	3.45

Figure 30.2 Egypt: 10 largest stocks by market capitalization

Chapter 31

Greece

Population:	10.1m
Gross national product:	$74.5bn
Market capitalization:	$9.9bn
Currency/US$:	236.5 drachma

Ancient Greece is the source of all our greatest philosophical and political ideas. Greek literature was the fountain of Latin and European poetry and history. Yet modern Greece, which became independent from the Ottoman Empire in the 1820s, has never been a brilliant star in the modern European firmament of nations. Its economy, too, has been slow to modernize.

The population of Greece is estimated at about ten million, of whom four million live in the area surrounding Athens. The long struggle for democracy in modern Greece had first to overcome the real threat of a Communist takeover in 1945, which was partly saved by Churchill's strong intervention, preventing Greece from being overwhelmed by the Communist tide in Eastern Europe. Then, in 1967, King Constantine was exiled and in 1973, Greece was declared a republic. Since the second World War, military government has been the rule rather than the exception. However, 1974 saw a new constitution with a 300-member parliament elected for four years.

The two main parties are the New Democracy Party, which is a centre right-party led by Constantine Mitsotakis and the Pan Hellenic Socialist Party (PASOK) led by Mr Papandreou who governed Greece between 1981-89, when it lost its majority. Mitsotakis formed a government in April 1990 and ruled for three years until October 1993, when Papandreou was re-elected. The Athens Stock Exchange reacted very positively to the election of the New Democracy Party in 1990 and hit an all-time high of 1684. However, the subsequent lack of improvement in the Greek economy disappointed investors' hopes and the index has dropped back to half this level.

Inflation has remained high at 16 per cent and the drachma has weakened by 10 per cent per annum against the dollar. Prospects for the Greek economy remain uninspiring, tied largely, as they are, to the European Community. However, the programme of privatization which was laun-

	1988	1989	1990	1991	1992	1993
Population (m)	10	10.04	10.12	10.06	10.08	10.12
GNP (US$bn)	50.5	55.7	65.8	73.2	73.8	74.5
Real GNP growth (%)	4.1	4.3	2	1.2	1.3	1.3
Per capita income (US$)	5050	5548	6502	7276	7321	7362
Exports (US$bn)	5.2	7.9	8	9.1	8.4	
Imports (US$bn)	10.5	14.9	17.4	19.8	18.3	
Foreign direct investment						
Inflation	13.5	13.7	20.4	18.9	16.3	11.5
Interest rates (lending)	22.9	23.3	27.6	29.5	28.7	28.7
Market capitalization (US$bn)	4.3	6.4	15.2	13.1	9.5	9.9
No. of listed companies	119	119	145	126	129	143
IFC Index performance in US$ (%)	-37.6	80.2	104.1	-19.3	-27	16.1
Price/earnings (P/E) ratios	10.6	9.8	13.5	10.4	11	9.4
Earnings per share (EPS) growth	28.8	76	38.7	24.6	-15.8	3.4
Turnover per annum (US$m)	313	549	3925	2443	1605	2200
Dividend yield	5.6	4.6	5	3.8	4.2	4.8
Currency to US$ (drachma)	147.7	156.3	159.5	175	215.3	236.5
Currency to US$ perf (%)	-18.2	-5.2	-2	-9.7	-23	-9.8

Figure 31.1 Greece: key statistics

ched by the New Democracy Party is a key aspect in attracting the attention of international investors. It started with the listing of the OTE (The Hellenic Telecommunications Organization) in late 1993.

The key sector of the Greek stock market is banking, with the National Bank of Greece having a market capitalization of nearly US$1bn. The other major banks are Ergo Bank, Commercial Bank, Credit Bank and Ionian Bank.

The stock market

The Athens Stock Exchange (ASE) was established in 1876 and is the only exchange in Greece. The ASE is a government institution which reports directly to the Ministry of National Economy and is supervised by the eleven-member Capital Markets Committee. Day-to-day management of the exchange is undertaken by a seven-member Stock Exchange Council.

Legislation introduced in 1988 established measures aimed at reforming and developing the capital market system in Greece. Among the major reforms included in this law is a provision for the creation of a parallel OTC market for smaller capitalization companies. Furthermore, the law allows

Company	**Market cap. (US$m)**	*Company*	**Volume (US$m)**
HBC	981	TCTSA Aemet	14.0
Intracom	928	Bank of Attica	11.2
National Bank	843	Greek Progress	9.4
Credit	832	Econ	
Ergo Bank	801	Attica Enterprises	7.5
Commercial Bank	738	Globe	
Greek Sugar Industry	507	Greek Sugar Industry	7.1
Heracles Cement	485	Allatini	6.2
Ionian Bank	477	Ideal Group	6.2
Delta Dairy	467	Ergoinvest	6.1
Titan Cement	333	Commercial Bank	5.3
Elais Oleaginous	284	Ergo Bank	4.8
Aktor	267	Heracles Cement	4.4
Aluminum of Greece	255	Intracom	4.3
Michaniki	241	Lavreotiki	4.3
Alpha Leasing	209	Balkan Export	3.9
Hellas Can	200	Petzetakis	3.6
National Mortgage Bank	183	Sheet Steel	3.5
Papastratos	172	St. George Mills	3.4
Alcatel Hellas	153	Hellenic Bottling	3.1

Figure 31.2 Greece: 20 largest stocks by market capitalization and average daily volume

for *Societes Anònymes* to function as brokers, thus paving the way for banks and other institutions to compete freely with existing brokers. To facilitate trading and settlement, a central depository, together with new and updated computer equipment, has been installed.

The rules and regulations governing the ASE are detailed and the requirements for new listings are comparable to those of other European countries. For example, two of the preconditions state that an existing company must have been profitable for a period of at least five years prior to listing and that any new issue must be accompanied by a minimum 25 per cent increase in share capital.

There are no restrictions on investment in Greek securities by foreign investors, who may freely buy and sell securities listed on the ASE. Foreign investors can, without restriction, repatriate capital invested in securities when liquidated plus any capital gains and dividends resulting from their investments. There is no capital gains tax in Greece.

Trading on the ASE is now fully computerized and the settlement period is two days on a cash basis for physical delivery. Official trading hours are from 11.00 to 13.30.

Exchange address

The Athens Stock Exchange
10 Sophocleous Street
Athens 10559
Greece

Tel: 30 1 321 1301 / Fax: 30 1 321 3938

Chapter 32

Israel

Population:	5.3m
Gross national product:	$68.7bn
Market capitalization:	$46.9bn
Currency/US$:	2.89 shekels

Israel became an independent state in 1948 after a terrorist campaign had been waged against the British who had held the League of Nations' mandate for Palestine following the Balfour Declaration. The years since 1948 have not been peaceful. In 1956, Israel captured the Sinai Peninsula from Egypt but agreed to hand it over to an United Nations peacekeeping force. In 1967, in the Six-Day War, Israel took the same area and defeated the attempt of the Egyptians to re-capture it in the Yom Kippur War of 1973. In 1967, it also gained the West Bank and East Jerusalem. It is over this area that it has now made peace with the PLO, having handed back the Sinai Peninsula as a consequence of the Camp David Agreement. The major outstanding territorial dispute is now with Syria over the Golan Heights.

As Israel's history has been steeped in conflict, it has not been allowed to trade with its Arab neighbours. This has led it to build up excellent trading relations with the rest of the world—it is the only country to have free trade agreements with the USA, Efta and the EC.

In the early 1980s, Israel suffered from hyperinflation—reaching 445 per cent in 1984. The government introduced a stabilization policy which led to a recession in the late 1980s due to the central bank's determination to protect the exchange rate through high interest rates. However, the government is determined to reduce its level of interference in the economy and aims to privatize many of its industrial holdings. It has already started this process but has much further to go, not least because of its ownership of the banks which, in turn, have large portfolios.

Israel has almost no raw materials and is therefore dependent on its ability to manufacture and trade. It has sizeable textile and high technology industries, both of which are helped by competitive labour rates. Pressure is kept on wage costs because of the high level of unemployment and of immigration—600,000 Russians have gone to Israel since 1989, bringing the

	1988	1989	1990	1991	1992	1993
Population (m)	4.44	4.52	4.66	4.97	5.1	5.3
GNP (US$bn)	54.44	55.3	58.12	61.53	65.59	68.7
Real GNP growth (%)	2.7	1.6	5.1	5.9	6.6	4.7
Per capita income (US$)	12260	12230	12470	12380	12860	12962
Exports (US$bn)	15.1	16.8	17.8	17.8	20.4	22.2
Imports (US$bn)	19.6	18.8	21.5	24.3	27.5	28.8
Foreign direct investment	169	87	-64	-161	-340	
Inflation	16.4	20.7	291	18	9.4	10.5
Interest rates	30.9	15	13	14.2	10.4	
Market capitalization (US$bn)	5.5	8.2	10.6	12.1	29.3	46.9
No. of listed companies	265	262	267	286	378	506
Index performance in US$ (%)						
Price/earnings (P/E) ratios						
Earnings per share (EPS) growth						
Turnover per annum (US$bn)	2.4	3.9	5.5	8.4	14.7	
Dividend yield						
Currency to US$ (shekel)	1.685	1.963	2.048	2.283	2.764	2.89

Figure 32.1 Israel: key statistics

total to 5.1m. Fortunately, this great wave has occurred at a time of fast economic expansion—7 per cent GDP growth in 1991, followed by 6.3 per cent in 1992—so unemployment is at the manageable rate of 11.2 per cent.

The stock market

An informal exchange was established by the Anglo-Palestine Bank in 1935, but the Tel-Aviv Stock Exchange (TASE) was formally established in 1953. There are 26 members of the TASE, 13 of which are banks, the rest being brokerage houses.

Recently, the exchange has grown rapidly, with the number of quoted companies more than doubling from 250 to over 500 in the past two and a half years. This has led to a division in the system of trading. The 100 most liquid companies are traded in a continuous series of rounds with a variety of prices being bargained each time. The other share prices are fixed once a day, with all transactions carried out at the same price. These prices may only fluctuate by 10 per cent either way per session each of which runs from 10.00 to 15.30, Sunday to Thursday. The top 100 companies account for 63 per cent of all trades. An options exchange was established in August 1993 to trade in the index of the top 25 companies.

	Market capitalization (NIS million)
Bezeq,The Israel Telecom Corp Ltd	4618
Dead Sea Works Ltd	3854
Israel Chemicals Ltd	3432
Teva Pharmaceutical Industries Ltd	3305
IDB Development Corp Ltd	2969
Clal Industries Ltd	2948
Clal (Israel) Ltd	2934
Koor Industries Ltd	2783
Discount Investment Corp Ltd	2593
IDB Bank Holding Corp Ltd	2539
Elbit Computers Ltd	2341
Clal Electronic Industries Ltd	1852
The First Int'l Bank of Israel Ltd	1774
Industrial Buildings Corp Ltd	1192
The Israel Corporation Ltd	1065
Africa-Israel Investment Ltd	1020
Elron, Electrical Industry Ltd	1018
FIBI Holdings Ltd	928
Super-Sol Ltd	863
Elite Industries Ltd	837

Figure 32.2 Israel: 20 largest stocks by market capitalization

The exchange's growth is also shown by the fact that $1.6bn was raised through new issues in 1992, with $1.2bn raised during the first six months of 1993 alone; similarly, turnover levels were $14bn and $12bn, respectively. It is worth noting that only 30 per cent of the total market capitalization is freely floating.

Technical notes

- Settlement is on the same day. Any buyer of shares has to have a bank account from which the money may be directly debited.
- The whole system is paperless with each company depositing a global share with the bank of its choice. No foreign banks provide a safe-custody service.
- Commissions are negotiable.
- Listing criteria: there are three options for companies wishing to be on the main list, these relate to years of activity, capital, profits, sales and added value. The requirements for the parallel list are less onerous demanding only one year of activity and a lower capital threshold. As a special concession companies with investment in research and development exceeding $0.5m may list straight away.

- There is no capital gains tax on stock exchange profits, but there is a 25 per cent withholding tax on dividends and a 35 per cent tax on interest. However, Israel has double-taxation treaties with many countries. Repatriation of capital, profits and dividends is allowed as long as the original investment came in as foreign currency.

Exchange address

The Tel Aviv Stock Exchange Ltd
54 Ahad Ha'am St
Tel Aviv 65202
PO Box 29060
Israel

Tel: 972 3 567 7411 / Fax: 972 3 510 5379

Chapter 33

Jordan

Population:	4.3m
Gross national product:	$4.64bn
Market capitalization:	$5.3m
Currency/US$:	1.4217 dinars

The Hashemite Kingdom of Jordan was carved out of the desert following the defeat of Turkey in the First World War. It remained under a British mandate until 1948, when it became an independent kingdom with the present King, Hussain, succeeding in 1952. The West Bank of the Jordan has been under Israeli occupation since the 1967 war, although Jordan has never formally renounced sovereignty over the area. As a result of the two Israeli-Arab wars of 1948 and 1967 there are nearly one million refugees living in Jordan, of an estimated total of 4.3m.

With its background, it is not a place one would expect to find the most efficient and most sophisticated stock market in the Arab world. Yet in the capital, the Amman Financial Market (AFM) has over 100 listed companies and market capitalization of about US$3bn. It benefits here from the advantage of a well-educated and talented population, two-thirds of whom are Palestinian.

The Amman Financial market was created in 1976 and started trading in 1978. Since its inception, it has shown its resilience in the face of various crises in the region including, most recently, the 1990-91 Gulf War with Iraq, its main trading partner. There are some leading blue chips, including the Arab Bank which accounts for over 30 per cent of total market capitalization. Typical of other listed Jordanian stocks, it is owned and managed by an Arab family, the descendants of Abdul Hamid Shoman, whose son and grandson still run the bank which has close connections to the Palestine Liberation Organization and assets of over US$10bn. Other leading stocks are the phosphate mines, cement factories and other banks including Jordanian National Bank, Commercial Bank of Jordan and no less than seventeen publicly-owned insurance companies, mostly founded in the 1970s.

	1988	1989	1990	1991	1992	1993
Population (m)	3.75	3.88	4.01	4.14	4.3	4.3
GNP (US$bn)	4.69	3.71	3.94	4.16	4.3	4.64
Real GNP growth (%)	1	10.6	0.1	0.5	2.0	2.5
Per capita income (US$)	1251	956	983	1005	1000	1080
Exports (US$m)	800	984	1062	1142	1200	n/a
Imports (US$bn)	2144	1898	2595	2521	3204	n/a
Foreign direct Investment	23.8	18.1	69.1	25.6	n/a	n/a
Inflation (1985 = 100)	106.4	133.8	155.4	168.1	174.8	n/a
Interest rates (discount)	6.25	8	8.5	8.5	8.5	n/a
International reserves(US$m)	247.9	573.2	949.4	929.6	868.6	n/a
Market capitalization (US$m)	2233	2162	2001	2512	3365	5.3
No. of listed companies	106	106	105	101	103	125
Index performance in US$ (%)	10.1	1.1	4.3	15.1	24.7	20.8
Price/earnings (P/E) ratios	14.2	14.4	7.8	10	14.5	n/a
Turnover per annum (US$m)	337	652	407	432	1317	n/a
Dividend yield	3.4	2.4	6.5	8.7	2.5	n/a
Currency to US$ (dinar)	2.0964	1.5432	1.5038	1.4815	1.4472	1.4217

Figure 33.1 Jordan: key statistics

	Market capitalization (US$ million)
Arab Bank	761.20
The Arab Potash	864.00
Jordan Phosphate Mines Co	150.48
The Jordan Cement Factories	132.00
Jordan Petroleum Refinery	75.20
The Arab Pharmaceuticals Man	82.44
Arab Aluminium Industry	45.60
Arab International Hotels	38.37
Housing Bank	75.60
Jordan National Bank	63.89
Arab-Jordan Inv Bank	22.45
Jordan Insurance	21.00
Jordan Tanning	8.00
Jordan Ceramic	19.30
Jordan Paper & Cardboard	13.80
National Cable & Wire	38.15
Cairo Amman Bank	42.00

Figure 33.2 Jordan: 17 largest stocks by market capitalization

The foreign element in the stock market is very small, at only 2 per cent, with 85 per cent held by Jordanian individuals and other Arab investors from the region.

Exchange address

Amman Financial Market
PO Box 8802
Amman, Jordan

Tel: 962 666 8404 / Fax: 962 668 6830 / Tlx: 21711 SUKMAL JO

Chapter 34

Kuwait

Population:	2.1m
Gross national product:	$24.6bn
Market capitalization:	$9.9bn
Currency/US$:	0.3 dinar

As a result of the Iraqi invasion of 1990, Kuwait has been much in the news in the past few years. Sited at the northern end of the Gulf, with a small land area and population, it had previously been a sleepy, but wealthy emirate. For 240 years, it has been ruled by the Al-Sabah family. Although a National Assembly existed it was not active and the Emir of Kuwait acted as a benevolent autocrat.

The strength of Kuwait's economy is almost entirely derived from its massive oil revenues which enabled the country to build up its overseas financial reserves—managed for the benefit of future generations by the Kuwait Investment Authority (KIA) and its London arm, the Kuwait Investment Office (KIO). Kuwait was invaded by Iraq on 2 August 1990 and liberated in February 1991 by the allied troops. The recovery of the economy in the last two and a half years has been gradual because of the destruction of many of Kuwait's oil wells.

The stock market

The Kuwait Stock Exchange was established in 1977 and enjoyed rapid growth in its early years. In 1981, it had become the world's ninth largest stock market and a highly speculative bubble had built up in the so-called *Soukh al Manakh* (the parallel over-the-counter market) which collapsed in the summer of 1982. The government intervened and purchased about 30 per cent of all listed shares in order to support the market, which did not recover for some years. Following the Iraqi invasion, the stock market opened only in September 1992 and is still rather quiet with only 37 listed companies.

	1988	1989	1990	1991	1992	1993
Population (m)	1.96	2.05	2.14	2.1	2.11	n/a
GNP (US$b)	27.5	32.8	26.4	16.6	24.6	n/a
Real GNP growth (%)	3.5	n/a	n/a	n/a	n/a	n/a
Per capita income (US$)	14031	16000	12336	7905	11659	n/a
Exports (US$m)	7736	11648	7254	888	6560	n/a
Imports (US$bn)	5311	5531	3548	4193	6363	n/a
Foreign direct investment						
Inflation	1.5	3.4	n/a	n/a	n/a	n/a
Interest rates (lending)	6.8	6.8	n/a	n/a	n/a	n/a
Currency to US$ (dinar)	0.28	0.29	n/a	0.28	0.3	0.3
Currency to US$ perf (%)	3.7	3.6	n/a	n/a	7.1	0

Figure 34.1 Kuwait: key statistics

Exchange address

Kuwait Stock Exchange
Mubarak Al Kabir Street
PO Box 22235, Safat
13063 Kuwait

Tel: 965 242 3130 / Fax: 965 243 9771

Chapter 35

Morocco

Population:	27m
Gross national product:	$28bn
Market capitalization:	$2bn
Currency/US$:	9.603 dirham

Morocco was ruled by a variety of dynasties from 681AD to 1912. Their powers during the 11th and 12th centuries extended over most of the Iberian peninsula and it is the only Arab country never to have been part of the Ottoman Empire. However, internal problems encouraged France and Spain to intervene in 1912. They ruled southern and northern Morocco respectively but left under pressure in 1956. The country has been politically stable since the beginning of King Hassan II's rule in 1961—there has been no attempt to overthrow him since 1972. The recent election has reinforced this appearance of stability with the right-wing conservative forces doing better than expected particularly in the indirect elections.

The population of 27.5m is almost entirely Moslem and reveres King Hassan not only as the political head, but also as a religious leader.

Morocco has an agrarian economy with 40 per cent of people employed on the land. Phosphates seemed to be the key to future prosperity and mining was greatly emphasized in the 1970s. Unfortunately, a decline in the world price made this project less than entirely successful. Tourism is becoming increasingly important and is strongly encouraged by the government. The money sent home by the 600,000 Moroccans working abroad is a great help to the economy. It is estimated that the drug industry could be worth $5bn or one-fifth of GDP: this undermines the value of many official statistics, particularly the unemployment rate, as many people are believed to work on the black market—which is estimated to be up to three times the size of the official economy.

In the last ten years, the Moroccan economy has been transformed and liberalized. During this time, the budget deficit has fallen from 15 per cent of GDP to 1.7 per cent and the current account deficit from 13 per cent to 2 per cent. The national debt has similarly fallen, from 125 per cent to 78 per cent and is planned to fall further, to 40 per cent. Foreign reserves have risen to $3bn, or five months' of imports, helped by foreign investment which has increased from $100m to $500m annually. Inflation has declined from 12 per cent to 5 per cent while, from 1985 to 1991, GDP grew by between 3-5 per cent per annum. Unfortunately, 1992 and 1993 have been drought years, to the detriment of the whole economy.

The privatization programme has not proceeded as quickly as initially intended. Between 1993 and 1995, 112 companies are scheduled for privatization. In a letter to the prime minister in June 1993, the King called for the process to be speeded up and he has subsequently called for audits of the telecommunications and phosphate companies, amongst others, as a preliminary to privatization. If all this does go ahead, then the stock market would become more liquid. However, privatization will not make the economy more efficient because the new owners have to agree to keep on staff as the government is worried about the unemployment rate.

There has been some speculation on the possibility of a further improvement in the relationship between Morocco and the EC. Morocco already has preferential access in areas other than agriculture. However, in the light of the greater pressure being exerted from Eastern Europe and the political realities of European trade, Morocco will not be high on the list for EC assistance or eventual membership.

The stock market

The Casablanca Exchange was established in 1929 and now has 69 companies listed on it. Of that number, no more than fifteen are reasonably liquid and, in an average month, there are only 10 to 15 trades averaging $25,000 to $50,000. Sessions are daily from 11.00 to 11.45, with the price usually being determined once with a 3 per cent limit between consecutive transactions. Only about 10 per cent of shares are freely floating and the best way to obtain a holding of any size is in a transaction off the floor of the exchange.

To facilitate the increase in business that ought to follow from the completion of the privatization programme, a number of reforms are in the pipeline. These include the introduction of higher reporting standards with more detailed information, the creation of an SEC-type body and a delivery against payment system.

Technical notes

- Settlement is one day after trading, but the physical transfer occurs once every two weeks. To remove uncertainty, all settlement is done through a custodian and a broker never receives either money or certificates.

	1988	1989	1990	1991	1992	1993
Population (m)	23.81	24.43	25.06	25.7	26.34	27
GNP (US$bn)	22.18	22.51	25.9	27.5	26.54	n/a
Real GNP growth (%)	10.4	2.5	3.7	5.1	2.9	3
Per capita income (US$)	932	921	1034	1070	1008	n/a
Exports (US$bn)	3.6	3.3	4.2	4.3	4	3.5
Imports (US$bn)	4.8	5.5	6.9	6.9	7.4	6.5
Foreign direct investment (US$m)	103	129	226	227	504	562
Inflation (1985 = 100)	114.3	117.9	126	136.1	142.8	n/a
Interest rates	9					
Market Cap (US$m)	446	621	966	1528	1876	n/a
No. of listed companies	71	71	71	67	62	n/a
Index performance in US$ (%)	22.6	26	30.7	16.6	4.2	n/a
Price/earnings (P/E) ratios						
Earnings per share (EPS) growth						
Turnover per annum (US$m)	33	16	62	49	70	n/a
Dividend yield	9.2	6.9	5.8	4.4	4.2	n/a
Currency to US$ (dirham)	8.211	8.122	8.043	8.15	11	n/a
Currency to US$ perf (%)	5.3	1.1	1	1.3	9.049	n/a

Figure 35.1 Morocco: key statistics

	Market capitalization (US$ million)
ONA	360.83
BCM	415.94
Credit du Maroc (CDM)	280.05
BMCE	246.90
Ciments du Maroc (CIOR)	100.31
Brasseries du Maroc	171.84
Wafabank	169.84
Lesieur	73.87
Asmar	70.67
BMCI	55.47
Cosumar	69.34
CGE Maroc	31.77
CTM	30.02
Credit Eqdom	26.82
SOFAC	24.11

Figure 35.2 Morrocco: 15 largest stocks by market capitalization

- Physical possession of stocks—no central depository.
- No foreign custodians, State Street and Barclays operate through BCM.
- Commissions: 1 per cent shared equally between the broker and the exchange.
- The stock exchange requires that a company must have been profitable for three years, issue at least 5 per cent of its capital and publish three years of financial information before it may be listed.
- Since 1990, foreign investment has been welcomed. Capital, profits and dividends may be repatriated freely as long as it is done through a reporting bank. There is no capital gains tax and the 15 per cent withholding tax on dividends is due to be abolished in 1994. Some companies do not want foreign investors to hold too many voting shares and are contemplating issuing special non-voting ones.

Exchange address

Casablanca Stock Exchange
98 Boulevard Mohammed V
Casablanca 01
Morocco

Tel: 212 2 204 110 / Fax: 212 2 200 365

Chapter 36

Portugal

Population:	10.58m
Gross national product:	$64.8bn
Market capitalization:	$10.6bn
Currency/US$:	167.5 escudos

Portugal is another small European nation with a long and brilliant history of exploration, empire and discovery. Since 1974, Portugal has undergone a complete metamorphosis (it is the only western European country to have experienced a revolution during this period). The population of about 10.6m is concentrated on the Atlantic coast around Lisbon and Oporto.

Portugal was under a military regime from 1932 onwards, when Antonio Salazar became prime minister, followed by Caetano in 1968. In 1974 the Communists, who had infiltrated the military which accounted for 20 per cent of the male population, took power in a bloodless revolution. The new left-wing government nationalized all banks, insurance, ship building, cement, brewery and transport companies. Large farms were also taken over by the workers and transformed into co-operatives. The African colonies of Mozambique and Angola were granted their independence. Only Macau, which the Chinese refused to take back, remains today a Portuguese colony until it is returned, by agreement with China, on 20 December 1999.

Political instability followed for several years while Portugal gradually moved away from left-wing policies. Two governments led by Mario Soares brought Portugal closer towards the European Community. The 1987 elections saw the Social Democrats emerge as the majority party under Cavaco Silva with Mario Soares becoming the first democratically-elected civilian president for 60 years.

The Portuguese economy has now moved back dramatically towards a free enterprise system. The most remarkable story perhaps is that of the Espirito Santo family who controlled one of the largest financial empires in Portugal prior to 1974. Although all their interests in the country were nationalized, they have been able to recover the bank and insurance company and today constitute again one of the largest financial groups in the nation.

	1988	1989	1990	1991	1992	1993
Population (m)	9.89	9.88	9.87	10.0	10.3	10.6
GNP (US$bn)	41.7	45.6	59.8	65.1	n/a	n/a
Real GNP growth (%)	4	4.9	4.1	2.1	1.5	0.5
Per capita income (US$)	4216	4615	6059	6510	n/a	n/a
Exports (US$m)	10.8	13.5	17.1	17.6	16.8	n/a
Imports (US$bn)	15.9	18.2	23.8	25.8	25.1	n/a
Foreign direct investment (US$m)	682	1517	3433	5045	4023	n/a
Inflation	9.6	12.6	13.4	11.4	8.9	7
Interest rates (discount)	13.7	14.3	14.5	14.5	14.5	13.5
Market capitalization (US$bn)	7.2	10.6	9.2	9.6	9.2	10.6
No. of listed companies	171	182	181	180	191	175
IFC Index performance in US$ (%)	28.3	40.1	29.8	1.7	19.4	30.9
Price/earnings (P/E) ratios	n/a	n/a	13.1	11.2	12.7	15.3
Earnings per share (EPS) growth	n/a	n/a	30.3	22.9	6.6	1.3
Turnover per annum (US$m)	1136	1912	1687	2818	3455	3600
Dividend yield	n/a	n/a	2.8	3.3	3.9	3.6
Currency to US$ (escudo)	146.7	149.6	136.6	133.6	146.9	167.5

Figure 36.1 Portugal: key statistics

The government's programme of privatization has brought a good deal of international capital back into the market. Foreign investment from other European countries has been growing year by year. Clearly, Portugal is a prime beneficiary of the European Community infrastructure programmes. The pro-business policies of the new government have resulted in steady improvements in the economy and unemployment.

The stock market, however, has never really recovered from the crash of 1987 and appears to offer quite good value at this level. Part of the reason for this under-performance lies in the weakness of the escudo. In addition, it is estimated that of the 30 per cent free float, half is held by overseas investors with many traditional investors in London. This has had a significant impact on the market with the sterling/escudo rate having a considerable influence.

The stock market

Since 1992, the Lisbon Stock Exchange's structural problems have seen some positive improvements. First, the market was divided into three markets: the Official Market, for the blue chip companies in the market and for the more liquid stocks, the Secondary Market for less liquid stocks, and the Unquoted Market for minor stocks.

Company	**Market cap. (US$m)**	*Company*	**Volume (US$m)**
Banco Commerical Português	1855	BCP	46.1
Banco Portugues do Atlantico	1458	Bank Totta	38.3
Banco Espirito Santo	1210	Bank Espirito Santo	31.4
Banco Totta	1206	BPI	25.6
Continente	861	Sonae	24.5
Banco Portugues de Investimiento	808	Radio Marconi	19.7
Sonae	748	Bank Manuf. Hanover	13.3
Marconi	486	Efacec	13.0
Jeronimo Martins	473	Soares de Costa	10.0
Modelo	420	Modelo	9.3
Unicer	334	Unicer	9.3
Soporcel	270	BPA	8.2
CPP	250	Jeronimo Martins	8.1
Tranquilidade	244	Lisnave	6.6
UBP	199	Engil	6.3
Soares Costa	195	Modelo Continente (SPCS)	6.1
Centralcer	189	Bank Espirito de Santo ('92 shares)	5.4
Corticeira Amorim	179	Radio Marconi (Normantiv)	5.1
BCI	165	BCI	5.1
Salvador Caetano	162	Corticeira	4.9

Figure 36.2 Portugal: 20 largest companies by market capitalization and average daily volume

A continuous trading system called TRADIS was also introduced, allowing the most liquid stocks on the Official Market to be traded continuously between 10.00 and 15.00. This system was based on the Rio de Janeiro Stock Exchange and there are now 48 shares being traded on the continuous system per day, representing 45 companies. Although the system saw a fairly slow introduction, it has performed smoothly, with shares on the system having their share prices synchronized between the Lisbon and Oporto Stock Exchanges.

Along with the continuous trading system, a central clearing house for all shares was established. Not only did this allow the elimination of costs associated with the physical delivery of stock certificates but, more importantly, it allowed shares to be traded 'delivery against payment'. The new system has resulted in improved clearing and settling, with settlement occurring at T+4.

The Sapateiro Law, named after its creator, has overhauled the legislation governing the market. Although the legislation is considered by many to be too cumbersome for the small Portuguese markets, it has taken many steps in the right direction. A Portuguese SEC, called the CMVM, has been created, and insider trading is now illegal. Companies are required to produce Annual Reports by 1 April and all companies were required to produce consolidated numbers as of financial year 1992.

Exchange address

Associacao da Bolsa de Valores de Lisboa
Gabinete de Estudos
Rua dos Fanqueiros, 10-1100 Lisboa
Portugal

Tel: 888 2738 or 888 3608 or 888 3237 / Fax: 877 402

Chapter 37

Tunisia

Population:	8.6m
Gross national product:	$12.9bn
Market capitalization:	$1.9bn
Currency/US$:	1.0458 dinars

Carthage was founded by Dido in 814BC. Its most famous general was Hannibal and the military threat that it posed to Rome was the reason for its destruction on the advice of the elder Cato. Since ancient times, Tunisia has had a variety of dynastic rulers, including the Ottomans. In 1881, a French protectorate was established until independence was achieved in 1956. Habib Bourguiba was the first president but was replaced, on the grounds of senility, by Zine El Abidine Ben Ali in 1987.

Tunisia is democratic but Ben Ali won 99 per cent of the vote in the 1989 elections and his RCD party won all 141 seats in the National Assembly, even though seven parties contested the election. Voting will take place again in 1994 and Ben Ali is expected to remain in control.

Economically, Tunisia has been flourishing. GDP grew at an average rate of 6.6 per cent in 1990-92. A restructuring programme to liberalize the economy has been taking place—tariffs have been reduced from 200 per cent to 43 per cent and subsidies have been cut from 3.3 per cent of GDP to 2 per cent. The tax system has been overhauled with more efficient collection at lower rates. This has led to a fall in the PSBR to 1.2 per cent of GDP. Moreover, the government's share of all economic activity has fallen from 40.5 per cent to 35 per cent. However, the current account deficit has grown considerably. The weather is crucial for the whole economy because of the importance of agriculture and tourism.

The government intends to embark on a far-reaching privatization programme. The Privatization Ministry has a clear idea of which companies it wants to float, but has not issued a list and needs higher political authority before it can take more action. Political opposition to privatization comes from those who feel that selling loss-making companies will lead to social problems and those who believe that losing profitable businesses is bad for the government's finances.

	1988	1989	1990	1991	1992
Population (m)	7.77	7.91	8.07	8.36	8.55
GNP (US$bn)	10.3	10.7	11.5	11.9	12.9
Real GNP growth (%)	0	3.9	7.5	3.5	8.4
Per capita income (US$)	1326	1353	1425	1423	1509
Exports (US$bn)	2.3	3.1	3.7	4	3.8
Imports (US$bn)	3.5	4.6	5.8	5.5	6
Foreign direct investment	63	74	75	147	
Inflation (1985 = 100)	120.6	129.5	138.3	149.7	157.8
Interest rates	9.15	9.4	11.53	11.79	11.73
Market capitalization (US$m)	510	556	622	643	817
No. of listed companies	13	13	13	13	16
Index performance in US$ (%)				29	5.2
Price/earnings (P/E) ratios					12
Earnings per share (EPS) growth					
Turnover per annum (US$m)	3.9	6.4	22.8	31.9	32.9
Currency to US$ (dinar)	0.8985	0.90406	0.8368	0.8645	0.9507
Currency to US$ perf (%)	15.5	6.8	7.5	3.3	10

Figure 37.1 Tunisia: key statistics

The stock market

The Tunis exchange, which operates from 10.30 to 12.30, Monday to Friday, was established in 1969. However, it was inactive for many years and, in 1989, a new financial market law was introduced to overhaul it. This law established a first and second market, depending on liquidity and the degree of information published. There is also an OTC market for unlisted securities.

Currently the market is small—with only seventeen companies listed at the end of 1992—and tightly-held. Most of the listed companies are banks which in turn own large amounts of the other listed companies. The privatization programme would improve this situation.

Technical notes

- Settlement is seven days after trading, but registration takes up to three months.
- Physical possession of shares—no central depository.
- No foreign custodians—Citibank has an office in Tunis and would become one if there were sufficient business.

- Commissions: under 50,000 dinars 0.2 per cent; over 50,000 dinars 0.1 per cent
- The stock exchange issues listing regulations for the two tiers which lay down specific reporting requirements and for a prospectus to be approved by the stock exchange before an issue.
- Foreign investment is encouraged: there are no taxes to pay on capital gains or dividends and repatriation of capital, profit and dividends is allowed.

Exchange address

Tunis Stock Exchange
19 bis, Rue Kamel Attaturk
1001 Tunis
Tunisia

Tel: 216 1 259 411 / Fax: 216 1 347 256

Chapter 38

Turkey

Population:	58.5m
Gross national product:	$120.7bn
Market capitalization:	$37.6bn
Currency:	14,050 lira

In some ways Turkey is similar to China, albeit on a smaller scale. It is undergoing a rapid transformation from an agricultural to a manufacturing economy, with all the social and economic pressures that implies. With a population of nearly 60m, Turkey is also strategically placed at the meeting point of Europe and Asia. With the break up of the former Soviet Union, new Turkish-speaking cities are emerging in the area of central Asia, centred on Uzbekistan. Turkey could well become a cultural and economic leader of these peoples. In addition, it is the only secular Muslim state, which enables it to provide a different model of development from those of the more strict Islamic nations. Besides this, the long centuries of the Ottoman Empire with its capital of Constantinople (now Istanbul) have left a tradition of sophisticated and cosmopolitan life and an active capital market.

The key date in modern Turkish history is 1923, when Atatürk abolished the Sultanate and was elected as the first president of the Republic. He instituted a series of sweeping social reforms which have in the last two generations transformed Turkey into a modern state. Changes were made in the legal, political, social and economic structures and even in the mode of dress and the alphabet. Certain Islamic traditions were outlawed and Islamic legal codes were replaced by Western laws. Kemal Atatürk's legacy is known as Kemalism and is still the dominant ideology in Turkey today.

Since 1946, Turkey has enjoyed a pluralist political system, although there have been three brief spells of military government, in 1960-61, 1971-73 and 1980-83. The army has historically been an important factor in Turkish politics. However, the periods of military rule have generally been brief and followed by a return to democracy. Since 1987, there has been steady progress towards a more liberal form of government, with checks and balances, but with a strong presidency and less parliamentary faction fighting.

	1988	1989	1990	1991	1992	1993
Population (m)	52.4	53.7	54.9	56.1	57.3	58.5
GNP (US$bn)	71.5	80.1	110.1	108.7	113.9	120.7
Real GNP growth (%)	3.8	1.9	9.2	0.3	5.3	4.7
Per capita income (US$)	1365	1492	2005	1938	1988	2063
Exports (US$m)	11662	11625	12959	13594	14716	n/a
Imports (US$bn)	13562	14940	21100	19912	21638	n/a
Inflation	75.4	63.3	60.3	66	70.1	75
Interest rates (discount)	54	54	45	45	51.9	65.0
Market capitalization (US$bn)	1.1	6.8	19.1	15.7	9.9	24.6
No. of listed companies	50	50	110	134	145	142
IFC Index performance in US$ (%)	61.1	502.4	2.8	41.8	52.8	213.7
Price/earnings (P/E) ratios	2	16.5	13.2	13.7	6.9	13.1
Earnings per share (EPS) growth	n/a	n/a	43.9	13.6	3.9	24.9
Turnover per annum (US$m)	101	798	5841	8571	8191	16568
Dividend yield	11.2	3.6	5.5	4.4	8.1	5.2
Currency to US$ (lira)	1805.1	2313.7	2930.1	5079.9	8564.4	14050
Currency to US$ perf (%)	76.8	28.2	26.7	73.4	68.6	64.1

Figure 38.1 Turkey: key statistics

There is a Grand National Assembly of 450 members elected for five-year terms.

President Turgut Ozal came to power in 1983 and continued as president until his death in April 1993. He was succeeded by Suleyman Demirel and the new prime minister elected at the same time was Mrs Tansu Ciller, formerly the finance minister. This has been a very popular choice and the stock market has reacted very positively to her appointment. Elections are expected to be held in 1994.

One of the major problems is that of inflation, currently running at about 70 per cent annually. Interest rates, on the other hand, are at an annual rate of 85 per cent and the Turkish lira has devalued at an average rate of 50 per cent p.a. against the US dollar. It is, however, noticeable that the currency, taking into account domestic inflation, has been appreciating in real terms against the US dollar, sterling and the Deutschemark. The Central Bank of Turkey has been successful in controlling currency depreciation and maintaining strong foreign currency reserves of about US$17bn.

As with the Brazilian market, the key analysis of the Turkish market is in timing the strong rallies in the Istanbul Stock Exchange compared with the lira/US dollar rate. There have been two recent booms in the market, in 1987 and again in 1989-90, when the market rose by nearly 600 per cent, in

US dollar terms. There is no doubt that the Turkish economy and stock market represent attractive prospects for the international investor and that Turkey should be part of every global emerging market portfolio. The main risk is in the inflation rate and the currency. There is a wide choice of stocks available and some strong groups such as Koc Holding and the Akbank group.

Developments in early 1994

The Turkish lira has further devalued in the last few months, from 14,582 per US dollar, down to the level of 34,000 lira in early May. This followed the increase in the rate of inflation from 71 per cent in 1993 to over 100 per cent by the spring of 1994. Three-month deposit rates also tripled between December and May, from 60 per cent to 180 per cent, and the Istanbul Stock Exchange Index collapsed, falling over 70 per cent, in US dollar terms, with the index going from a high of 28,883 down to 15,000. The prime minister, Mrs Tansu Ciller, nevertheless, maintained her position in the mayoral elections in March, although both Istanbul and Ankara were won by Muslim fundamentalist candidates. The government announced an austerity package on 5 April but the market has not reacted positively and is waiting to see whether the IMF will support the Turkish government in its economic reform plans.

The stock market

The history of the Turkish stock market dates back to the 19th century, when the Dersaadet Securities Exchange was one of the most active exchanges in the world after Paris, London and Berlin. However, activity slowed down after World War I and it was not until early 1986 that the market was officially re-inaugurated as the Istanbul Stock Exchange.

The securities industry in Turkey is regulated and supervised by the Capital Markets Board (CMB) which was established in 1981. The ISE is an autonomous professional public organization which is run by a board of directors and an executive council, whose members are elected in the general assembly by the members of the exchange. The chairman is appointed by the government.

Trading and settlement

Trading on the ISE takes places between Monday to Friday from 10.30-12.30. There is a continuous trading system on the trading floor of the exchange building which is located in the heart of the old town. Trading is not computerized at present but the management have plans to introduce a

Company	Market cap. (US$m)	Company	Volume (US$m)
Tofas Oto Fabrika	3315	Eregli Demir Celik	4.6
Koc Holding	1997	Dogan Holding	3.1
Tupras	1710	Cukrova Elektrik	3.0
Akbank	1664	Cimentas	3.0
Eregli Demir Celik	1104	Mardin Cimento	2.6
Arcelik	1093	Otosan	2.6
T. Garantibank	1052	Petrol Ofisi	2.5
Petrol Ofisi	973	Yapi Kredi Bank	2.4
Otosan	805	Tofas Oto	2.4
Netas	536	T. Is Bank	2.3
Yapi Kredi Bank	509	Akal Tekstil	2.2
Aksa	503	Adana Cimento	2.2
Ege Biracilik	456	Netas	2.0
Cukurova Elektrik	427	Tupras	1.8
Turcas	347	Arcelik	1.8
Turk Demir Dokum	308	T. Sise Cemi	1.5
Koc Yatrim	308	Bagfas	1.5
Alarko Holding	268	Metas	1.5
Migros	266	Aksa	1.4
Eczacbasi Ilac	246	T. Is Bank (B)	1.4

Figure 38.2 Turkey: 20 largest companies by market capitalization and average daily volume

screen-based trading system, similar to that of the Vancouver Stock Exchange, when the exchange moves to larger premises in the new financial centre in the near future.

Settlement is T+1 and the system is run by a sister company of the exchange owned by the members. The same company also acts as the central custodian for equity shares in the Turkish market. Besides the central custody system, Citibank, Chase and Ottoman Bank (a subsidiary of Paribas) render professional custodial services to foreign investors.

Regulatory framework

Foreign investors are allowed to buy and sell any listed Turkish securities through financial intermediaries, in compliance with the provisions of the Capital Markets Law and repatriate their principal and income from such investments without any restrictions.

Foreign shareholders of Turkish companies have to register their holdings with the Foreign Investment Directorate of the State Planning Organization if they wish to exercise their voting rights, i.e. if they wish to become involved in the management of the company. Permission is always granted as the procedure is for registration purposes rather than to secure approval.

Foreign and domestic investment companies and mutual funds are not subject to capital gains tax. Dividends (including stock dividends) are exempt from withholding tax for both domestic and foreign shareholders.

Minimum dividend rule and rights issues

Turkish capital market legislation differs from general market practice in two main ways: firstly, distribution of the dividends is not left to the discretion of the companies; and secondly, rights issues are launched at the par value of the security rather than at a discount to the market value.

The Capital Markets Law requires companies to distribute at least 50 per cent of the distributable profits at the end of each year. In return, companies tend to recover these dividends through rights issues each year. With regard to the procedure involving rights issues in Turkey, the Corporate Law requires companies to issue new capital at par value, which is TL1000 in 99 per cent of cases. These two requirements lead to a dilution of capital in Turkish-listed companies. The CMB is studying this situation and is expected to propose a solution shortly.

Exchange address

Istanbul Stock Exchange
(Istanbul Menkul Kiymetler Borsasi)
Borsasi
Rihtim C, 245, Karakoy
Istanbul 80030

Tel: 90 1 252 4800 & 251 7390 / Fax: 90 1 243 7243 & 252 4915

PART VI

Africa

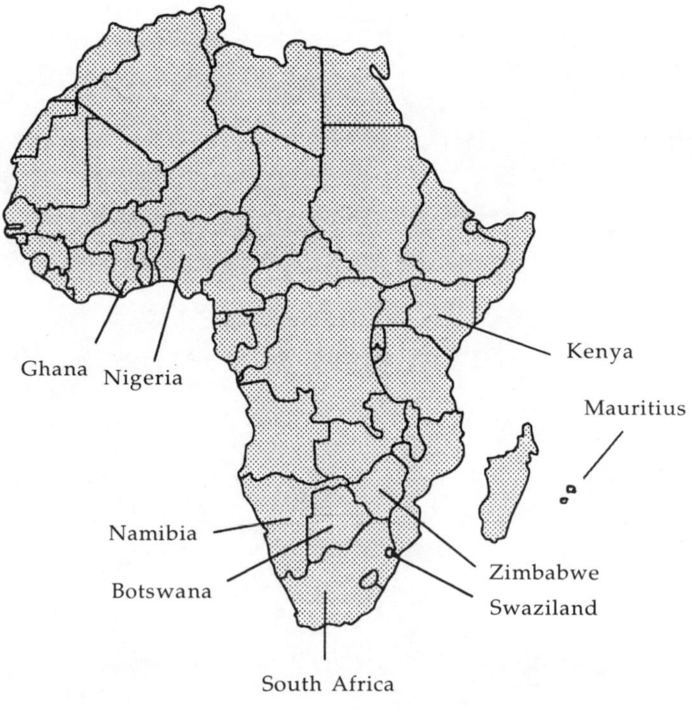

THE EMERGING MARKETS OF AFRICA

Chapter 39

Africa - Introduction

One hundred years ago there was a scramble for Africa by European powers such as Britain, Germany and France. In the 1960s, nearly all the European colonies were given independence and there was great optimism about the economic potential for the new African nations. It has taken over a generation of economic and political decline for reality to be faced. Africa, also had the misfortune to be drawn into the Cold War, so that Soviet military and economic aid came to influence countries such as Ethiopia, Angola and Mozambique, with the consequence that civil wars in these countries dragged on for many years and impoverished their peoples. Now the last of the colonial powers, Russia, has also withdrawn from Africa as the British and the Portuguese did twenty years before.

No longer is Africa seen as a place to settle issues of power politics. As at the beginning of the 'scramble' in the 1890s, so too in the 1990s Africa now appears to be a continent of hope. It still has great natural resources, cheap labour and, in parts, fertile soil and a pleasant climate. It has fallen behind the rest of the world since the end of the colonial period mainly because of incompetent and despotic government. This seems to be changing. There is a recognition that the state cannot solve all the people's problems and that interaction with the rest of the world does not mean subservience, but can mean wealth. Many countries are now implementing market reforms and are lifting exchange controls to welcome foreign investment.

There are, however, still major problems. Many parts of Africa are stricken by violence. Africa also suffers from many killer diseases, cerebral malaria makes tourists nervous and the scourge of Aids could wipe out millions.

It needs to be recognized that if South Africa degenerates into civil war, then the evil consequences will reverberate around the continent. Zimbabwe, Botswana, Namibia and Mozambique would be the worst affected. Yet, if all goes well, then South Africa will be the engine of growth for the whole region. It is potentially a vast market which could require goods and services from the whole of the region. With the prospect of foreign investment the process could advance apace—electrifying the area—in some parts literally as well as metaphorically. The opening up of all these markets, the abandoning of government-inspired programmes for import substitution

	S. Africa	Kenya	Botswana	Nigeria	Zimbabwe	Mauritius	Swaziland	Ghana	Namibia
Population (m)	37.63	26.98	1.39	115.43	10.45	1.08	0.84	15.51	1.45
GNP (US$bn)	110.4	11.82	3.89	20.31	5	2.78	-	-	2.47
Real GNP growth (%)									
1992	-2.1	-	6.5	4.3	-8.3	5.8	-	-	3.5
1993	0.4	-	-	-	-	-	-	-	-
Per capita income (US$)	2934	456	2802	175	478	2573	-	-	1700
Exports (US$bn)	23.38	1.08	2.19	10.46	1.45	1.17	-	-	-
Imports (US$bn)	17.92	1.75	2.3	7.29	1.85	1.18	-	-	-
Foreign direct investment (US$m)	-	38.9	-	-	-	-	-	22.5	156
Inflation	9.8	19.8	16.2	44.6	46.2	4.6	9.3	10.1	17.9
Interest rates	15.25	20.3	14.25	24.8	22 - 48	8.3	15	30	-
Market capitalization (US$bn)	216.3	1055	258	-	1431	770	296	124	350
No. listed companies	647	49	11	-	62	30	4	15	5
Index performance in '93 (%)	39	64.3	-11.5	-	74.5	42.2	-15	36.9	-
Price/earnings (P/E) ratios									
1993[e]	18.2	15.6	7.7	-	7.4	-	-	6.7	-
Earnings per share (EPS) growth									
1992	-1	-	-	-	-	-	-	-	-
Turnover per annum (US$m)	12.9	-	18.7	-	49	36	0.295	4.1	10
Dividend yield	2.4	3.6	5.8	-	4.9	-	-	5.5	-
Stock market performance, '88-'93 (%)	221.9	18.9	125.8	-	14.8	99.5	-24.9	-18.8	-
Currency to US$ perf., '88-'93 (%)	-30.2	-72.8	-25.1	-75.7	-77	-28.6	-30.2	-72	-30.2

Note: Economic statistics for South Africa are for 1993, Kenya for 1991 and the remainder for 1992 except Swaziland and Ghana for which reliable up-to-date figure are unavailable

Figure 39.1 Africa: country statistics (31 December 1993)

and the odd drop of rain, could see a plethora of small stock markets blooming.

Just as peace in the Middle East has been a side-effect of the end of the Cold War, so the end of apartheid in South Africa has resulted from the collapse of communism, US sanctions and the need for South Africa, like all other economies, to open up to trade and investment. By the end of 1994, South Africa will have a new multi-racial government and its relations with black Africa should, therefore, improve rapidly. The developed infrastructure of finance and mining houses, amongst other sectors, will benefit not only the new South Africa, but also its black African neighbours. Zimbabwe is likely to be the first beneficiary of this northern move of capital and technology. Amongst other countries with considerable natural resources are Zambia and Tanzania, Kenya with its very successful tourism industry, and Ghana and Nigeria with their mineral and petroleum resources. After a generation of corruption, economic contraction and political dictatorship, the Africans have also learned the lesson that they will need to give foreign investors a fair deal in order to attract their share of foreign investment.

Chapter 40

Botswana

Population:	1.44m
Gross national product:	$3.6bn
Market capitalization:	$300m
Currency/US$:	2.8 pula

Since independence in 1966, Botswana, the former Bechanaland Protectorate, has gone from being one of the poorest countries in the world to being one of the richest in Africa. It has had an annual average GDP per capita growth rate faster than that of Taiwan, Indonesia, Hong Kong, Singapore or Kuwait. It is a large country with 224,607 square miles and a population of only 1.44m people and 2.8m cattle. There are also 2.3m goats and 349,000 sheep. Almost three-quarters of the country is desert—the Kalahari—and rainfall is low in the whole of the country, nowhere has more than 30 inches per annum.

When the Protectorate ended, Botswana had no infrastructure at all. It did not have any public secondary education and its whole economy was based on subsistence farming. The key to its economic success has been diamonds—and the De Beers organization. The government, unlike some of its neighbours, was happy to welcome overseas expertise in exploiting the huge resource which it happened to find in 1967 at Orapa. This has made it one of the world's most important diamond suppliers and it has provided money to build roads, an airport and to turn Gabarone from a minor town into a city. Diamonds still make up over 75 per cent of exports and their abundance has allowed the government to run a consistently balanced budget with comparatively low tax rates. It is the intention of the current government—which has been in office since independence, although Botswana is genuinely democratic—to reduce taxes further.

The development of the economy away from the dependence on one commodity is hoped for. Little employment is created by the mining sector and the government is prepared to offer incentives through the National Development Bank and the Financial Assistance Policy. However, utility prices are high and the population is not trained in modern skills. Therefore, it is intended to encourage foreigners to come to Botswana to provide

	1988	1989	1990	1991	1992
Population (m)	1.21	1.26	1.3	1.35	1.39
GNP (US$bn)	2.03	2.68	3.15	3.43	3.89
Real GNP growth (%)	14	13.2	5.7	8.9	6.5
Per capita income (US$)	1676	2108	2420	2547	2802
Exports (US$bn)	1.38	2	1.8	2.47	2.19
Imports (US$bn)	1.12	1.62	1.97	2.63	2.3
Foreign direct investment	-	-	-	-	-
Inflation (1985 = 100)	130.9	146	162.7	181.8	211.2
Interest rates (bank rate)	6.5	6.5	8.5	12	14.25
International reserves (US$bn)	2.26	2.84	3.39	3.77	3.84
Market capitalization (US$bn)	-	128	228	270	309
No. of listed companies	-	5	6	8	11
IFC Index performance in US$ (%)	-	66.4	54.4	5.4	5.8
Price/earnings (P/E) ratios	-	-	-	-	-
Earnings per share (EPS) growth	-	-	-	-	-
Turnover per annum (US$m)	-	1.8	4.2	8.5	15
Dividend yield	-	-	-	-	-
Currency to US$ (pula)	1.94	1.87	1.87	2.07	2.26
Currency to US$ perf (%)	19.1	3.4	0	9.7	8.2

Figure 40.1 Botswana: key statistics

services to the whole of southern Africa. The importance to this economy of a peaceful transition in its neighbour, South Africa, cannot be overestimated and any visitor to Botswana would immediately be aware of this as it is a main topic of conversation.

Botswana has lifted all exchange controls for foreign investors up to 50m pula (US$20m) for any one transaction. Assuming that an investment is sold to another foreigner, then no permission is needed for the repatriation of capital or profit. If it were sold to a local, then approval would be needed from the authorities. However, the permanent secretary to the Ministry of Finance has indicated that this permission would almost certainly be granted. Botswana has had a prudent fiscal and monetary policy and therefore the pula, which had the same value as the rand in the early years of independence, is the strongest currency in the region.

The stock market

The Botswana Stock Exchange was established in 1989. Initially, it had five companies quoted—a figure which has now increased to eleven, with a market capitalization of US$309m. There is one stock broker, the founding firm of Stockbrokers Botswana Ltd., who act as agent for their clients but do not take positions themselves. The market is as yet not established by legislation, but the Stock Exchange Act has been prepared in draft form and the Ministry of Finance expects to see it passed in 1994.

The founders of this stock market are regularly consulted by other African states who are considering the same process. It is widely regarded as having been a successful experiment and a number of highly respectable companies like Barclays Bank are quoted on it.

Technical notes

- Settlement is 3 days after trade for overseas clients within 14 days for local clients.
- Physical possession of stocks—no central depository.
- Both Barclays Bank of Botswana and Standard Chartered Bank of Botswana offer custodian services for overseas clients and are prepared to act as sub-custodians where necessary.
- Commissions:

1-50,000 pula	2%
50,001-100,000 pula	1.5%
100,001+ pula	1%

  Additionally, there is a handling fee of 15 pula per purchase and 10 pula per sale.
- Listing requirements will be formally established in the Stock Exchange Act, it is currently subject to approval by the Interim Stock Exchange Committee which will consider granting permission to any reasonable company. It is particularly encouraging smaller firms to list.
- Foreign investors may not own more than 5 per cent of the total issued share capital of a public company without permission nor may a total of more than 49 per cent of the free float be owned by external investors. Capital gains tax was abolished for quoted companies in 1991, dividends are subject to a 15 per cent withholding tax but the corporate tax rate for quoted companies is 35 per cent, against 40 per cent for private ones.

Exchange address

Stockbrokers Botswana
5/F Barclays House, Khama Crescent
PO Box 41015, Gaborone,
Botswana

Tel: 267 357 900 / Fax: 267 357 901

Chapter 41

Ghana

Population:	15m
Gross national product:	$6.3bn
Market capitalization:	$110m
Currency/US$:	550 cedi

Ghana, which covers the same area as the United Kingdom, was formerly known as the Gold Coast. First visited by Europeans in the 15th century it became, in part, a British Colony in 1874, with the rest following either in 1901 or in the post Great War mandate given to Britain. In 1957, it was granted independence and has subsequently been governed by the military with occasional outbreaks of civilian rule.

Seventy per cent of the population is employed in the agricultural sector. The main revenue producing crop is cocoa and attempts are being made to focus on other cash crops. The rest of the economy is comparatively small, but the mineral deposits around Dunkwa are important. Gold and manganese are mined with 30,000 people being employed in the industry. Reliance on commodity products has led to a weak economic performance in the last few years.

However, an economic reform programme has been in place for some years involving devaluation, deregulation and tax cuts. The IMF is believed to be pleased with progress and with taxes down 15 per cent to 35 per cent and inflation less than a tenth of its 1983 level of 142 per cent the foundation for economic reform has been established. This process is being encouraged both by facilitating investment in Ghana and through a privatization process. Immigration rules for a minimum investment of $10,000 are welcoming and the draft Investment Bill currently before Parliament allows unconditional repatriation. Capital allowances on machinery and equipment are 50 per cent per annum and 20 per cent per annum for buildings. However, not all the bureaucratic hurdles have been removed.

	1988	1989	1990	1991	1992
Population (m)	14.13	14.57	15.03	15.51	-
GNP (US$bn)	4.57	4.68	5.89	-	-
Real GNP growth (%)	5.6	5.1	3.3	-	-
Per capita income (US$)	323	321	392	-	-
Exports (US$bn)	0.89	0.91	n/a	n/a	n/a
Imports (US$bn)	0.81	1.15	n/a	n/a	n/a
Foreign direct investment (US$m)	5	15	14.8	20	22.5
Inflation (1985 = 100)	228.8	286.5	393.2	464.1	510.8
Interest rates (discount)	26	26	33	20	30
International reserves (US$bn)	298.8	425.6	282.1	624.2	398
Market capitalization (US$bn)	-	-	n/a	117	84
No. of listed companies	-	-	11	16	15
IFC Index performance in US$ (%)	-	-	-	27.2	18.5
Average daily turnover (US$m)	-	-	-	0.5	0.44
Currency to US$ perf (cedi)	229.89	303.03	344.83	390.63	520.83
Currency to US$ (%)	23.4	24.1	12.1	11.7	25

Figure 41.1 Ghana: key statistics

	Market capitalization (US$ million)
Unilever	45.5
Standard Chartered	16.0
Guinness	9.7
Pioneer Tobacco	7.7
Mobil Oil	5.4
Fan Milk	5.1
Accra Brewery	4.9
Super Paper Products	4.8
Kumasi Brewery	1.5
UTC	1.4
CFAO	1.3
Enterprise Insurance	1.2
SCOA	0.7
Metalloplastica	0.5
Paterson Zochonis	0.4

Figure 41.2 Ghana: 15 largest stocks by market capitalization

The stock market

1971 saw the passing of the Stock Exchange Act, but the Ghana Stock Exchange did not actually open until 1990. There are three stockbroking firms to cater for 15 listed companies, several of which carry internationally-recognizable names, such as Guinness and Standard Chartered. Trading takes place on Tuesdays and Fridays between 10.00 and 11.00. Volumes have been improving as the government has been selling off some of its holdings, while it also has plans for a broad privatization programme.

Technical notes

- Settlement is fourteen days after trading.
- Physical possession of stocks—no central depository.
- Standard Chartered of Ghana offers safe custody services.
- Commissions:

4-5m cedi	1.75 per cent
5-10m cedi	1.5 per cent
over 10m cedi	1 per cent
Basic charge	850 cedi

- Listing requirements: first list minimum capital 100m cedis, of which at least 30m must list, and five years of audited accounts. Second list: 50m cedis, 15m and three years respectively.
- Foreign investors may not own more than 10 per cent individually, or 74 per cent severally, of a company's outstanding shares. Dividends, capital and profit may only be repatriated with approval. Dividends are subject to a 10 per cent tax rate but capital gains are tax-free.

Exchange address

Ghana Stock Exchange
2/F Kingsway Building
Kwame Nkrumah Avenue
PO Box 1849, Accra
Ghana

Tel: 233 21 669 908 / Fax: 233 21 669 913

Chapter 42

Kenya

Population:	24m
Gross national product:	$8.8bn
Market capitalization:	$700m
Currency/US$:	32.2 shillings

Kenya gained independence from Britain in 1963. It was one of the few colonies to have suffered from serious internal strife under the Crown, during the course of the Mau-Mau Rebellion. In 1982, the government introduced a new constitution making it a one-party state, with Kenya African National Union being the only legal party. Subsequently, there have been free and democratic elections. These saw Daniel Arap Moi remain in power with the benefit of a popular mandate.

Economically, Kenya is heavily dependent on agriculture which provides over half the total export earnings. This covers a wide range of products owing to the wide variety of growing conditions in Kenya. Since Moi took office there has been considerable industrial development including tyre manufacture, textiles and steel. Thanks to the East Indian business community, light manufacturing in this country is better than anywhere else in East Africa. Additionally, Kenya's 224,961 square miles is one of the most glorious tourist destinations in the world.

Kenya has been going through a structural adjustment programme, although it did threaten to stop it because of the suspension of all aid. Nevertheless, taxes have been reduced on companies from 50 per cent to 37 per cent, tariffs have been slashed from 140 per cent to 30 per cent and capital gains tax has been abolished. Exchange controls have been weakened, but not entirely removed, while privatization is proceeding. Inflation is a problem which has been temporarily exacerbated by the lifting of price controls. However, real GDP growth is impressive at 5 per cent per annum through 1988-1992. Many serious and respected commentators believe that the prospects are better in Kenya than for anywhere else in the region.

	1988	1989	1990	1991	1992
Population (m)	23.88	24.87	24.03	25.91	26.98
GNP (US$bn)	11.45	11.01	12.46	11.82	n/a
Real GNP growth (%)**	2.4	4	2.9	8.4	n/a
Per capita income (US$)	479	443	431	456	n/a
Exports (US$bn)	1.02	0.92	0.98	1.08	n/a
Imports (US$bn)	1.89	2.05	2.02	1.75	n/a
Foreign direct investment (US$m)	1.8	60.8	47.7	38.9	n/a
Inflation (1985 = 100)	124.4	140.5	162.4	194.6	269.9*
Interest rates (discount)	16.02	16.5	19.43	20.27	20.37*
International reserves(US$m)	280.6	299.1	218.9	131.9	65.2
Market capitalization (US$bn)	474	499	453	638	607
No. of listed companies	55	57	54	53	57
Index performance in US$ (%)	3.7	18.2	0.6	10.2	5.6
Price/earnings (P/E) ratios	7			5.2	5.8
Turnover per annum (US$m)		229	10	11	12
Dividend yield	8.4	12.3	12.3	15.7	11.1
Currency to US$ (shilling)	18.599	21.601	24.084	28.074	32.216
Currency to US$ perf (%)	11.2	13.9	10.3	14.2	22.5

**to end of 3rd quarter*
***using the CPI as a proxy for the GDP deflator*

Figure 42.1 Kenya: key statistics

The stock market

The Nairobi Stock Exchange, which has six firms represented on it, was established in 1954. It operates every weekday on a open-outcry system between the hours of 10.00 and noon. Several of the quoted companies have large foreign partners like Brooke Bond, British American Tobacco and Standard Chartered. Indeed, the top fifteen companies account for 89 per cent of turnover and six of these are in the financial sector. Unfortunately, of these fifteen companies' total capitalization, 55 per cent is held by immovable holders, a fact which considerably restricts the market's liquidity.

Technical notes

- Settlement is ten days after trading.
- Physical possession of stocks—no central depository.
- Barclays Bank of Kenya and Standard Chartered Bank of Kenya both offer safe custody services.

- Commissions: 2 per cent for both buying and selling plus a registration fee of 2.5 shillings.
- Foreign investors are only allowed to buy shares once they have received official approval and require authority to repatriate capital, profit or dividends. There is no capital gains tax but there is a 10 per cent dividends tax.

Exchange address

Nairobi Stock Exchange
2/F IPS Building
Kimathi Street
PO Box 43633
Nairobi

Tel: 254 2 230 692 / Fax: 254 2 224 200

	Market capitalization (US$ million)
Brooke Bond	98.6
BAT	86.8
Barclays Bank	83.3
Standard Chartered Bank	51.1
Kenya Breweries	31.3
Diamond Trust	27.9
Total Kenya	22.4
Kenya Commercial Bank	19.4
Bamburi Portland Cement	12.6
Uchumi Supermarkets	11.9
Motor Mart	11.9
Jubilee Insurance	9.9
Kakuzi	9.6
Nat'l Industrial Credit	9.6
Credit Finance	7.5
Housing Finance	6.7
Sasini Tea & Coffee	6.3
East African Cables	5.0
Crown Berger	4.9
East African Oxygen	4.3

Figure 42.2 Kenya: 20 largest stocks by market capitalization

Chapter 43

Mauritius

Population:	1.09m
Gross national product:	$2.78bn
Market capitalization:	$600m
Currency/US$:	19.36 rupees

Mauritius was discovered by the Portuguese, named by the Dutch after Prince Maurice of Nassar, had a century as a Dutch colony (1638-1710) and then a century as a French colony (1715-1810). Captured by the British in 1810, it remained a British Crown colony for 158 years although the French language and French law were preserved during this period. Since independence in 1960, Mauritius has flourished and most recently has become an offshore financial centre, which will begin slowly to provide an additional source of income to the other main revenue earners of sugar and tourism. Manufacturing has also begun to grow, with investments being made by Hong Kong textile entrepreneurs among others.

The population is just over 1m and is composed of nearly 70 per cent Indians (52.6 per cent Hindus, 16.5 per cent Muslims) with the balance of nearly 30 per cent being made up of Mauritians of African, European and Chinese origin. Despite its remote location, Mauritius has managed to draw investors, initially because of its proximity to South Africa, as a transit point for airlines from the orient and as an efficient tax-free centre. More recently it has become an advantageous point from which to invest in India. It has a small but efficient business community, with lawyers, accountants and several major international banks in the capital, Port Louis.

The Mauritian Stock Exchange was inaugurated in July 1989, but has already developed quickly with government support—by the end of 1993 market capitalization was nearly US$600m and the number of listed companies was 25, with an additional 71 companies traded in the over-the-counter market. The Mauritian government has offered several inducements to companies to list on the exchange, such as reducing corporate taxes from 35 per cent to 25 per cent, although those in the export processing zone already benefit from a tax rate of 15 per cent.

	1988	1989	1990	1991	1992	1993
Population (m)	1.02	1.03	1.07	1.07	1.08	1.09
GNP (US$bn)	2.01	2.15	2.67	2.89	2.78	
Real GNP growth (%)	6.8	4.6	7.1	4.1	5.8	
Per capita income (US$)	1971	2087	2495	2701	2573	
Exports (US$bn)	0.97	1	1.23	1.26	1.17	
Imports (US$bn)	1.25	1.35	1.68	1.67	1.18	
Foreign direct investment (US$m)	23.6	35.1	40.4	8.1		
Inflation (1985 = 100)	111.5	125.6	142.6	152.6	159.6	176.9
Interest rates (discount)	10	12	12	11.3	8.3	8.25
International reserves(US$m)	446.4	523.6	742.6	898.1	824.3	741.8
Market capitalization (US$bn)	-	-	265	324	377	520
No. of listed companies	-	-	13	20	22	
Index performance in US$ (%)	-	-	65.7	16.7	6.8	
Price/earnings (P/E) ratios	-	-	8	7	11.6	
Earnings per share (EPS) growth	-	-	-	-	-	
Turnover per annum (US$m)	-	-	6	5	10	7
Dividend yield	-	-	6.5	6.1	1.4	
Currency to US$ (rupees)	13.834	14.996	14.322	14.794	16.998	19.366
Currency to US$ performance	12	7.7	4.7	3.2	13	13.9

Figure 43.1 Mauritius: key statistics

In 1992, the Mauritian government announced the establishment of a national investment trust to enable the Mauritian public to be shareholders in government-owned companies. This represents an ambitious programme of privatization which will include some major banks and commercial companies, such as the State Commercial Bank Ltd., Air Mauritius and several hotels. This has given considerable impetus to the development of the stock exchange in the last twelve months. International recognition of these changes was achieved by the flotation of the US$25m Mauritius Fund Ltd, which was listed on the London Stock Exchange in December 1992 and supported by the Commonwealth Development Corporation and the Mauritius Commercial Bank, which is the island's largest commercial bank with assets of US$1.2bn. The potential for this small emerging market appears to be attractive considering that the island's economy has a total GNP of nearly US$3bn. Risks might include political change in the island, although this seems unlikely; also, a successful conclusion to the Uruguay round of GATT talks may have adverse consequences for the sugar and textile industries in Mauritius. Thus, the development of the island as an offshore financial centre will be critical to its future prosperity.

	Market capitalization (US$ million)
Rogers	77.4
Maur. Commercial Bank	71.5
Sun Resorts	55.7
Shell (Mauritius)	34.7
Mon Tresor & Mon Desert	30.8
Maur. Dev. Invest. Trust	26.2
Harel Mallac	23.0
United Basalt Products	21.7
Harel Freres	19.5
Maur. Chem. & Fertilizer	19.0
United Docks	16.9
Swan Insurance	16.5
Courts	16.2
Mount Sugar Estates	14.7
Savannah Sugar Estates	14.1
Maur. Stationery Manuf.	13.7
BA Insurance	12.2
Con. Invest. Trust	NA
Maur. Oil Refineries	5.5
Com. des Mag. Populaires	5.5

Figure 43.2 Mauritius: 20 largest stocks by market capitalization

Exchange address

The Mauritius Stock Exchange Commission
9/F SICOM Building
Sir Celicourt Antelme Street
Port Louis
Mauritius

Tel: 230 208 8735 / Fax: 230 208 8676

Exchange address

Chapter 44

Namibia

Population:	1.8m
Gross domestic product:	$1.2bn
Market capitalization:	$300m
Currency/US$:	N$ 3.4 (pegged to SA rand)

Namibia, which covers 318,261 square miles, was the German Protectorate of South West Africa from 1880 to 1915 and, until 1920, was administered by South Africa which was then entrusted to look after the country according to the terms of the Treaty of Versailles. In 1990, it became the last African country to be granted independence. In the first election, 96 per cent of the electorate took part and the South West Africa People's Organization won nearly 60 per cent of the vote. Upon independence, Namibia was welcomed into the Commonwealth. The government is democratic with an executive president, a post held by Dr Sam Nujoma since February 1990.

Almost all the work-force are tied to the land, but diamonds and uranium are an important source of foreign exchange, with the former accounting for 35.9 per cent of exports in 1992. The control of the coast gained since independence has been a great help to the national economy as earnings from fishing have boomed and now account for around 15 per cent of exports. Corporate taxes have been significantly reduced from 42 per cent to 32 per cent making them some of the most competitive in Africa. Personal taxes have also been cut and it is hoped that this will help reduce urban unemployment which currently stands at 20 per cent. Education in Namibia has been more successful than in most of this continent with 80 per cent able to read and write.

The stock market

The Namibian Stock Exchange was established in 1992 and the only broker is Simpson, McKie, which acts as an agent between buyers and sellers without taking positions for its own book. Trading is computerized and takes

	1988	1989	1990	1991	1992
Population (m)	1.28	1.32	1.36	1.4	145
GNP (US$bn)	2	1.98	2.13	2.25	2.47
Real GNP growth (%)	6.2	0.4	3	5.1	3.5
Per capita income (US$)	1562	1500	1566	1608	1700
Exports (US$m)	1086	1135	1101	1245	1264
Imports (US$bn)	913	1028	1118	1110	1178
Foreign direct investment (US$m)			92	275	156
Inflation	12.9	15.1	12	11.9	17.9
Market capitalization (US$m)	n/a	n/a	n/a	n/a	250
No. of listed companies	n/a	n/a	n/a	n/a	5
Index performance in US$ (%)	n/a	n/a	n/a	n/a	n/a
Price/earnings (P/E) ratios	n/a	n/a	n/a	n/a	n/a
Earnings per share (EPS) growth	n/a	n/a	n/a	n/a	n/a
Weekly turnover (US$ 000s)	n/a	n/a	n/a	n/a	100
Dividend yield	n/a	n/a	n/a	n/a	n/a
Currency to US$ (rand)	2.38	2.54	2.56	2.74	3.05
Currency to US$ perf (%)	18.83	6.24	1.03	6.58	10.15

Figure 44.1 Namibia: key statistics

place on weekdays between 10.00 and noon. Turnover has been surprisingly large, considering that only five companies are listed, at US$25,000 a day.

Technical notes

- Settlement is seven days after trading.
- Physical possession of stocks—no central depository.
- No foreign bank offers safe custody services currently.
- Commissions:

N$1-10,000	1%
N$10,001-20,000	0.85%
N$20,001-100,000	0.65%
N$100,001-500,00	0.5%
N$500,001-1,000,000	0.4%
N$1,000,001 and above	0.2%

  There is an additional charge of N$15 per transaction.
- Foreign investment is encouraged and repatriation of capital, profits and dividends is allowed through the financial rand system. There is no capital gains tax but a withholding tax of 10 per cent on dividends.

Exchange address

The Namibian Stock Exchange
PO Box 196
Windhoek
Namibia

Tel: 264 61 239 708 / Fax: 264 61 32 513

	Market capitalization (US$)
Standard Bank	3.5 bn
Nam Sea Products	12.5m
Nam Fishing	4.4m
Metje & Ziegler	1.9m
Nictua Limited	0.5m

Figure 44.2 Namibia: five largest stocks by market capitalization

Chapter 45

Nigeria

Population:	108.6m
Gross domestic product:	$37.5bn
Market capitalization:	$1.2bn
Currency/US$:	24 naira

Nigeria became independent in 1960, since which time it has not seen stable democratic rule. The military took over in 1966 and again in 1985. In 1989, General Babangida issued a new constitution which was supposed to lead to civilian rule. However, he did not like the result of subsequent elections and imposed a puppet government. This faced a degree of popular opposition and was declared illegal by the courts. However, the rule of law does not count for much and the *vox populi* is not heard. Military rule has been reimposed and the future of democracy is, at best, uncertain.

The main export from Nigeria is oil, which provides 90 per cent of foreign earnings. Agriculture, although employing half the labour force, now only provides 20 per cent of GDP. The government has been implementing a structural adjustment programme for the last seven years. Many businesses have been privatized and the free market is generally being encouraged. Unfortunately, oil subsidies are still very expensive, with a gallon of petrol being cheaper than the same quantity of filtered water, and an attempt to raise prices caused public order problems. This led to a week long general strike and was the proximate cause of the military coup. This subsidy is partly responsible for the large government deficit, which for 1992 was 9.8 per cent of GDP, and this has in turn pushed inflation up to 48 per cent. Owing to the government's failure to satisfy the IMF that its economic policies were sensible, it was not possible to reschedule $17bn of the $30bn outstanding foreign debt and interest arrears are high at $1.6bn. In some ways, Nigeria's economic story is one of the gross mismanagement of initially promising material.

Nigeria is not generally considered to be an attractive tourist destination. Too much of its 356,669 square miles are mangrove swamp or desert and there is a degree of lawlessness which not only makes many people somewhat nervous, but is also rather discouraging for potential visitors.

	1988	1989	1990	1991	1992
Population (m)	104.96	105.02	108.54	112.16	115.43
GNP (US$bn)	25.15	27.07	26.52	26.82	20.31
Real GNP growth (%)	9.9	7.4	8.2	4.5	4.3
Per capita income (US$)	235	258	245	239	175
Exports (US$bn)	5.83	7.58	12.21	12.33	10.46
Imports (US$bn)	4.01	4.03	5.08	9.07	7.29
Foreign direct investment	377	1882	588	712	n/a
Inflation (1985 = 100)	181.8	273.5	293.7	331.9	479.8
Interest rates (prime)	16.62	20.44	25.3	20.04	24.76
International reserves (US$bn)	0.655	1.768	3.818	4.439	0.969
Market capitalization (US$m)	960	1005	1372	1882	1243
No. of listed companies	102	111	131	142	153
Index performance in US$ (%)	7	21.1	40.5	37.8	34.9
Price/earnings (P/E) ratios	5.6	6.5	6	10.6	9
Turnover per annum (US$m)	5	4	11	9	23
Dividend yield	9	7.3	12	6.8	5.1
Currency to US$ (naira)	5.353	7.651	9.001	9.862	19.646
Currency to US$ perf (%)	22.6	30	15	8.7	49.8

Figure 45.1 Nigeria: key statistics

The stock market

The stock market was established in 1960. There are 134 brokers in Nigeria and 163 quoted companies, divided into two tiers. Some of the first tier companies are the offshoots of major multinationals like Guinness, Cadbury, Mobil and Nestlé. The market is open each week day between 11.00 and 13.00, so it seems rather unlikely that all these brokers can be kept busy. Trading is done using a call-over system and average turnover is about $400,000 a week, which represents an annual turnover of less than 2 per cent of total market capitalization. Were it not for the political problems, Nigeria would have the second most important stock exchange in Africa. Their intractability will prevent this happening.

Technical notes

- Settlement is supposed to be made two days after trading, but is generally made two weeks late.
- Physical possession of shares—no central depository.
- No foreign banks currently offer safe custody services.

	Market capitalization (US$ million)
Nigerian Breweries	92.0
UAC	88.0
Lever Brothers	80.0
Patterson & Zochonis	68.0
Nigeria Tobacco	48.0
Guinness	40.0
Nigeria Bottling	39.7
Ashaka	34.9
Total	32.4
Cadbury	31.0
Mobil	30.6
United Nigerian Textile	29.4
Nestle	28.1
African Petroleum	27.5
National Oil	25.9
SK-Beecham	25.4
Benue Cement	23.8
W A P Cement	19.7
Dunlop	18.6
J Berger	18.4

Figure 45.2 Nigeria: 20 largest stocks by market capitalization

- Commissions: 3 per cent to the stockbroker. Exchange fee: 1 per cent. Stamp duty: 0.075 per cent.
- Foreign investment is only allowed after permission has been granted while dividends, capital and profit may only be repatriated after official approval has been granted. Dividends are subject to 5 per cent tax and capital gains tax is 20 per cent.

Exchange address

The Nigerian Stock Exchange
Stock Exchange House
2-4 Customs House
PO Box 2457
Lagos
Nigeria

Tel: 234 1 266 0287& 0305 / Fax: 234 1 266 8724

Chapter 46

South Africa

Population:	37.63m
Gross domestic product:	$110bn
Market capitalization:	$151bn
Currency/US$:	3.4 rand

With a population of 37.63m people and an area of 471,445 square miles, South Africa is one of the most fertile and potentially most prosperous countries in Africa and, indeed, the world. Blessed with a favourable climate and mineral deposits, which include gold and diamonds in prodigious quantities, South Africa should have had a wonderful history.

Sadly, South Africa's history is one of trouble and bloodshed. From Isandlwana to Ulundi through to Bergendal and the years of apartheid, South Africa has seen internal strife, thereby reducing its opportunities for economic development. The final Boer War settlement of 1909 made provision for the racial inequality that proved such a problem after its rigorous extension by the post-Second World War Afrikaner governments. All this is now changing.

The key event was the election in April 1994. The ANC emerged as the largest party and is now committed to a modern capitalist-style economy—having abandoned most of its Marxist philosophy. This will allow the next government to continue the important reforms of the recently 'retired' finance minister, Derek Keyes. He has been the moving force behind the National Economic Forum—which represents the government, business and trade unions—that has agreed a broad programme of economic reform. Fiscally the NEF has agreed to stop borrowing to meet current expenditure programmes and to relax the annual budget deficit from its current level of 7 per cent of GDP. It aims to alter the balance of taxation from direct to indirect with a top marginal rate of 40 per cent. Corporate tax is viewed as a greater priority than personal tax. Combined with this is a tough monetary policy implemented by the central bank to defeat inflation. Positive real interest rates have led to negative real money growth and the money supply is now growing more slowly than desired. Inflation continues to fall and this is allowing some easing of interest rates.

	1988	1989	1990	1991	1992	1993
Population (m)	33.75	34.51	35.28	36.07	36.85	37.63
GNP (US$bn)	83.24	91.93	102.95	108.15	108.35	110.4
Real GNP growth (%)	4.2	2.3	0.5	0.6	2.1	0.4
Per capita income (US$)	2466	2664	2918	2998	2940	2934
Exports (US$bn)	20.68	23.03	23.83	24.36	22.3	23.38
Imports (US$bn)	17.97	19.09	18.43	18.92	19.93	17.92
Foreign direct investment (US$m)	98	10	5	8	n/a	n/a
Inflation (1985 =100)	155.4	178.2	203.8	235	267.7	293.9
Interest rates (prime)	18	21	21	20.25	17.25	15.25
International reserves (US$bn)	2.74	2.1	2.42	2.4	3.19	2.58
Market capitalization (US$bn)	126.1	131.1	137.5	123.9	150.7	n/a
No. of listed companies	754	748	740	728	652	n/a
Index performance in US$ (%)	3.5	53.9	14.3	47.1	29.1	n/a
Price/earnings (P/E) ratios	5.6	6.9	7.5	11.8	9.1	n/a
Turnover per annum (US$bn)	4.9	7.1	8.2	8.1	7.8	n/a
Dividend yield	7	5.2	5.2	3.5	4.6	n/a
Currency to US$ (rand)	2.38	2.54	2.56	2.74	3.05	3.3
Currency to US$ perf (%)	18.83	6.24	1.03	6.58	10.15	8.2

Figure 46.1 South Africa: key statistics

Additionally, it wants to reduce the government's involvement in the market-place and to make its redistribution efforts more effective. There is an industrial strategy which aims to move South African industry from being a self-sufficient economy to being competitive on a world level. There is also a desire for a job creation programme. Unemployment in the legitimate economy is over 40 per cent and, with a 2.75 per cent growth in the economically-active population each year, GDP growth of at least 4 per cent per annum is required to reduce this level of unemployment.

In spite of the need for these reforms, South Africa is economically the most advanced nation in Africa. It accounts for 75 per cent of sub-Saharan Africa's GDP and benefits from a good infrastructure, a wealth of mineral resources and a sophisticated business community. However, the rate of economic growth has slowed over recent decades. In the 1960s, it averaged 6 per cent per annum, in the 1970s 3 per cent, but in the 1980s a mere 1 per cent. So far, the 1990s has seen an economic contraction. Part of the reason for this has been the general decline in commodity prices, but South Africa has also suffered from a lack of investment which runs at 14 per cent of GDP against a desired rate of 25 per cent. The isolation of the country led to expensive attempts at import substitution which was somewhat opposed to Ricardo's helpful recommendations. The final years of white minority rule have not been economically successful. Inflation has been over 18 per cent—although it is now back under 10 per cent—and wages rose continually every year from 1987-92; meanwhile, the currency declined in value.

Nevertheless, there have been some successes: the current account since 1985 has been in surplus, at around 2.5 per cent of GDP, allowing much of the foreign debt to be paid off—only $5bn of the rescheduled debt is left. Interest rates have begun to come down—although, at 17 per cent they are still high. Indeed, except in the area of wages which rise in spite of high levels of unemployment, the South African economy has taken the unpleasant medicine and is now ready—*ceteris paribus*—for strong economic growth. This would obviously be helped by foreign investment which the ANC in principle welcomes. This will not flow in until the financial and commercial rand are merged. All parties wish to do this but none promises a date and, sadly, it is unlikely to happen soon. The issue of exchange controls is tied up with the financial rand and it will probably follow the abolition of the dual-rate system.

Recent developments

The successful outcome of the 27 April historic election in South Africa, giving the ANC a clear overall majority and making Nelson Mandela the first black president of South Africa, is a watershed in the history of the country. The fact that this election proceeded peacefully and without widespread bloodshed is a good harbinger for the future. Investors are now clearly looking at South Africa as a major new emerging market. With over US$100bn market capitalization, it is far and away the largest African stock market.

The success or failure of South Africa's economy in the next few years will have enormous implications for the rest of the continent. Trade and investment between South Africa and its African neighbours may be expected to grow rapidly. International, particularly US, capital will flow first towards South Africa, with its well established infrastructure, mining industry, financial market, etc., and then north towards Zimbabwe, Zambia, Tanzania and the French-speaking countries of West Africa. With political stability, there is no question that the enormous central reserves of the continent, especially mineral reserves, can be well developed and will be reflected in a new importance given to South Africa by global emerging market managers. The first announcements by President Mandela have generally been favourable towards investors and towards preserving the free market system of the South African economy.

The stock market

The Johannesburg Stock Exchange was established in 1886 and, until the 1970s, was one of the major stock markets of the world. It is still one of the top dozen.

The overseas investor currently buys South African stocks at a notable discount owing to the difference between the financial and commercial rand. The financial rand is used for all capital investment in South Africa according to the regulations issued by the central bank. The commercial rand is used for all trade-related transactions. The discount fluctuates according to the market's perception of the country, the intention being that the financial rand should take the strain of political uncertainty. In this way, it has been from 10-50 per cent cheaper than the commercial rand. Dividends are paid in commercial rand—hence foreign investors receive a much better yield than their South African counterparts.

South Africa has operated a system of stringent exchange controls for many years but has companies with considerable earning power. This has severely limited their investment opportunity and they have, therefore, tended to invest in the Johannesburg market. This leads to a complicated inter-relationship between companies—essentially big fleas have lesser fleas upon their backs to bite 'em and little fleas have smaller fleas, and so on *ad infinitum*. This makes the structure of the market difficult to understand.

Although over eighty companies on the Johannesburg Stock Exchange have market capitalizations above US$200m, it is widely seen as being dominated by a handful of major conglomerates. This is not misleading as Anglo and De Beers account for 18.1 per cent of the All-Share Index. Recently, there has been interest in the question of 'unbundling'. There are two reasons for this, one is the belief that the sum of the parts is greater than the whole. The second is the hostility of the ANC to these great corporations or monopolies—Anglovaal and SAB invoke its special ire.

There are two types of 'bundled' company. The first is where a founding family with a relatively small stake—often no more than 10 per cent—maintains control through layers of holding companies—in this way, the Oppenheimers kept control of Anglo. The second is where fund management companies have reached such a size that their holding gives them managerial control—Old Mutual and Sanlam have holdings in Barlows and Gencor, both of which are being unbundled. In both cases, a minority shareholder manages to exercise control almost regardless of the other shareholders.

The unbundling process naturally appeals more to the second group because control is not an object in itself and their stakes are large enough to continue their control, if they wish, of the unbundled companies. The point of unbundling—other than to placate the ANC—is to reduce the discount to net asset value at which the parent company's shares often sell. By simplifying the situation, it ought to make it easier for the market to evaluate the true worth of a company correctly. It is not yet clear whether this theory actually works. Gencor saw its discount narrow from 30 per cent to 19 per cent after it became tax efficient to unbundle and before its announcement. However, this still meant that it underperformed the mining sector as a whole. The real impetus for further unbundling will be political—Anglo and others wish to remain firmly bundled. One of the real advantages of unbundling could be a major boost to the liquidity of the stock market.

Possibly the greatest interest and excitement in the South African market is aroused by the mining sector, although it is only 13 per cent of GDP, and most particularly gold. From before time immemorial, gold has been a symbol of wealth and an acceptable form of payment for all manner of goods and services. South Africa provides nearly 50 per cent of the world's total gold production. A sensible way to look at gold shares is through an international comparison. The new FT Gold Mines Index only looks at the biggest mines—those producing over 300,000 ounces a year. It showed the following geographic distribution during 1993.

	South Africa	Canada	USA	Australia
Market capitalization(%)	27.0	42.2	19.5	11.2
Production(%)	53.8	22.6	12.6	11.0
Reserves(%)	59.5	23.9	8.7	7.9
Profitability(%)	44.7	32.0	12.7	10.6
Market capitalization (% per oz)	22.6	43.7	13.7	20.0

Figure 46.2 FT Gold Mines Index: distribution of gold mines in 1993
Source: Mercury Asset Management

South Africa may be compared with America from the above figures: on the basis of reserves, the USA is 4.9 times more expensive and on profitability—2.5 times.

It is difficult to forecast the price of gold, but the fact that fabrication demand has been greater than supply since 1980 is not unduly important because new supply is only a small percentage of the potentially available stock. The gold price really depends on inflationary expectations and on the continuation of confidence in paper money, based on nothing other than people's preparedness to accept it. South African gold shares are attractive because they provide a relatively high yield and a greater gearing to the gold price. Production costs are, surprisingly, the highest of the major producing nations. This is mainly because of the increase in wages given to rather aggressive unions. The steady devaluation of the rand has helped offset this to some degree.

Platinum is another important metal for South Africa. It is the world's largest producer. Platinum is not normally used as a store of value but is needed for catalytic converters and jewellery. World recession has been bad for car manufacture and Japanese ladies have been buying less jewellery, which has not been good for the platinum price. However, as the economy generally recovers, so will the demand for platinum. In this respect, it is like a base metal; it does not have the special quality of gold. Nevertheless, any investor who wishes to buy platinum shares needs to do so through South Africa.

Technical notes

- Settlement: This is done on a weekly basis with all brokers settling their net balances through the clearing house on the immediately following Monday. Individual investors must settle within seven days. It is possible to arrange payment against delivery.
- Physical possession of shares—no central depository.
- Safe custody is offered by South African banks but because of sanctions, no foreign banks do this yet.
- Commissions:

over 200 rand	flat charge 30 rand
up to 5000 rand	1.2%
5001-10,000 rand	0.85%
10,001-100,000 rand	0.75%
100,001-250,000 rand	0.65%
250,001-500,000 rand	0.55%
500,001-1,000,000 rand	0.45%
1,000,001-1,500,000 rand	0.35%
over 1,500,001 rand	0.20%

These rates apply to an aggregate day's transactions to buy or sell per account.

Marketable securities tax: 1%

- The stock exchange issues a lengthy booklet detailing the listing requirements which is available on application and payment of the appropriate fee. However, the essentials are: 3 years of profit with the current year being more than 1m rand; 30 per cent of the first million shares to be held by the public and an agreed percentage of the rest; at least 300 shareholders and a subsidized capital of not less than 2m rand.

- Foreign investment through the financial rand is encouraged and will continue to be so under the new regime. Profits and dividends may be freely repatriated. The latter are subject to a 15 per cent non-resident shareholders tax (NRST).

Exchange address

Johannesburg Stock Exchange
PO Box 1174
Johannesburg 2000

Company	**Market cap. (US$bn)**	*Company*	**Volume (US$m per mth.)**
Anglo American Corp	10.8	De Beers Cons Mines	68.2
De Beers Cons Mines	9.5	Vaal Reefs	34.3
Richemont	5.9	Richemont	32.4
SA Breweries	5.8	Anglo American Corp	27.5
Liberty Life	4.7	Amgold	25.6
Rembrandt	4.4	Driefontein	23.2
Minorco	4.2	Kloof	19.9
SBIC	3.4	Minorco	16.6
JCI	3.4	Barlows	15.3
SASOL	3.2	Gencor	14.8
Driefontein	3.0	SA Breweries	14.3
Gencor	2.8	Rusplat	13.6
Amgold	2.6	SASOL	12.5
Barlows	2.6	Western Deeps	12.1
Rusplat	2.5	Fregold	11.8
Fregold	2.2	Liberty Life	11.5
Vaal Reefs	2.2	Rembrandt	10.6
First Bank	2.1	South Vaal	10.2
Tiger Oats	2.0	ABSA	9.1
Kloof	1.8	JCI	8.2

Notes:
P/Es are those for local investors
Gold share earnings are after capital expenditure hence the relatively high multiples

Figure 46.3 South Africa: 20 largest companies by market capitalization and average daily volume

Chapter 47

Swaziland

Population:	760,000
Gross domestic product:	$581.6m
Market capitalization:	US$107m
Currency/US$:	3.4 emalangeni

The Kingdom of Swaziland, with the splendid national anthem 'Ingoma Yesive', was established in April 1967. There are no legal political parties, but the country has been stable under the legitimate monarch who rules as well as reigns. It is not an advanced nation and is still governed on tribal lines.

Both in terms of population and area—a mere 6704 square miles or less than the English county of Somerset—Swaziland is a small country. The main economic activity since 1988 has been manufacturing, before then it was agriculture which would primarily have been sugar, cotton and pineapples. It is a completely land-locked country surrounded by South Africa to the north, west and south and Mozambique to the east. It is, obviously, therefore, highly dependent on South Africa for its future economic prosperity.

The stock market

The stock market was opened in 1990 on the initiative of the government and the Commonwealth Development Co-operation. It trades daily between 10.00 and noon. There is only one stockbroking firm, Swaziland Stockbrokers, which acts as an agent between buyers and sellers. It is a very small market, with only three companies listed and an average daily turnover of under $1000. It is, however, efficiently organized and responds quickly to enquiries.

Technical notes

- Settlement is immediate.
- Physical possession of shares—no central depository.

- Standard Chartered of Swaziland will offer safe custody services.
- Commissions:

1-49,999 emal	2 per cent
50,000-99,000 emal	1.5 per cent
over 100,000 emal	1 per cent

  plus a transaction fee of 20 emal for both buyers and sellers.
- Listing requirements: a company needs to be approved by the Stock Exchange Committee and the Listing Committee. Swaziland Stockbrokers assist with this process. It evaluates companies and then acts as the sponsoring broker.
- Foreign investment is subject to exchange control approval, but repatriation of dividends, capital and profit is unrestricted. There is no capital gains tax, but there is a dividend tax of 15 per cent.

	1988	1989	1990	1991	1992
Population ('000s)	740	760	770	820	840
GNP (US$m)	581.6	n/a	n/a	n/a	n/a
Real GNP growth (%)	5.2	n/a	n/a	n/a	n/a
Per capita income (US$)	786	n/a	n/a	n/a	n/a
Exports (US$bn)	430.7	491.1	529	n/a	n/a
Imports (US$bn)	490.6	600.2	687.6	751	n/a
Foreign direct investment	38	56.9	40.7	14.5	
Inflation (1985 = 100)	149.9	157.9	178.1	198.1	216.5
Interest rates (prime)	15	14.5	14.5	16.25	15
International reserves (US$m)	140.1	180.61	216.47	171.93	309.1
Market capitalization (US$m)	-	-	17.2	27.2	107
No. of listed companies	-	-	1	2	3
Index performance in US$ (%)	-	-	16.5	9.8	15.9
Currency to US$ (emalangeni)	2.38	2.54	2.56	2.74	3.05
Currency to US$ perf (%)	18.83	6.24	1.03	6.58	10.15

Figure 47.1 Swaziland: key statistics

	Market capitalization (US$ million)
Royal Swaziland Sugar	78.3
Standard Chartered	11.5
Swazi-Spa	7.5

Figure 47.2 Swaziland: three largest companies by market capitalization

Exchange address

The Swaziland Stock Market
c/o Swaziland Stockbrokers Ltd.
Suite 205, 2/F, Dhianu'ubeka House
Walker Street
Mbabane, Swaziland

Tel & Fax: 268 46163

Chapter 48

Zimbabwe

Population:	11m
Gross domestic product:	US$5bn
Market capitalization:	US$1bn
Currency/US$:	Z$6.67

Zimbabwe is the home of the Ndebele and Shona tribes. In 1890, it was named Southern Rhodesia after Cecil Rhodes, the British adventurer. From 1923 until Ian Smith's Unilateral Declaration of Independence in 1965, Southern Rhodesia was a self-governing British colony. Ian Smith wanted to preserve white minority rule against the wishes of the then British government, led by Harold Wilson. This was a key event in the nation's history, and it led to fourteen years of economic isolation during which the Smith regime encouraged import substitution and the authorities directed a siege economy.

The 1979 Lancaster House agreement negotiated by Lord Carrington led to independence in 1980 and Comrade Mugabe—as he is referred to by television announcers—took charge. When communism failed in many parts of the world, Mugabe allowed his highly-regarded finance minister to implement a series of market-orientated reforms. From 1989, many price controls have been scrapped, while employment regulations and exchange controls have even been partially lifted. Tariffs are being reduced and foreign investment is encouraged. The IMF has been influential in the process, as has the World Bank, and the country has been supported by some international aid.

The economic reform package is real and unlikely to be reversed. First, exchange controls have been lifted entirely for foreign investors. Capital, profits and dividends may be freely repatriated. Second, government spending has been cut. The deficit is now 4 per cent of GDP, with the total debt being around 100 per cent of GDP of which 35 per cent is foreign. Some 40 per cent of government spending is debt servicing. There is no welfare benefit and the policy is to cut current spending but to keep capital programmes. Third, almost all wage and price controls have been lifted, although there is still a vestigial minimum wage. Fourth, together with

	1988	1989	1990	1991	1992
Population (m)	8.88	9.12	9.37	10.02	10.45
GNP (US$bn)	5.6	5.8	6	5.6	5
Real GNP growth (%)	7.2	4.7	2.3	3.6	-8.3
Per capita income (US$)	636	636	640	559	478
Exports (US$bn)	1.3	1.4	1.6	1.6	1.45
Imports (US$bn)	1.4	1.5	1.7	1.7	1.85
Foreign direct investment (US$bn)	4.1	n/a	n/a	n/a	n/a
Inflation (1985=100)	138.1	155.9	183	227.5	332.7
Interest rates (base)	13	11.5-13	11.5-12	12-17.25	21.75-47.5
International reserves (US$m)	257.7	176.8	218.8	217.6	310.3
Market capitalization (US$m)	772	1055	2684	1406	626
No. of listed companies	53	54	577	60	62
Index performance in US$	25	40.8	94.9	-52.3	-59.8
Price/earnings ratios (P/E)	3.2	4.4	8.3	7	2
Turnover per annum (US$m)	38.4	35.5	51.3	84.4	18.4
Dividend yield	7.8	9.8	4	5.8	6.1
Currency to US$ (Z dollar)	1.94	2.27	2.64	5.05	5.48
Currency to US$ performance	-14.4	-14.4	-13.9	-47.8	-7.9

Note: GDP figures published by the Reserve Bank are only available to 1989. Later years are extrapolations and are no more than indicative. Trade figures are provisional 1991 and estimated for 1992.

Figure 48.1 Zimbabwe: key statistics

other factors, this liberalization led to inflation which peaked at 50 per cent but fell to about 15 per cent and is expected to be less than 10 per cent next year. High real interest rates to clamp down on monetary growth and a tight fiscal policy have both improved the position, although the currency has continued to depreciate. Fifth, economic growth is expected to be about about 6 per cent in 1994.

Politically, Zimbabwe is stable. Although Zanu PF has 147 out of 150 seats in Parliament, it is not a one-party state and it is obvious from reading Zimbabwe's Hansard that debate is free and government policy is criticized harshly on occasions. Elections have to be held by 1995 and there is no doubt that the status quo will hold. The only fly in the ointment is the question of property redistribution which has been legislated for and is seen to be important. It does undermine property rights in a fairly arbitrary way, but there is not thought to be the money to proceed with it on a significant scale. With a large share of the national wealth, the government intends to privatize some of its holdings, but it is reluctant to sell profitable companies and the unprofitable ones are firmly in the 'barge-pole' category.

Zimbabwe inherited a solid basic infrastructure second only to South Africa's. The country also has one of the highest literary rates in the developing world—greater than South Africa's, at 85 per cent—and Zimbabweans have a good command of English.

With a land area three times the size of England, and a population of around 11m, Zimbabwe enjoys both a delightful climate and fertile soil. It has suffered from serious drought during recent years, particularly in 1991/2, which harmed the whole economy; agriculture accounts for 15 per cent of GDP and agri-business much more. However, rain will eventually fall and, when it does, the economy will be greatly helped. Zimbabwe has excellent tourist opportunities and can offer safari-adventure holidays as well as visits to Victoria Falls.

The stock market

The first stock exchange in Zimbabwe opened in 1896 in Bulawayo, but it closed down in 1902. The exchange was re-established in 1946 with its Harare floor following in 1951. It is regulated by the 1974 Act. The market operates daily and prices are set according to a call-over system, which is a scaled-down open-outcry.

The market is tightly-held because, in the past, local institutions and individuals were not able to obtain overseas currency to fund the purchase of assets and, therefore, tend to view investments as very long-term. Recently, exchange controls have been eased, allowing residents to have foreign currency-denominated accounts but the Zimbabwe dollar is not freely convertible for locals. This ought to change in 1995. From 1984 to 1993 no foreign investors were allowed to own shares.

The market is in two main sections, industrial and mining, for each of which an index is calculated. Domestic investors do not generally like investing in the mining stocks which they regard as too volatile. This is particularly true of the large institutions.

Technical notes

- Settlement is on the basis of cash against delivery which must be made within 14 days of the trade.
- Physical possession of shares—no central depository.
- Both Barclays Bank of Zimbabwe and Standard Chartered of Zimbabwe offer safe-custody services.
- Fixed commissions:

up to Z$50,000	2%
next Z$50,000	1.5%
over Z$100,000	1%

minimum charge:	Z$15 per transaction
basic charge:	Z$20 per transaction
registration charge:	Z$20 per transaction
safe-custody charge:	Z$50 per annum, waivable at broker's discretion.
Stamp duty:	0.3 per cent.

- Listing requirements are detailed and include a minimum offering of 30 per cent of the outstanding shares with an 'adequate' spread of shareholders. Financial information must not be more than six months old.
- Foreign investment is now welcome; however, it is limited to 25 per cent in total and 5 per cent individually. Profits, dividends and capital may be freely repatriated subject to a 15 per cent dividend withholding tax and a 10 per cent capital gains tax.

	Market capitalization (US$ million)
Delta	231.6
Zimbabwe Sun	106.5
Barclays Bank	62.3
National Foods	39.5
TSL	53.6
PG Industries	39.3
Hippo Valley	40.4
Rio Tinto	30.8
FSI	40.4
Cluff Resources	26.8
Bindura Nickel	22.8
Dunlop	23.0
Tanganda Tea	17.5
Falcon Gold	18.7
Edgars Stores	16.2
Colcom	17.0
David Whitehead	20.0
Portland	31.6
Wankie	19.8
Zimbabwe Financial Holdings	21.3

Figure 48.2 Zimbabwe: 20 largest stocks by market capitalization

Exchange address

Zimbabwe Stock Exchange
8/F Southampton House
Union Avenue
Harare
Zimbabwe

Tel: 263 4 736 861 / Fax: 263 4 791 045

PART VII

Russia & Eastern Europe

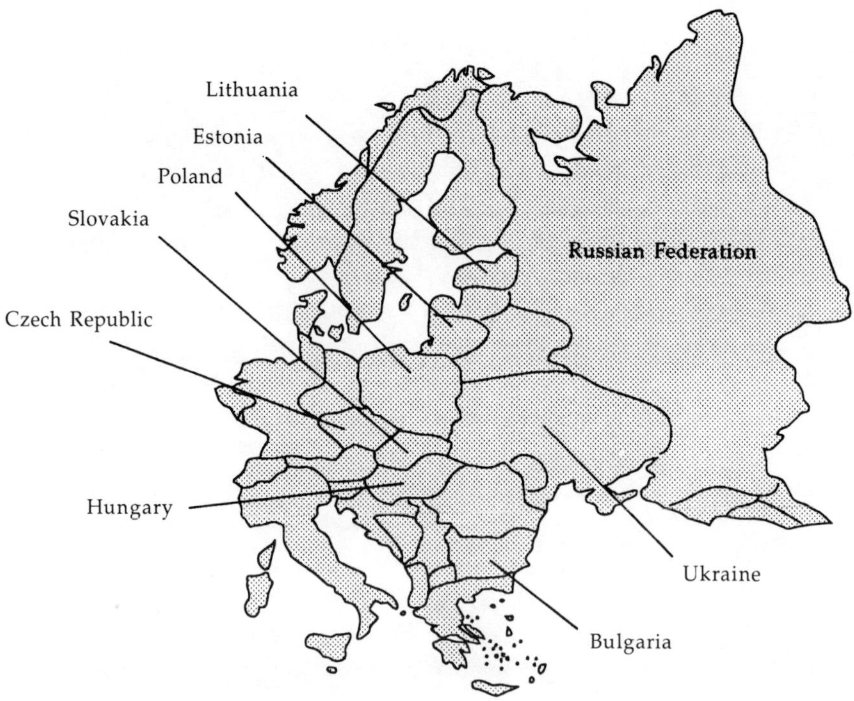

THE EMERGING MARKETS OF EASTERN EUROPE

Chapter 49

Russia & Eastern Europe - Introduction

From the ashes of disaster grow the roses of success

The experience of Germany after the Second World War has given rise to great hope for the whole of Eastern Europe. Peoples whose lives have been ruled for them, yet whom tyrants could not wholly crush are now liberated from communism in the way Germany was liberated from National Socialism. Countries whose industrial base had been destroyed by years of neglect and whose entrepreneurial spirit had been removed by state control must see the similarities with Germany after total defeat. From that base has grown one of the most powerful economies in the world. It has developed not through aid programmes which were limited in the early years—the Marshall Plan is often exaggerated—but through its own endeavours. The question is can the Eastern Europeans do the same?

The people are similar—indeed some Eastern European countries are basically Germanic. Their histories until 1914 are similar, they were parts of the great continental empires. However, there is some sign that the political will to accept the necessary changes is not there. This is shown by the election of former communists.

The difficulties are immense—in Russia Peter the Great tried and failed to prepare his country for the 18th century. Yet in earlier times these countries did not have democracy or capitalism to help them succeed. Looking at what a powerful combination these two have been—especially when capitalism takes the lead—indicates that there is a good chance that these nations will finally triumph. The fact that they have already introduced stock markets, which is one of the purest signs of capitalism, is encouraging and the speed with which Germany returned to the fore offers a guiding light.

As an *aide-memoire* it is worth pointing out that economic statistics of Eastern European countries are unreliable. The means of collecting them are not satisfactory and, because of the dramatic changes, many of these places have seen large black markets grow up. Such figures ought, therefore, to be considered indicative and not absolute.

	Poland	Czech Republic	Hungary
Population (m)	38.5	10.3	10.3
GNP (US$bn)	80.1	30.8	33.0
Real GNP growth (%)			
1992	1	-	-
1993	2	-	-
Per capita income (US$)	2080	2990	3204
Exports (US$bn)	14.21	12.77	10.04
Imports (US$bn)	19.12	12.56	10.46
Foreign direct investment (US$m)	577	-	2339
Inflation	36.9	20.8	22.5
Interest rates	35.0	11.5	25.4
Market capitalization (US$m)	2139	1000	659
No. listed companies	22	953	28
Index performance in '93 (%)	739.6	128**	24.6
Price/earnings (P/E) ratios			
1993[e]	31.5	14	52.4
Turnover per annum (US$m)	1598	1800	75
Dividend yield	0.4	-	2.7
Stock market performance, '88-'93 (%)	262.9	128	-29.9
Currency to US$ performance, '88-'93 (%)	-97.4	-	-47.8

Notes: The above figures are not wholly reliable as authoritative sources differ and refer to the latest information only
**From the establishment of a stock market*
***HN Wood 30 Index established September 1993*

Figure 49.1 Eastern Europe: country statistics (31 December 1993)

Chapter 50

Czech Republic

Population:	10.3m
Gross domestic product:	$14.2bn
Market capitalization:	See Figure 50.1 overleaf
Currency/US$:	31 koruna

The Czech Republic was established on 1 January 1993. It had been ruled jointly with Slovakia under the Austro-Hungarian Empire until 1918. It was then independent, before the Nazis invaded in 1938. After the War, the Russians took control which they brutally reinforced in 1968. 1990 saw free elections and in 1992 it was decided to divide the country in two.

Economically, the Czech Republic was the workshop of the Soviet Empire, famous for the quality of its engineering including weaponry, textiles and footwear, with the largest shoe factory in the world. However, the drawbacks of a planned economy, a lack of investment and the collapse of its major markets caused a slump. In 1985, the former Soviet Union accounted for 44 per cent of the Czech Republic's exports. This trade collapsed in 1991 as it lost the ability to pay for its requirements. Unemployment—officially non-existent under the Communist regime—is still growing, having reached 4.1 per cent by the end of 1991 (11.8 per cent in Slovakia). The abolition of price control and the removal of subsidies led to raging inflation—58 per cent in December 1991.

However, for the coming years, the Czech Republic has some natural advantages. A land-locked nation, geographically at the heart of Europe and a neighbour of Germany, it has low labour rates—estimated to be one-twentieth of Germany's level—a stable political outlook and an enthusiastic policy towards foreign investment. Moreover, although the Commission of the EC has been grudging in its efforts so far, there is a strong moral pressure on the Community to open its markets to its most immediate poor relations.

	1992	1993
Population (m)	10.3	10.3
GNP (US$bn)	-	30.8
Real GNP growth (%)	n/a	n/a
Per capita income (US$)	-	2990
Exports (US$bn)	8.23	12.77
Imports (US$bn)	8.89	12.56
Foreign direct investment	n/a	-
Inflation	11.1	20.8
Interest rates	9.5	11.5
Market capitalization	-	1000
No. of listed companies	-	953
Index performance in US$ (%)	-	128
Price/earnings (P/E) ratios	-	14
Turnover per annum (US$m)	-	1800
Dividend yield	-	-
Currency to US$ (koruna)	-	31

Note: 1993 import and export figures include Slovakia

Figure 50.1 Czech Republic: key statistics

The stock market

The origins of a Prague stock market may be found in the 1850s, with official recognition being granted by the Austrian Ministry of Finance and Commerce in 1871. The German invasion brought trading to a halt in 1938 and the exchange was formally abolished in 1952. This was reversed in 1992 when the Prague Stock Exchange was officially founded, with trading beginning in 1993. The government's privatization programme was an important motivator. In the first wave, over 950 companies were issued to the public in exchange for vouchers which both Czechs and Slovaks were able to buy and exchange for companies. Many investors put their vouchers into mutual funds which currently own 70 per cent of the market. Second and third waves of privatization are planned.

Trading on the exchange happens once a week—this is expected to increase to three times by the end of the year. Prices are set to maximize the number of orders filled each session and all trading takes place at that price, which may not move by more than 50 per cent between sessions. Volume is low, with only forty companies traded in an average day, of which 25 to 30 are regulars.

	Market capitalization (US$m)	% of index
CEZ	103.5	30.73
Ceska Sporitelna	51.0	15.12
Komercni Banka	36.0	10.69
Cokoladovny	23.3	6.92
TABAK	20.4	6.05
Cesk Pojistovna	17,2	5.10
Investicni Bank	10.6	3.13
Skoda Pizen	6.6	1.95
Zivno Bank	6.0	1.78
Pizenske Pivovary	5.5	1.63
Sklo Union Teplice	5.3	1.59
Barum	5.0	1.49
FINOP	4.7	1.38
Prazska Teplar	3.9	1.15
CKD Praha	3.7	1.11
Spolana	3.5	1.04
Trinecke Zel	3.2	0.94
Hotel Forum	2.9	0.86
Zapad Keram Zav	2.7	0.81
Pivovar Radegast	2.4	0.70

Figure 50.2 Prague Stock Exchange: 20 largest stocks by market capitalization (as at 11 January 1994)

The large number of small private investors has meant the continuation of the 'RM system' which was initially set up to gain bids for the original privatization. It has low commission cost and trades once a month. Individuals have direct access to the RM system and turnover in individual companies can be very small. About 500 stocks are traded each month in this way.

The main bulk of trading does not take place either across the floor of the exchange or on the RM system. Direct trades, which currently do not have to be made public, are the only way in which it is possible to buy any quantities of shares. Essentially, the good brokers know which of the funds own what and deal directly with them when they have a foreign purchaser. This makes the listed prices no more than a general guide and could present some liquidity problems in the event of a market crash.

Technical notes

- Settlement on the exchange is three days after trading.
- There is no physical possession of stocks, the Stock Exchange Securities Register ensures that the Centre for Securities is notified of all changes of ownership.

- Citibank and Chase Manhattan are setting up custodian services.
- Commissions:

  1 per cent on RM system
  0.5-1.25 per cent Exchange costs
  Negotiable brokers' charges
  No stamp duty

- Listing criteria: The exchange lays down detailed regulations which include the issuing of a prospectus. It is important to note that to September 1993, *no* shares were officially listed and the number expected to list shortly is in single figures. This makes no difference to the ability of shares to be traded, but it does mean that much less information is available.
- Foreign investment is generally welcomed. Companies may limit the amount owned by foreigners and the breweries, particularly, have done so. Repatriation of capital and profit is allowed, although dividends are taxed at 25 per cent and have to be collected via a Czech address. CGT at 45 per cent is charged on investments held for under one year.

Exchange address

Prague Stock Exchange
Namustka 3
110 00 Praha 1

Tel: 2423 0176. Fax: 2421 9187

Chapter 51

Hungary

Population:	10.3m
Gross domestic product:	$33bn
Market capitalization:	$812m
Currency/US$:	100.7 forints

Hungarian history has been one of tumult: The 13th century saw the Mongol hordes invading and destroying. Then, 200 years later, came the Ottoman Empire which, after the death of Suleiman the Magnificent, slowly declined to make way for the Hapsburgs. The Treaty of Versailles removed the Hapsburgs and Transylvania while between the wars Hungary was independent. The Russians took control after World War II which, hidden from the world's attention by Suez, they strengthened in 1956. 1990 saw democratic elections and 1991 the final withdrawal of the Soviets.

Hungary has two main rivers, the Danube and Tisza, and is at the centre of Europe. It borders Austria, various parts of the former Yugoslavia, Romania, the Ukraine and Slovakia. Although, theoretically, on a major trade route—the Danube—the Yugoslavian war has recently removed this advantage. Hungary was the major tourist destination of the Soviet Empire and a stopping place for Germans en route to Greece and Yugoslavia. Neither of these markets now exist.

As with other planned economies, the switch to a market one has not been easy. 1990-92 saw a cumulative fall in industrial production of 32 per cent and 1993 is expected to be another bad year. Exports have been hit by the division of the Soviet Empire. In 1989, 40.1 per cent of all exports went to Eastern Europe. By 1992, it was 21.3 per cent. Inflation has been a problem, reaching 135 per cent in 1991, while the government's fiscal deficit was 7 per cent of GDP in 1992 and is expected to be 11 per cent in 1993. Moreover, the individual worker bears a heavy yoke. Each 100 workers support 143 dependents, with income and social security taxes being 36.9 per cent of GDP, which is higher than all 12 member nations of the EC.

The hope for this economy, with a population of 10.3m in 36,000 square miles, is that trade to the West ought to open up. Foreign investment has started to flow in—more was received in 1991-2 by Hungary than by Po-

	1988	1989	1990	1991	1992	1993
Population (m)	10.44	10.4	10.36	10.35	10.32	10.3
GDP (US$bn)	34.8	35.1	33.8	29.8	33.4	33.0
Real GDP growth (%)	5.5	0.9	-3.7	-11.8	-	-
Per capita income (US$)	3333	3375	3263	2879	3236	3204
Exports (US$bn)	9.6	9.13	7.98	10.11	10.04	-
Imports (US$bn)	8.99	8.29	8.87	11.31	10.46	-
Foreign direct investment	0	0	0	1462	1479	2339
Inflation (1985 = 100)	132.5	154.8	199.5	279.5	331.2	405.7
Interest rates	13	17	28	35.2	33.1	25.4
Market capitalization (US$bn)	-	-	-	505	562	812
No. of listed companies	-	-	-	21	23	28
IFC Index performance in US$ (%)	-	-	-	37.8	9.5	28.6
Price/earnings (P/E) ratios	-	-	-	12.7	-	52.4
Average daily turnover (US$m)	-	-	-	117	38	99
Dividend yield	-	-	-	8.8	-	2.7
Currency to US$ (forint)	52.537	62.543	61.449	75.62	83.97	100.7
Currency to US$ perf (%)	13.3	-19	1.7	-23.1	-11	-16.6

Note: GDP 1988-1991 at 1990 price. 1992 and 1993 money GDP converted at year-end exchange rate

Figure 51.1 Hungary : key statistics

land and the Czech Republic combined—and this should continue to be so, especially from Austria. Furthermore, Hungary's GDP per capita, at a 1993 estimate of $3204, is higher than the Czech Republic at $2909 and Poland at $2080, not to mention Romania at $610.

Politically, Hungary appears to be stable. The elections which are to be held next year are not expected to see a major shift in power. There are, however, two caveats. To the left it is possible that continued economic hardship may—as in Poland—reinvigorate the former communists. To the right there is a greater danger represented by Mr Gheorghe Funar. He is a Romanian-Hungarian who is calling for the Budapest government to support its people in Transylvania. Some senior politicians have responded to his call by saying that Hungary's borders ought to be changed. Bearing in mind the troubles of its neighbour, the Transylvanian issue is of concern.

The stock market

The Budapest Commodities and Stock Exchange was opened in 1867 and traded actively in times of peace. It was closed in 1948 by the communists.

The re-establishment of a securities market started in 1983, but the new stock market was formally set up in 1990.

To date, ten stocks are listed on the exchange and 15 more are traded. Only six companies have so far been privatized, but the government intends to speed it up by swapping equity for compensation certificates, which are already actively traded. The exchange trades each week day from 11.00 to 12.30 on both an open-outcry and public order-book system. There are 46 brokers who do most of their business in government securities. The volume of stocks traded has fallen from $160m in 1991, to $76m in 1992. It was down again in the first quarter 1993, but picked up in the summer on the back of foreign buying. Some stocks trade infrequently—six traded in less than one-third of all sessions in 1992.

Technical notes

- Settlement on the exchange is 5 days after trading.
- A separate depository and clearing house are to be set up shortly to hold securities and arrange settlement for the stock exchange and the OTC market.
- Commission: 1.5-2 per cent to buy or sell. No stamp duty.
- Listing criteria: Detailed regulations are laid down by the stock exchange and backed up by legislation. A prospectus has to be issued and 'issuers should also meet the obligation of a continuous disclosure of information'. Traded securities have to meet less stringent criteria—only 10 per cent need be issued on a one-year trading history against 20 per cent and 3 years.
- Foreign investment is welcomed, however, they may only buy registered shares. Repatriation of dividends, capital and profits is allowed. Dividends are subject to tax at 10 per cent, capital gains 20 per cent, but foreigners will not be further taxed and the capital gains rate is supposed to decline to 10 per cent.

Exchange address

Budapest Stock Exchange
Deak Ferenc utca 5
H-1052 Budapest
PO Box Pf 24 1364
Hungary

Tel: 361 226 2635 / Fax: 361 118 1737

Chapter 52

Poland

Population:	38.36m
Gross national product:	$84bn
Market capitalization:	$2139m
Currency/US$:	9900 zloty

'Poland is indestructible: she will rise again like a rock, which may for a time be submerged, by a tidal wave, but which remains a rock...'

Winston Churchill

Poland was the favourite playing-field of the Prussians, Russians and Hapsburgs from the 18th century. It was officially abolished in the 1790s and removed from the map. It gained a short-lived independence after the Great War, but the Molotov-Ribentrop pact repeated the usual pattern. After the Second World War, the Russians assumed sole command which they relinquished after being pushed and harried by the Solidarity movement.

The frequent carving and re-carving of the map of Poland has left the potential for diplomatic squabbles. However, Germany has agreed not to ask for any of the land it lost after World War II to be returned, while Poland currently shows no inclination to demand segments of its neighbours. Thus, its current size of 121,000 square miles is unlikely to change.

The Polish economy under communism concentrated on heavy industry such as steel and ship building. It also had a large agrarian economy providing 9 per cent of GDP but, more importantly, 25 per cent of employment. Both these areas were inefficient and the opening up of the economy has led to great hardship. Unemployment rose from 0.5 per cent in 1989 to 13.6 per cent by 1992. Inflation raged as widespread government subsidies were removed: it rose to 585 per cent in 1990, although in 1993 it fell to around 30 per cent.

The response of the electorate, in September 1993's voting, was a partial return to the former communists. This was not as serious as it appeared for three reasons. First, the former communists do not have an overall majority:

	1988	1989	1990	1991	1992	1993
Population (m)	37.86	37.96	38.12	38.24	38.36	38.5
GNP (zlotys trillion)	29.6	118.3	606.7	824.3	1145	1593.6
Real GNP growth (%)	4	0.2	-11.6	-7	1	2
Per capita income (US$)	1814	2166	1675	2038	2191	2080
Exports (US$bn)	11.95	3	13.63	14.39	15.79	14.21
Imports (US$bn)	10.88	2.37	8.41	15.22	16.15	19.12
Foreign direct investment (US$m)	7	7	89	300	577	n/a
Inflation (1985 = 100)	236.1	828.9	5684.3	9680.2	13,846.8	18,953.1
Interest rates	6	140	55	40	38	35
Market capitalization (US$m)	-	-	-	144	222	2139
No. of listed companies	-	-	-	9	16	22
Index performance in US$ (%)	-	-	-	-25.1	-42.3	739.6
Price/earnings (P/E) ratios	-	-	-	4.5	3.7	31.5
Turnover per annum (US$m)	-	-	-	28	164	1598
Dividend yield	-	-	-	-	5.5	0.4
Currency to US$ (zlotys)	503	6500	9500	10957	15767	19900
Currency to US$ perf (%)	-59	-1192	-46	-15	-44	-26

Note: Owing to the high rate of inflation which is lagged—sometimes to a great extent—by alterations in the zloty/dollar exchange rate, no meaningful figures can be provided for GNP in US dollar terms. Therefore,GDP is given in zlotys while GDP per capita is given in US dollars converted at the average exchange rates. Significant fluctuations can thus be seen.

Figure 52.1 Poland: key statistics

they have 171 out of 460 seats on 16.4 per cent of the vote. Second, they have changed since their previous time in office and accept many of the recent reforms. Third, the electorate cast about a third of its votes for a plethora of right-wing parties that did not individually reach the 5 per cent minimum and so received no seats in parliament. If these parties were to merge, then the right would be much better represented. In fact, these results may indicate no more than that the Poles have rejected communism but do not like the full rigours of capitalism and so continue to seek the phantasmagoric middle way.

Regarding the political outlook, there are, currently, reasons for optimism. Out of a total population of 38.5m—which, unlike most European countries, is growing—24 per cent of those over 15 have received tertiary education, whilst 44.4 per cent of those not involved in agriculture are employed by the private sector. Moreover, because of its geographical position, Poland has access to the European market. Since 1989, exports have grown by 56 per cent and there has been a dramatic shift from East to West.

The former Soviet Union now only accounts for one-eighth of Poland's trade against over one-third with Germany. It is significant that Polish wage rates are under one-twentieth of Germany's.

These encouraging factors are bolstered by some of the reforms already implemented and unlikely to be reversed by the left-wing government. The budget deficit is being brought down and ought to remain at around 5 per cent of GDP. Pressure for additional social spending is strong, but the tax base is being widened with the introduction of VAT. However, it would be wrong to imply that the transition to capitalism will be easy and smooth.

The stock market

The Warsaw Stock Exchange was founded in 1817, but was closed in 1939. It was reopened in July 1991 and is symbolically housed in the old Communist Party Headquarters. 1993 was an incredibly good year for this market, rising more than five times in US dollar terms, based on P/Es expanding from under four times to over twenty-two times.

Just over 20 companies are listed on the exchange. These were all privatized through public offerings and a few more are expected to be issued. This process will continue, but the key event will be the 'mass privatization'. Groups of companies will be put into National Investment Funds. These will be holding companies which will manage, develop and provide capital for their groups. All adult Poles will be given an opportunity to acquire shares in these funds. Employees will hold 15 per cent of their own companies and the state will retain 25 per cent leaving 60 per cent with the funds.

The law relating to the mass privatization has been passed. Commentators believe that the new government could delay but will not stop this process. Assuming it does go ahead, then the current market capitalization would increase several times as each fund is anticipated to have assets of several hundred million dollars. The Warsaw Stock Exchange has already been much more liquid than those in Prague or Budapest.

Trading is order-driven, with a single price being set each session. These are now daily. The price is set to maximize the number of transactions and minimize the price fluctuation which is limited to ten per cent either way. The whole process is paperless with the National Depository of Securities recording changes to brokers' accounts, who it turn record changes to their clients' accounts. The correct registration of shares is highly important. No transfer of shares may take place except across the floor of the exchange. Even a minor technical error is difficult to correct while the re-registration of shares in the name of a new custodian is not allowed: they must go across the floor and could end up in the possession of someone else.

	Market capitalization (US$m)	Daily turnover (US$ '000s)
Electrim	441.8	4612
Wedel	318.3	1126
WBK	249.2	1857
Slaskibank	178.6	0
BRE	161.5	1692
BIG	153.8	887
Zywiec	135.9	1288
Universal	123.6	568
Polifarb	116.6	4141
Okocim	111.4	984
Mostostal	88.7	1418
Exbud	78.4	1154
Vistula	73.9	0
Prochnik	42.6	465
Wolczanka	38.8	730
Krosno	33.2	551
Sokolow	29.3	0
Swarzedz	28.4	829
Irena	21.5	639
Mostl Warsaw	20.9	0
Slaski Kabli	19.2	595
Tonsil	19.2	197

Figure 52.2 Warsaw Stock Exchange: stocks by market capitalization and turnover

Technical notes

- Settlement is three days after trading.
- No physical possession of stocks. The National Depository of Securities holds global certificates and issues a depository receipt through a broker.
- Citibank acts as a safe-custodian, but PKO brokers have agreements with BBH, Chase Manhattan, State Street and Deutsche Bank.
- Commissions:

  1.2 per cent up to $5,000. These are negotiable
  1.0 per cent up to $10,000
  0.8 per cent up to $50,000
  No stamp duty
- Listing criteria: detailed regulations are laid down which require inter alia accurate and timely publication of information and unlimited transferability for shares. The rates for the parallel market are less stringent.

- Foreign investment is welcomed. Except when double taxation agreements exist, taxation is the same as for Poles. No capital gains until 1995 except if share trading is your business (unclear if this applies to people managing money for third parties) 20 per cent tax on dividends. Repatriation of dividends and profits allowed. Interest may not be repatriated.

Exchange address

Warsaw Stock Exchange
ul Nowy Swiat 6/12
00-920 Warszawa
Poland

Tel: 02 628 3232 / Fax: 02 628 8191

Chapter 53

Russia

Population:	148m
Gross national product:	$700bn
Market capitalization:	$10bn (est.)
Currency/US$:	2100 roubles

Russia is the wounded giant of the global economy. It has potentially the greatest riches of any country, with the largest surface area but probably the worst management. With an estimated GNP of US$1400bn (for the former Soviet Union as a whole), it has a small securities market compared to its economic size. Yet in the past two years, more than 70 per cent of the whole Russian economy has been privatized. At the same time, the rouble has lost 90 per cent of its value against the dollar and domestic inflation has exceeded 1000 per cent annually. It presents a contrast to foreign investors of enormous potential and chaotic, often lawless, conditions for business. Yet there is little doubt that a period of stable and enlightened government would quickly show results in tapping this potential and attracting capital.

In the report that follows we have concentrated first on Russian history and culture, secondly on the western provinces and the stock markets of Moscow and St. Petersburg and, lastly, on what we believe is the most promising area, Siberia, with the new open cities of Novosibirsk and Vladivostok highlighted in particular. This last mentioned port is the gateway to the Pacific and Russia's trade with Japan, China, Korea and the United States. It also happens to have the fastest-growing stock exchange in the whole of the country.

Investing in Russia

Russia is chiefly important in the world today for the wealth of its natural resources and the threat of what could happen if its reforms fail. This is a sea-change from only a few years ago. The old Soviet Union restricted outside trade contacts to what was necessary to fulfill its 5-year plans. There was no talk of reform, let alone of what could go wrong with an economy which was in the process of perfecting socialist history. Now there is no

	1994
Population (m)	148
GNP (US$bn)	700 (est.)
Per capita income (US$)	4700 (est.)
Exports (US$bn)	108.6
Imports (US$bn)	114
Foreign direct investment (US$bn)	n/a
Inflation	250% p.a. (est.)
Interest rates (lending)	n/a
International reserves (US$bn)	n/a
Market capitalization (US$bn)	10 (est.)
No. of listed companies	(1400 privatized)
Currency to US$ (rouble)	2100

Figure 53.1 Russia: key statistics

Soviet Union, and no lack of interest in making money from the country's patrimony. From being one of the world's most secretive, guarded and paranoid societies, it has become in less than 10 years one of the world's most unguarded, freewheeling and vociferous. This is more than revolutionary, it is an overwhelming development because never in Russian history have people at all levels had a chance to participate so freely in their own destiny.

The history of Russia and the experience of its peoples does not fit neatly into our usual categories of East and West. Russia is a mixture of both, as well as large enough to deserve its own categorization. It remained close to its landlocked central Asian roots until the Eighteenth Century, when the European Enlightenment attracted the attention of the Court and brought about the first reforms to the savagely antiquated basis of Russian life. In the process, the capital moved to St Petersburg, physically turning its back on the old order in Moscow.

Before the reforms, not only the serfs, but the gentry as well, were tied to the land at the sovereign's pleasure. Freedom of movement, let alone of expression, which Europeans have taken for granted since Roman times, did not exist. Instead, the Tsar ruled with the complete authority of a tribal chief, in whom both the race, the mythologies and the laws of the nation were all mixed together. Those reforms which did occur were quite limited by western standards and, at the opening of the twentieth century, the country still had no system of elected parliament, no independent system of laws, no middle class, and hence none of the basics of democracy which the

West takes for granted. The only major reform had been the abolition of serfdom, which western Europe had achieved centuries before.

Not surprisingly, the Russian intelligentsia at the turn of the century was inclined to read history as a succession of stages in which Russia was stuck in the Middle Ages, whilst the West was embarking on a stage of development, approximate to its industrial revolution, which was set to embrace the workers themselves. As if to leap-frog the natural course of history, these Marxist historians became social engineers on an unprecedented scale and began a furious race with the West, the goal being to surpass the capitalist stage and create the new world order as promised by Marxism, in Russia first. This proto-nationalism became the private obsession of Stalin, who devised the command economy believing such a massive concentration of resources would yield greater economies of scale than anything available to the free-market system of the West.

This strategy proved effective only so long as production was driven by demand for basic capital goods, but was a total failure at producing goods which people wanted. It says something about the long-suffering nature of the people that the system did not collapse sooner. It was kept going artificially by the explosion in oil prices in the 1970s; as they receded in the 1980s the Soviet economy was left painfully exposed.

The current reforms date from Gorbachev's declaration of *perestroika* in 1985 when he became general secretary of the Party. By going further and introducing *glasnost* (openness), Gorbachev let the genie out of the bottle. After five years of making compromises with reformists and hardliners, he was swept away at the end of 1991 along with the Soviet Union, the Communist Party, and the ideological support for the command economy.

The changes are so recent, the situation so fluid, and events so compressed that it is at best risky to anticipate the direction in which they are moving. The most surprising thing, however, is that they seem to concern the general population so little. This may have something to do with Russian fatalism, or a complete loss of confidence in any solution to Russia's intractable woes. At any rate, both major attempts by hardliners to derail the reform process—in August 1991 when Gorbachev was briefly detained in his holiday bungalow, and October 1993 when the parliament tried to encourage armed resistance to Yeltsin—failed to attract popular support. Most opinion polls suggest rather that Russians are non-committal about what is promised to them by either side. The one link with the past is the strong leadership of Yeltsin, which is in keeping with the Russian cult of the leader. Russia post-Yeltsin is harder to imagine therefore than China post-Deng, and this contributes to the instability of the political situation.

With no history of popular elections—the first elections in Russian history took place in 1989—the political situation is extremely fragile. There are plenty of political parties, but they lack experience of working together.

With this weakness in view, it is likely that the executive powers of the president will continue to direct events in an atmosphere of quasi-crisis, at least while the economic and social problems are so desperate.

Just as it is remarkable that there are so many political parties coming into existence to represent ideas that would have seemed totally suppressed, so it is with the number of entrepreneurs who have taken up a calling which previously barely existed. There were nearly one million new business entities registered as of March 1993, employing 16m people (22 per cent of the work-force). Many had spun off from state firms but over one-quarter were brand new start-ups. The private sector therefore, as distinct from the privatizing former state sector, is growing very rapidly.

Many opportunities are emerging for new businesses to service the gap in demand opening up between the old command economy, and the new economy that is learning to respond flexibly to price signals. This new activity is not showing up in official statistics, however, which still reflect mainly the painful passing away of the old economy and not the promise of the new.

The point at which the old and new economies interact is a grey area where sales are not recorded, taxes not paid, and goods sold for barter or dollars rather than for cash. The authorities unwittingly encouraged the growth of this grey market: first under Gorbachev, when managers were allowed to set their own budgets and sell excess production outside the state system, and then under the more recent reforms, when all companies were compulsorily turned into joint stock companies, which enabled them to devise new structures to hide more and more of their activities and profits. The grey market has therefore become a transit stop between the black market, which flourished under the command economy, and the market economy which the reformist government is trying to create.

The full transition to a market economy has been held up by the compromises the reformists have had to strike with the bureaucracy. It has left the unreformed central bank, which was at the core of the old Soviet economy, free to allocate credits and subsidies to its traditional wards. This has kept them from going bankrupt, but at the price of massive inflation. If this financial flow were switched off and normal commercial criteria applied, a large proportion of Russian industry would be bankrupt by now and the work-force put out of work, as in Poland and East Germany.

A stabilizing factor for the government has been its ability to maintain hard-currency sales of natural resources (mostly oil and gas) to pay for basic consumer goods. With oil production itself falling, it has only been able to do this by diverting sales from the former Soviet republics to the open market. The relatively well-stocked shelves have blunted any opposition to the reforms among the general public just as effectively as the pri-

Company	**Employment**	**Management & workers**	**Workers**	**Management**	**CEO**	**Outsiders**	**Block-holders**	**Property Fund**	**Variant**
Food	130	80	20	60	60	20	5	0	2
Zil	103,000	40	35	5	n/a	35	20	25	1
Machine tools	1500	60	n/a	n/a	n/a	10	0	30	2
Radio	5000	60	55	5	0	20	0	20	1
Trucking	n/a	93	90	3	1	7	4	0	1
Chalk	120	60	55	5	n/a	9	9	31	1
Trucking	80	80	n/a	n/a	n/a	0	0	20	1
Steel	181	100	89	11	8	0	0	0	lease
Steel	342	64	29	35	1.5	26	23	10	2
Metal	350	84	66	18	10	16	1.4	0	2
Furniture	1200	51	46	5	*no voucher auction yet*				2
Textiles	1200	97	92	5	small	3	0	0	?
Women's wear	2300	90	90	0	0	0	0	10	1
Machine tools	3500	51	33	18	small	19	17.5	30	2
Pasta	320	61	57	4	small	18	n/a	20	2
Wheat	2000	73	28	45	2.5	9	1	18	2
Department store	1100	40	10	30	n/a	40	28.4	20	1
Trucking	526	75	45	30	n/a	3	1	22	1
Trucking	1300	63	58	5	3	7	1	30	2
MEAN	6897.17	69.58	52.82	16.71	9.56	13.44	6.55	15.89	

Figure 53.2 **Workers, management and outside ownership in Russian privatized firms.**
Note: Data based on a survey of companies which have been privatized

vatization process—by creating quasi-worker cooperatives—has deflected criticism among the work-force.

Russia is extremely rich in natural resources, but not in the ability to extract them. It is also suffering from severe internal tensions between the centre and the local regions, which having been exploited for so long under the Soviet system, are now seeking to gain more control over their own fortunes. Because of the wealth locked up in their territories, the central government has had to compromise with the leaders of these regions, many of whom are the old party *aparatachiki* rather than a new brand of nationalist.

The importance of Moscow is further diminished because it does not have the funds to maintain and develop the various regions' natural resources any more. It is here that foreign investment can make a critical difference, yet foreigners have been unwilling to invest because of broken contracts in the past, and hostile legislation designed to thwart foreign control. In 1993, a breakthrough occurred when a major international oil consortium began drilling off Sakhalin in the Far East. If this project progresses smoothly, other oil majors are expected to begin investing too.

In 1992, foreign companies made only $100m of direct investment in Russia, which in statistical terms is hardly more than an accounting error. Towards the end of 1993, the first large investments in consumer goods manufacturing by western multinationals were announced after a lull of several years during which foreign capital had refrained from any kind of investment except short-term trade finance.

Foreign capital is also needed to smooth the transition to a market economy. The G7 nations have pledged large sums: $25bn on a bilateral basis, and over $18bn from multilateral aid agencies. The Japanese, who have had the least friendly relations with Russia up to now, are sceptical that aid will be used to restructure the economy, rather they think it will be used to buy political time. They argue that Russia's potential economic refugees are concentrated on Europe's borders and that Japan can live without Russia.

Inflation took off after the government liberalized price controls in January 1992. To counter the extreme hostility this provoked among the parliamentary opposition, the government switched attention to privatization in order to regain the reform momentum. In June 1992, President Yeltsin persuaded parliament to pass a privatization programme which obliged all firms with over 1000 workers, or with a capitalization of Rb50m, to convert themselves into joint stock companies with freely-tradeable shares. A smaller-scale privatization programme was already underway to auction all shops and other small businesses. The first pilot auction was held in March 1992. By August 1993, 60 per cent of all shops had been transferred into private ownership, and 30 per cent of other service outlets, mostly purchased by their former owners.

The government began issuing vouchers for the main privatization programme in November 1992, setting an ambitious target of auctioning 5600 companies by the end of 1993. By the autumn, it was clear that the government was on course to achieve its target, thus making its privatization the most successful as well as the most ambitious ever attempted. None of the newly-independent states have had half the success with their own versions and none of the East European programmes have achieved the same degree of transfer or breadth of ownership.

The privatization programme is also a political compromise, which though it may prove astute in the long-term, could also backfire. To win over managers and workers, the government has allowed them to maintain control over a majority (51 per cent) of the shares in their company. (Companies had two other options available to them, but since workers and management had to decide privatization terms themselves, not surprisingly the majority—two-thirds up to the end of 1993—chose the option which offered least control to outside shareholders who could shake up their business or close them down.) Even if the new owners are the work-force, the government still deems it a major blow against the old system of party bureaucrats, and an opening towards a market economy.

The other hopeful force for change is the generational shift from those born before the war during the Stalinist era and those born after Stalin died in 1953. In between a generation is effectively missing, corresponding to the estimated 40m people, mainly of child-bearing age, who died either of Stalin's purges, famines or in the Second World War. This is, therefore, a youth revolution with a totally new meaning. It provides Russian society with great potential dynamism. This was clear to see in the speed with which the privatization programme was carried out, as government officials, mostly under 35 years of age, achieved timetables thought impossible by the western experts advising them.

The voucher scheme is ingenious because it co-opts the population (approximately 148m people) and makes them stakeholders in Russian industry. Voucher bearers have the choice to sell their voucher for cash (when the vouchers were issued in the second half of 1992 they were equivalent to about four months' salary) or swap them for shares in a voucher fund which invests the vouchers in a spread of companies in the same way as a mutual fund. Ownership of state enterprises was transferred to State Property Funds which are responsible for conducting auctions. In most cases, the funds hold a minimum of 29 per cent of the shares to be privatized and the government retains 20 per cent, which it will sell or transfer at a later stage. Only 400-500 of the largest and best-known companies are auctioned on a national basis; all other companies are offered at auction in the city or region where they are based. This has been useful in co-opting support at the local level too. Roughly six months after the programme

Name	No. employees	Industry	Implied $ value of enterprise
Zil	103,000	Truck mfg.	15,857,826
Preobrazhenskaya	44,817	Fishing	118,477
Rostselmash	42,928	Auto mfg.	771,477
Permsky Motors	35,000	Engine mfg.	6,276,015
Uralmash	34,041	Machine prod.	3,908,214
Zapadno-Sibirsky Metallurgical Plant	32,769	Metal prod.	3,890,820
Ribinsky Motors	27,351	-	988,241
Volgograd Tractor Factory	26,417	Tractor mfg.	570,747
Pervouralsky Novotrubny Factory	24,198	Metal prod.	2,548,514
Dalnevostochnoi Morskoi Parochodstvo	17,942	Shipping	-

Figure 53.3 Russia: 10 largest Russian enterprises sold in voucher auctions by employment and value

began, some 60 per cent of companies scheduled for privatization had presented their plans to the Property Funds for approval.

In this start-up phase, vouchers have served as a proxy for valuing Russian industry and evaluating the reform process. They had a face value of Rb10,000 at the time of issue, though this was purely notional as no money changed hands. The value of vouchers has since fluctuated up and down according to the supply and demand for them, as well as to how many vouchers investors are willing to submit to acquire shares in a company (investors have to use vouchers to buy shares). During this phase of the privatization process, vouchers have been generally the only liquid security available to trade. By the end of 1993, around 150,000 voucher certificates were being traded daily on the largest Moscow exchange. The price of the voucher had climbed steeply to Rb32,000 from less than Rb7000 in the summer, when the reform process was stalled by the parliamentary opposition. This is a sharp increase in four months, but less spectacular over the course of a year during which monthly inflation has been running at over 20 per cent.

The almost frightening point about inflation is how cheap it has made the companies which are being auctioned off. Companies were capitalized based on their book values at January 1992 which, after two years of annual inflation rates of 2000 per cent, are now meaningless. In dollar value terms, the rouble fell over the period when the first auctions commenced at the end of 1992 from around Rb500 to over Rb1,000 in the second half of 1993. The combination of these two factors means that a major industrial conglomerate like Zil was valued at only $16m, based on the market valuation after it had issued its first shares at auction. Based on the voucher prices achieved for other companies auctioned prior to July 1993, the implied value of the whole of Russian industry was only $5-10bn, which is less than the valuation of a large Fortune 500 company. The fear that outside shareholders would not be able to prevent the management running the companies for their own benefit is one reason given for these low valuations. With few exceptions therefore, neither Russian flight capital, nor foreign portfolio investors, participated in these early auctions. Hyperinflation in 1993 finally killed any enthusiasm for high-risk investment which was left.

A lack of information further compounds the investment risk. Companies provide only the barest information about themselves ahead of the privatization auction. There is not that much to say about them anyway. Most companies, if they are not actual monopolists, occupy a highly-protected niche within the structure of the pre-privatization economy. Meanwhile, the sophisticated financial intermediaries that stalk the privatization market are not so much interested in value as in strategic control. For this, it is important to have a wider view of the opportunities for the restructuring of whole industries, rather than companies alone, by seeing the possibility of redistributing business activities among different participants, developing new business lines, or drawing in foreign joint venture partners to provide capital and know-how. The reformists trust that these would-be corporate raiders will overcome the barriers managers and workers erect to outside control (which includes the purchase of more shares in their own company from financial intermediaries). To help them, the government is planning to lift the 10 per cent ceiling on the number of shares any one fund may own in a company. Once the government tightens credit, even well-defended companies will be prepared to strike deals with outside investors who have access to finance, new markets or partners. The driving force for most such deals will therefore be survival rather than control.

Out of this privatization process, new forms of holding company are also emerging, linking companies both horizontally and vertically through cross-shareholdings. The new financial institutions are also seeking to find ways to help these Russian versions of *keiretsu* to reorganize and refocus. Grouping together for self-defence, though contrary to the spirit of the capitalism taught by western advisers to the privatization process, may nevertheless be a necessary form of management in the special conditions of Russia's fragile economy. At the next stage, western capital could be introduced into these structures, largely through the financial entrepreneurs which are trying to restructure them.

There is much to attract foreign capital. There is an internal market of 150m people, with material needs which have been neglected for decades. The enthusiasm for change among the young and educated is strong and driven by a potent mix of national shame and the will to survive. There is a large pool of well-educated people. The undeveloped state of the market is also an opportunity for western know-how and capital to make a disproportionate impact.

Confronting this is the lack of a properly-functioning banking system, an inexperienced legal system to protect investors, an undependable transport-distribution system and raging inflation. The banking system is at least innovative, with companies free to form their own bank entities in order to expedite business and foreign banks allowed to set up in competition. Investment protection will never be as secure as westerners would like, but Russians are closer to orientals in their attitude to laws, honouring them in the spirit rather than the letter. The rail system is over-loaded and under-maintained and must be an important priority for western aid. The air transport system could develop rapidly if private capital were made available to invest in new aircraft and, more importantly, improved airport handling facilities. Inflation has remained persistently high through 1993 but would start to fall if the political situation allows the government a freer hand with the economy, though the price is bound to be more social hardship.

Currently, it is less the falling value of their purchasing power which worries Russians—since at least they now have things to buy—as the issue of law and order. This can still play into the hands of the conservative hardliners for whom public ownership is the only safeguard against private theft. The reform government's hope is that once the economy is stabilized much of the grey market activity like street trading, which now sustains a hotchpotch of Mafia types as well as legitimate aspiring businessmen, will disappear and in its place will develop a normal market for goods and services.

Where does all this leave would-be portfolio investors? Stock market activity is so low that most investment must effectively be development or venture capital that is willing to wait patiently for an exit route once stock markets have developed. Buying shares in funds is one way of diversifying risk, but it is difficult to evaluate performance as none of the funds have had time to develop a track record. In spite of these drawbacks, there are enough opportunities to justify a limited investment on the grounds of starting early on the learning curve and there are now enough people and sources of information to guide the novice investor around. Most of the best opportunities are in the service sector and consumer goods field, which includes real estate, office development, housing, retail, distribution, banking, food processing and energy.

There were an estimated 100 licenced stock exchanges in Russia when trading first began in vouchers, but the number is contracting fast as smaller ones merge with larger ones. The main centres of activity are Moscow, St Petersburg, Novosibirsk (in Western Siberia) and Vladivostok (covering the Russian Far East). The number of listed shares on these markets was still very small at the end of 1993. Vladivostok had the most (at around 160). Other exchanges, even in Moscow, still only had a handful. This does not limit trading activity however, most of which is conducted on an OTC basis in an unregulated environment. In fact, the concept of a central exchange is at such an embryonic stage that outside investors must avoid making too harsh a comparison with established practice elsewhere. For the moment, trading via an exchange is only one of several options open to buyers and sellers. The physical location may even be unimportant once telephone trading is replaced by computer terminals. The Vladivostok Exchange is in fact a bank of computer terminals already. By the beginning of 1994, it is planning to provide on-line access to members so that they can trade from anywhere in the region or beyond, providing that they have the necessary terminal connections and software.

The Stock Department of the Moscow Raw Materials and Commodities Exchange, which is the most active of the local exchanges in Moscow, did not have any listing regulations in 1993 and will trade in the shares of any joint stock company. Other exchanges may operate a listing procedure but with so few shares traded, other than vouchers, there are few incentives for companies to join. Listing requirements are not uniform. Some exchanges operate a dual-listing process designed to distinguish larger companies from the rest. Also, as there is generally more than one exchange competing for business, the same stocks are generally traded on any or all of them. (Vladivostok is an exception, although it must compete with Nakhodka which is not far away in Russian terms).

Vladivostok has one of the most progressive exchanges, which is somehow befitting a city on the dynamic Pacific seaboard. There are over 200 members but only 25 active participants. About 20-25 stocks are actively traded although, as elsewhere, only 20 per cent of this trading is done through the exchange. One of the large fishery companies raised Rb1.2bn through a public offering in which a Japanese company made the highest bid. There were four more issues in the pipeline in the last quarter of 1993. Through its on-line computer network the exchange plans to make settlement and registration much more efficient too.

Nobosibirsk is interesting for the way it is becoming the regional exchange for the western Siberian region and beyond. The city is already the transport hub for the region, a major industrial centre and home to the prestigious Siberian branch of the Russian Academy of Sciences. As a result it does not lack for rocket scientists. The two main exchanges are due to merge by the beginning of 1994. Both are already large by Russian standards, though neither had more than half-a-dozen stocks listed in 1993. The larger Siberian exchange conducts an open telephone trading system with five other regional centres on two mornings of the week. Trading is mostly

	Dec	Jan	Feb	Mar	Apr	May	Jun	Total
No. of enterprises sold	18	105	188	416	582	477	632	2418
No. of regions participating	8	19	29	51	58	48	61	75
No. of employees ('000s)	47	191	181	651	898	511	692	3171
Charter cap. sold (Rbls m)	513	607	1375	5318	7.57	4193	6102	25,165
Weighted av. % of charter cap. sold	17%	11%	23%	20%	24%	21%	23%	21%
Vouchers accepted ('000s)	158	150	501	2188	4854	2666	3526	14,043
Weighted av. auction rate, 1000 rouble shares per voucher	3.2	4	2.7	2.4	1.5	1.6	1.7	1.8

Figure 53.4 Voucher auctions, December 1992 - June 1993

in vouchers, but trading in stocks is also increasing, as is new issue activity. One of the largest local voucher funds is due to list its stock. Eventually, it is clear the exchange will become the main trading centre for the whole of Siberia, which will then make trading in the underlying wealth of the region much more accessible.

Vouchers tend to account for 80 per cent or more of the trading on exchanges. Prices doubled at the end of October 1993 in the first sign of a bull market. Trading volume also doubled on the main Moscow exchanges. Vouchers are in limited supply and had to be redeemed by July 1994, when the mass privatization programme was completed. Nationwide, some 550 funds had collected 25m vouchers by the middle of 1993 and had a total of 12m shareholders. These funds speculate in vouchers in addition to buying shares at auction. Some funds are pure speculators who buy shares to sell back to the management in a Russian version of green mailing. Many larger funds aim to influence corporate governance by having themselves voted on to the board of directors. They will become more active once the restriction on how many shares they can buy in a company is lifted. Banks and financial intermediaries have been the other active constituents of the market, issuing various kinds of securities to raise capital for their operations.

Stock market activity will grow as companies recognize the benefits of raising capital more efficiently through a market. Already a major reason for listing shares is to enhance the impression of openness for the purposes of improving credit standing. A handful of non-bank companies have already raised capital from the market and all the major exchanges have issues in the pipeline. Activity will also increase once markets become better regulated and when the process of consolidation among the exchanges is completed. Liquidity will be a problem because many shares will be held in large blocks, notably by the work-force. Once the market is well developed, some workers will themselves become mini-capitalists, selling their shares and buying shares in other companies or in professionally-managed funds. This will take two or three years at least, but investors in the meantime should begin climbing the learning curve by testing the market.

Technical notes

- Settlement dates are unreliable because of the malfunctioning banking system.
- A separate depository system and clearing house are to be set up by each of the major exchanges.
- Commission—1.0 per cent to buy and sell, but in most cases the rate is negotiable.
  No stamp duty.
- Listing criteria: Various, but typically require authorized capital of between Rb50m or Rb100m depending on whether the company is qualifying for a main listing or simply registering its shares, between 2500-5000 shareholders, and a minimum period of trading as a joint stock company of one year.
- Foreign investment is welcome. There is no restriction on repatriation of profits, no capital gains tax, and only a 10 per cent withholding tax on dividends.

A visit to the Vladivostok Stock Exchange

Vladivostok (whose name means 'Ruler of the East') is the principal Russian port on the Pacific Ocean and the natural entrepôt for all Russia's trade with Japan, Korea and China. As Hong Kong is to China, so Vladivostok could become to Russia. It is the Far Eastern terminus of the Trans-Siberian Railway and, as such, has a great strategic importance. US-Russian trade also flows largely across the Pacific and through this point. The port remains open virtually the whole year. The city has a pleasant maritime air and the landscape is somewhat reminiscent of both San Francisco and Hong Kong. There is clearly a large and growing foreign presence here, with Asians and Westerners mingling with the mainly Russian population of 700,000.

The stock exchange is located in a large, newish red brick building near the railway station. It was formerly owned by the local communist party. The floor of the exchange looks like a large school gymnasium. In the middle stand three rows of computer terminals, fifteen in all, which were standing idle as we entered. The director of the exchange is a dynamic and powerfully-built man in his mid-thirties, named Victor Sakharov. Like many in the new generation of entrepreneurs in Russia, he is not popular with the older generation of communists but he has clearly been largely responsible for creating this new Far Eastern stock exchange. There are already 200 shares listed, of which about 25 are actively traded. The most promising sectors are shipping stocks such as FESCO (the Far Eastern Shipping Company), ports and fisheries. There are also some mines and forestry companies representing the enormous natural wealth of Siberia. The average daily turnover in October 1993 was running at about 40m roubles a day or, at current exchange rates, US$40,000, about the same as the other Siberian exchange in Novosibirsk. The exchange has just held one public offering and four more companies are due to list before the end of 1993. Futures trading in rouble/dollar contracts has just started. Mr Sakharov was somewhat vague about listing requirements. There are 200 stockbroking members but only 25 active participants, including one or two foreign firms. A Korean company is apparently interested in broking Russian shares in the Hong Kong market, but the Russian Ministry of Finance is not yet ready for this. Commission rates are 1 per cent for buying and selling. A new computer was installed in early 1994, with an online network linking the brokers and a central settlement and registry system. It has real time connections with all the main exchanges in the Russian Far East. There is plenty of foreign advice available from accounting firms, lawyers and stock brokers. One cannot help believing that, in these unpromising and modest beginnings, there could be the seat of a dynamic emerging market which will reflect the growing flows of trade and capital between the Far East of Russia, with its great natural resources and the manufacturing nations of Asia.

Chapter 54

Other Eastern European markets

As the wind of change has blown across Eastern Europe, more and more nations have suddenly opened stock markets. Some of these are in countries which, for centuries, have not had an independent existence but now wish to anchor themselves in the bay of capitalism, hoping that it will provide shelter against any further storms of tyranny.

Bulgaria

Population:	9.01m
Gross domestic product:	$20.5bn
Currency/US$:	26.6 lev

Victor Parazov, funded by ten shareholders and almost $600,000, founded the First Bulgarian Stock Exchange shortly before the end of 1991. The market currently exists without any securities law and only one company—the trading firm Lear—is officially listed. However, others are planning to list and twelve companies trade in a usual week. Volumes are not large at under $200,000 a week by the middle of 1993, but subsequently lower. Initially trading sessions were only held once a week, but this has been increased and the market is now open on Tuesdays and Thursdays. There is a second stock market in Bulgaria, but it is very small with $12,000 turnover a week.

Bulgaria is waiting for the implementation of its privatization law which ought to see a considerable increase in the number of listed companies. The current regime encourages foreign investment and has occasional campaigns to further this objective. The currency has been floated and, in spite of high inflation, has performed satisfactorily.

Estonia

Population:	1.576m
Gross domestic product:	$12bn
Currency/US$:	13.7 kroon

The Estonian government approved a bill on 6 April 1993 to control the country's stock exchange and 'to create a legal framework for establishing a stock market in Estonia and guarantee for all investors equal conditions', in the words of Madis Uurike, the minister of finance.

Although Estonia is regarded as being ahead of other members of the former Soviet Union and some of the other Eastern European countries, it is a small country with few sizeable companies. In spite of its name, the Tallinn International Stock Exchange is a tiny outfit and even faces competition from others who wish to run Estonia's stock market. However, a privatization scheme—based on restoration of confiscated property—is in hand. The currency is sound in as much as it is fixed to the Deutschemark and foreign investment is broadly welcomed.

Lithuania

Population:	3.723m
Gross domestic product:	$28bn
Currency/US$:	3.9 litas

The Stock Exchange in Vilnius was launched with a flourish on 14 September 1993. Nineteen securities were listed, of which three offered both preferred and ordinary shares. As in many Eastern European countries, trading is based on the French system with a 10 per cent movement limit. Settlements take four days to clear and transactions are recorded by a book-entry system.

Turnover to date has been minute; however, a large number of companies have been privatized—nearly 1600—and some of these will eventually be quoted. This process may jolt the Lithuanian market into life.

Slovakia

Population:	5.3m
Gross domestic product:	$10bn
Currency/US$:	32.9 koruna

Regarded as the poor relation of the Czech Republic, Slovakia has been ignored since the split took place on 1 January 1993. Nevertheless, the stock market opened its trading floor on 6 April and, on 1 July, it moved to a book-entry form for trading listed securities which are the product of the first wave of privatization.

Seven companies are listed on the Bratislava Stock Exchange and 13 brokers compete with each other to trade in them. The market operates on Tuesdays and Wednesdays—initially it only opened alternate Tuesdays—and will trade more regularly as demand requires.

The government has liberalized the rules for foreign investors and importance is attached to relations with bodies like the IMF, the World Bank and the European Bank for Reconstruction and Development. Foreign investors are given equal treatment with local ones in terms of taxation and eligibility for subsidies.

Ukraine

Population:	51.471m
Gross domestic product:	n/a
Currency/US$:	30,968.8 karbovanets

The third of January 1992 saw a Ukrainian Stock Exchange open in Kiev incorporating a number of state and private agencies. However, there are sixty other registered stock exchanges of which only fourteen others are at all active. The Kiev operation is the most important of these and it is modelling its systems on the French ones.

Again, the stock exchange will have to wait upon the privatization programme which is progressing slowly. Foreign investment is encouraged, with no specific investment restrictions and the availability of five-year tax holidays or only 15 per cent tax on repatriated profits which is waived if the investment were in a high technology area. However, there is some political opposition to foreign money.

PART VIII

Other emerging markets

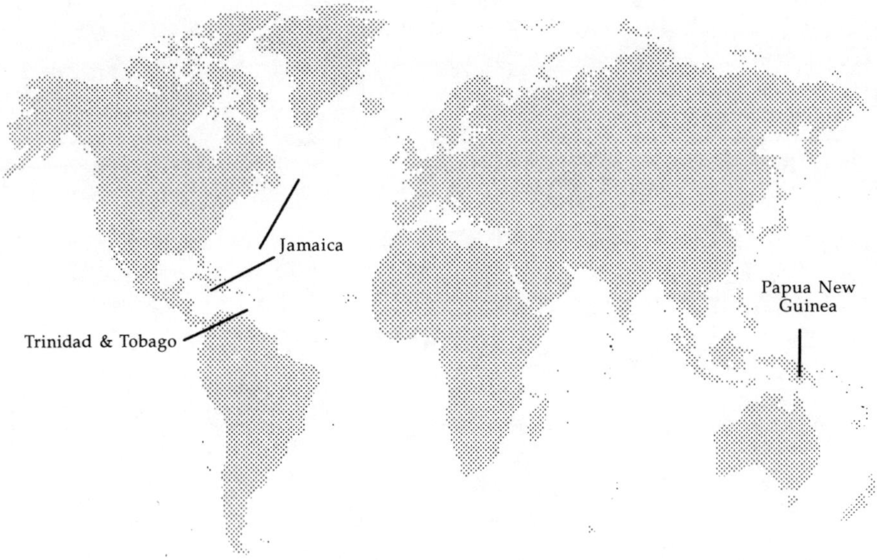

OTHER EMERGING MARKETS

Chapter 55

Jamaica

Population:	2.53m
Gross domestic product:	$3.514bn
Market capitalization:	$4.1bn
Currency/US$:	32.475 Jamaican dollars

Although Jamaica was discovered by Columbus as early as 1494, it became a British colony in 1655 and was one of the most successful colonies economically over the next three centuries, with its rich sugar plantations. It achieved independence from Britain in 1962 and has since had a colourful parliamentary democracy. The population is relatively small at about 2.6m and centred on the capital, Kingston. Major exports are alumina, bananas, bauxite and sugar, although the largest source of foreign exchange receipts comes from tourism. Jamaica attracts nearly 1.4m visitors a year.

The stock market

The Kingston Stock Market Committee was established in 1961, under the auspices of the Bank of Jamaica. The Jamaica Stock Exchange itself started trading in 1969 and by 1992, the capitalization had increased at an impressive rate to J$76.8bn (US$3.5bn). The total value of listed shares represents 130 per cent of GNP. The market is very concentrated with one company, Telecommunications of Jamaica, a subsidiary of Cable & Wireless, accounting for 14 per cent of total market value and over 15 per cent of trading volume. The Bank of Nova Scotia also has a large market value of US$370m. These two stocks alone account for 25 per cent of the market. In this sense, Jamaica has some distinct advantages over other emerging markets, with leading blue chips forming the core of the market.

There are, in fact, only about 40 companies listed on the exchange and nine stockbrokers actively involved in daily trading activities. One of the major problems with the Jamaican economy has been the rate of inflation which has, nevertheless, come down from the 80 per cent of two years ago to approximately 30 per cent today, leading to a rapid devaluation of the Jamaican dollar.

	1988	1989	1990	1991	1992	1993
Population (m)	2.36	2.39	2.42	2.48	2.51	2.53
GNP (US$m)	3416	3334	3606	3497	3514	n/a
Per capita income (US$)	1447	1395	1490	1410	1400	n/a
Exports (US$m)	896	887	1033	608	116	n/a
Imports (US$bn)	1300	1445	1467	827	1381	n/a
Foreign direct investment (US$m)	-12	57.1	137.9	127.0	86.5	n/a
Inflation	8.3	14.3	22	51.1	77.3	73.1
Interest rates (lending)	23	25.6	34.2	35.6	53.4	44.2
International reserves(US$m)	147.2	107.5	168.2	106.1	n/a	n/a
Market capitalization (US$m)	796	957	911	1034	3227	4100
No. of listed companies	44	45	44	44	48	50
IFC Index performance in US$ (%)	4.8	20	1.4	12.1	182.6	n/a
Price/earnings (P/E) ratios	5.7	7	7	13.4	22	n/a
Earnings per share (EPS) growth					87.7	n/a
Avg daily turnover (US$000)	100	360	128	384	820	n/a
Dividend yield	2.5	3.4	3.9	2.8	2.6	2.7
Currency to US$ (J dollars)	5.391	6.48	8.038	21.4925	22.185	32.475

Figure 55.1 Jamaica: key statistics

Exchange address

The Jamaica Stock Exchange
3/F Bank of Jamaica Tower
Nethersole Place
PO Box 621
Kingston

Tel: 1 809 922 0806 / Fax: 1 809 922 3868 / Tlx: 2165 & 2167

	Market capitalization (J$ million)
Telecommunications of Jamaica	11,202
Bank of Nova Scotia	8172
NCB Group	6720
CIBC (Ja) Ltd	5413
Lascelles DeMercado	4992
Carreras Group Ltd	4976
Desnoes & Geddes	4246
Mutual Security Bank	3604
Life of Jamaica	2981
Grace Kennedy & Co	2859
Carib Cement Company	2501
Island Life	2400
Jamaica Producers Group	2174
Jamaica Flour Mills	2050
Seprod	1991
Trafalgar Development Bank	1222
Goodyear (Ja) Ltd	1218
Jamaica Citizens Bank	896
ICD Group	891
Jamaica Broilers Group	656

Figure 55.2 Jamaica: 20 largest stocks by market capitalization

Chapter 56

Papua New Guinea

Population:	3.9m
Gross national product:	$4.8bn
Currency/US$:	0.97 kina

Papua New Guinea is a well-known destination for anthropologists, but less well-known for investment managers. It is reputed to have half of the world's language groups in its narrow secluded valleys, with stone age tribes who have still not been contacted by the modern world. Historically, it was a British territory which came under Australian administration. Papua New Guinea achieved full independence in 1975. It is rich in both agricultural and mineral resources. The massive Bougainville mine, part of Rio Tinto Zinc Group (RTZ), has huge resources of copper, silver and gold. In the Western provinces, the most important new development is of large copper and gold deposits at Ok Tedi.

There have recently been political disturbances and, in 1989, the Bougaineville mine was closed down and has not re-opened since. The government has started to increase its stake in several large mining projects which has created uncertainty among foreign investors as well as concerns about law and order. However, there is now a move afoot to establish a stock exchange, closely linked to the Australian Stock Exchange and this was announced in the 1993-94 budget. It is estimated that the Papua New Guinea Stock Exchange could attract more than thirty companies including the nine companies already listed on the Australian Stock Exchange. The three biggest—Highlands Gold, Niugini Mining and Oil Research—have a combined market capitalization of more than 1.1bn. This could, therefore, be an interesting emerging market for investors wishing to diversify into gold and other natural resources in the Asia Pacific region.

	1988	1989	1990	1991	1992	1993
Population (m)	3.56	3.63	3.7	3.77	3.84	3.91
GNP (US$bn)	3.8	3.7	3.5	4.1	4.3	4.8
Real GNP growth (%)	2.9	1.4	3.7	9	5.6	10.3
Per capita income (US$)	1067	1019	946	1087	1120	1228
Exports (US$m)	1461	1308	1181	1356	1803	2226
Imports (US$bn)	1394	1355	1010	1407	1330	990
Inflation	5.4	4.5	6.9	5.3	5.5	5
Interest rates (lending)	12.7	14.6	15.5	14.2	14.5	11.1
International reserves(US$m)	393	384	403	323	239	141
Currency to US$ (kina)	0.86	0.85	0.96	0.95	0.96	0.97

Figure 56.1 Papua New Guinea: key statistics

Chapter 57

Trinidad & Tobago

Population:	1.27m
Gross national product:	$5.8bn
Market capitalization:	$550m
Currency/US$:	5.81 TT dollars

Trinidad lies only seven miles off the coast of Venezuela and is the most southern part of the West Indies. It has a population of about 1.3m. Trinidad itself was a British colony from 1802 onwards and was joined by Tobago in 1888. The joint territories became an independent member of the British Commonwealth in 1962. The major source of revenue is from oil production, which is 55m barrels a year. Trinidad also has large reserves of natural gas, estimated at 100 years' production at current rates.

The stock market

The stock exchange was opened in 1981 and has grown rapidly with government support, so that today there are 27 companies quoted and a market capitalization of approximately US$525m. As in Jamaica, the five largest companies account for over 50 per cent of total market capitalization, with the Republic Bank Ltd., accounting for 13 per cent alone. Trinidad and Tobago is a member of the Caribbean Community (Caricom) which aims to create a Caribbean common market. Although economic growth has been sluggish in recent years, both oil and tourism contribute to a steady improvement in living standards and education.

Exchange address

Trinidad and Tobago Stock Exchange
65 Independent Square
Port of Spain
Trinidad

Tel: 1 809 625 5107 / Fax: 1 809 623 0089 / Tlx: 22532

	1988	1989	1990	1991	1992	1993
Population (m)	1.21	1.22	1.23	1.25	1.26	1.27
GNP (US$m)	4067	4323	5121	5279	5442	5750
Real GNP growth (%)	n/a	n/a	n/a	n/a	n/a	n/a
Per capita income (US$)	3361	3543	4163	4223	4319	4528
Exports (US$m)	1276	1578	2080	1983	1850	1428
Imports (US$bn)	913	1099	1136	1497	1287	959
Foreign direct investment	n/a	n/a	n/a	n/a	n/a	n/a
Inflation	7.8	11.4	11	3.8	6.5	4.8
Interest rates (lending)	12.6	13.3	12.9	13.2	15.3	15.5
International reserves (US$m)	127.1	246.5	492	338.6	172.2	149.7
Market capitalization (US$m)	268	411	696	671	514	550
No. of listed companies	33	31	30	29	27	28
Index performance in US$ (%)	31.1	50.1	70.6	1.6	26.4	n/a
Price/earnings (P/E) ratios	8.3	7.8	11.4	10.3	n/a	n/a
Earnings per share (EPS) growth	n/a	n/a	n/a	n/a	n/a	n/a
Avg daily turnover (US$ '000s)	88	276	220	320	88	n/a
Dividend yield	4.5	3.6	2.7	5.1	n/a	n/a
Currency to US$ (TT dollars)	4.25	4.25	4.25	4.25	4.25	5.81

Figure 57.1 Trinidad & Tobago: key statistics

	Market capitalization (TT$m)
Republic Bank Ltd	277.4
West Indian Tobacco Co Ltd	242.2
Neal & Massy	229.8
Royal Bank Ltd	202.0
Bank of Nova Scotia	177.6
Angostura Holdings	175.5
Ansa Mc Al	156.9
Bank of Commerce	146.8
Geddes Grant	134.0
Trinidad Cement Ltd	130.0
Lever Brothers	66.9
Guardian Life of the Caribbean	64.4
Trinidad Co-operative Bank	24.8
Agostini's Limited	24.3
Caribbean Communications Network	22.7
National Commercial Bank	21.1
Valpark	18.5
Trinidad Publishing Company	17.5
Furness Trinidad Ltd	15.7
Readymix (WI) Ltd	9.1

Figure 57.2 Trinidad & Tobago: 20 largest stocks by market capitalization

The Publisher....

Probus is a major force on the international business and finance publishing scene. We are committed to publishing the very finest books and information products. Our range of quality books in core business subjects such as investments, banking, the capital markets, accountancy, taxation, property, insurance, sales management, marketing and healthcare, is second to none. We believe that you will find many other titles in our range to be of interest. Are you a writer? If so, please feel free to refer potential publications to us.

You may wish to contact Probus direct at:

Probus Publishing Company
1925 North Clybourn Avenue
Chicago
Illinois 60614
USA
Tel: (312) 868-1100
Tel [Sales]: 1-800-PROBUS-1
Fax: (312) 868-6250

OR

Probus Europe
11 Millers Yard
Mill Lane
Cambridge CB2 1RQ
England
Tel: (0223) 322018
Fax: (0223) 61149

The World's Futures & Options Markets, Nick Battley (Ed.)
1029pp, Probus Europe, 1994. ISBN 1 55738 513 0

Where in the world can you trade Biotechnology Index options? What are the component stocks of the FT-SE 100 Index? Which is the most heavily-traded of the world's five eurodollar futures contracts? The answers to all these questions—and more—can be found in this fully classified directory, making it **the** essential reference work for everyone with a professional or personal interest in futures and options. This major publication features detailed information on over 550 contracts, categorized by type and listed alphabetically for ease of reference. Of course, in addition to the contracts, the 51 exchanges on which they are traded are covered in full detail.

For those with an appetite for statistics, the appendices contain 7-year historical volume figures, not only for almost every contract, but also for each exchange.

To bring the world of international futures and options directly to your your desk, place an order with your bookseller, or call (0223) 322018 in the UK or (312) 868 1100 in the United States.